Human Resource Management and the Institutional Perspective

One of the most influential debates across business and management studies has centered on the relative impact of institutions on the fortunes of firms and nations. However, analyses have primarily focused on institutional effects on societal features, rather than actual firm practices. This volume brings together recent trends in comparative institutional analysis with a rich body of data on firm-level human resource management practice, consolidating and extending more than a decade of research on the topic.

Human Resource Management and the Institutional Perspective explores the overlapping and distinct elements in work and employment relations both within and across country lines. The authors focus on intra-firm relations, internal diversity within varieties of capitalism, and the uneven and experimental nature of systemic change, all the while employing an impressive level of theoretical rigor and empirical evidence. In a single volume, this text unites soundly based, theoretically strong and empirically new chapters that bring advances in institutional theory to bear on the subject of international and comparative human resource management.

This book is a valuable resource for students and scholars interested in contemporary developments in institutional theory, the relationship between regulation and practice, and innovation and continuity in human resource management.

Geoffrey Wood is Professor and Associate Dean at Warwick Business School, University of Warwick, UK. He is also Adjunct Professor at Griffith University, Australia, and Visiting Professor at Pecs University, Hungary, and Nelson Mandela Metropolitan University, South Africa.

Chris Brewster is Professor at Henley Business School, University of Reading, UK and Visiting Professor at the University of Nijmegen, Netherlands and Vaasa University, Finland. He researches international and comparative human resource management and has published over twenty-five books and more than 175 articles.

Michael Brookes is Reader at Middlesex University, UK, as well as Director of the Khanyisa Project, a non-profit partnership seeking to address employability issues in the Eastern Cape of South Africa. His research interests include labor market discrimination, industrial relations and comparative human resource management.

Routledge Global Human Resource Management Series

Edited by Randall S. Schuler, Susan E. Jackson, Paul Sparrow and Michael Poole

Routledge Global Human Resource Management is an important new series that examines human resources in its global context. The series is organized into three strands: Content and issues in global human resource management (HRM); Specific HR functions in a global context; and comparative HRM. Authored by some of the world's leading authorities on HRM, each book in the series aims to give readers comprehensive, in-depth and accessible texts that combine essential theory and best practice. Topics covered include cross-border alliances, global leadership, global legal systems, HRM in Asia, Africa and the Americas, industrial relations, and global staffing.

Managing Human Resources in Cross-Border Alliances
Randall S. Schuler, Susan E. Jackson and Yadong Luo

Managing Human Resources in Africa
Edited by Ken N. Kamoche, Yaw A. Debrah, Frank M. Horwitz and Gerry Nkombo Muuka

Globalizing Human Resource Management
Paul Sparrow, Chris Brewster and Hilary Harris

Managing Human Resources in Asia-Pacific
Edited by Pawan S. Budhwar

International Human Resource Management (second edition)
Policy and practice for the global enterprise
Dennis R. Briscoe and Randall S. Schuler

Managing Human Resources in Latin America
An agenda for international leaders
Edited by Marta M. Elvira and Anabella Davila

Global Staffing
Edited by Hugh Scullion and David G. Collings

Managing Human Resources in Europe
A thematic approach
Edited by Henrik Holt Larsen and Wolfgang Mayrhofer

Managing Human Resources in the Middle-East
Edited by Pawan S. Budhwar and Kamel Mellahi

Managing Global Legal Systems
International employment regulation and competitive advantage
Gary W. Florkowski

Global Industrial Relations
Edited by Michael J. Morley, Patrick Gunnigle and David G. Collings

Managing Human Resources in North America
Current issues and perspectives
Edited by Steve Werner

Global Leadership
Research, Practice, Development
Edited by Mark Mendenhall, Gary Oddou, Allan Bird and Martha Maznevski

Global Compensation
Foundations and Perspectives
Edited by Luis Gomez-Mejia and Steve Werner

Performance Management Systems: A Global Perspective
Edited by Arup Varma, Pawan S. Budhwar and Angelo DeNisi

Managing Human Resources in Central and Eastern Europe
Edited by Michael J. Morley, Noreen Heraty and Snejina Michailova

Global Careers
Michael Dickmann and Yehuda Baruch

Global Leadership (second edition)
Research, practice, development
Mark E. Mendenhall, Joyce S. Osland, Allan Bird, Gary Oddou,
Martha L. Maznevski, Michael J. Stevens, Günter K. Stahl

Manager–Subordinate Trust
A global perspective
Edited by Pablo Cardona and Michael J. Morley

Managing Human Resources in Asia-Pacific (second edition)
Edited by Arup Varma and Pawan S. Budhwar

Human Resource Management and the Institutional Perspective

Edited by Geoffrey Wood, Chris Brewster and Michael Brookes

Routledge
Taylor & Francis Group

NEW YORK AND LONDON

Please see the series website at:
http://www.routledge.com/cw/globalhrm/

First published 2014
by Routledge
711 Third Avenue, New York, NY 10017

and by Routledge
2 Park Square, Milton Park, Abingdon, Oxon OX14 4RN

Routledge is an imprint of the Taylor & Francis Group, an informa business

Library of Congress Cataloging in Publication Data
Human resource management and the institutional perspective / edited by Geoffrey Wood,
Chris Brewster, Michael Brookes.
pages cm. — (Global HRM)
Includes bibliographical references and index.
1. Personnel management. 2. Organizational sociology. I. Wood, Geoffrey, editor of
compilation. II. Brewster, Chris, editor of compilation. III. Brookes, Michael.
HF5549.H78436 2014
331.2—dc23
2013040817

ISBN: 978–0–415–89692–4 (hbk)
ISBN: 978–0–415–89693–1 (pbk)
ISBN: 978–1–315–79607–9 (ebk)

Typeset in Times New Roman
by Swales & Willis Ltd, Exeter, Devon

Printed and bound by CPI Group (UK) Ltd, Croydon, CR0 4YY

Dedication

We are grateful to our colleagues in the Cranet network around the world who collected the data, discussions with whom have informed our understanding of developments in various countries and our analyses. We are also grateful to Cranfield School of Management in the UK for coordinating the network.

Contents

Figures

Tables

Contributors

Richard Croucher is Professor of Comparative Employment Relations and Director of Research at Middlesex University Business School, London; he is visiting professor at Cranfield School of Management. He has led research funded by the Low Pay Commission, the ILO, the ESRC and many other sources. He has published over 50 refereed articles in journals such as *Human Relations, Industrial Relations, A Journal of Economy and Society* and elsewhere.

Mehmet Demirbag is Professor of International Business in Strathclyde Business School at University of Strathclyde. He researches in the area of international business and has a particular interest in strategic decision making, high performance work systems, people management in emerging market MNEs, and outsourcing decisions in MNEs. Recent research interests have been focused around the internationalisation of R&D activities, product/regional diversification strategies of MNEs, and MNEs from emerging markets.

Marc Goergen holds a Chair in Finance at Cardiff Business School. His previous employment includes the Universities of Manchester, Reading and Sheffield as well as UMIST. Marc is also a Research Associate of the Brussels based European Corporate Governance Institute. His research interests are in corporate finance and corporate governance, in particular, initial public offerings, corporate control, mergers and acquisitions, and boards of directors. He is widely published and his research has appeared in the *Journal of Finance*, *Journal of Corporate Finance*, and *Journal of Law, Economics, and Organization*.

Dr Michael J. Mol is Professor of Strategic Management at Warwick Business School. His research focuses on the strategic management of larger firms, with particular interests in management innovation (the creation of new management practices) and sourcing strategy (outsourcing and offshoring). His numerous publications have appeared in, among others, *Academy of Management Review, Journal of the Academy of Marketing Science, Research Policy,*

MIT Sloan Management Review and *Strategic Management Journal*. He has also co-authored four books. He serves on the editorial boards of a number of journals such as the *Journal of International Business Studies*. He has won several awards for his work including the best article award from *Academy of Management Review*. Michael holds a PhD from Erasmus University, Rotterdam.

Suzanne Richbell was formerly Senior Lecturer in Human Resource Management at Sheffield University's Management School. She remains active in both teaching and research. Her current research interests include: non-standard working time (especially permanent night working), travel plans and absenteeism, and HRM in both retailing and the SME sector.

Marian Rizov is Professor of Economics at Middlesex University Business School. He has previously held full time research positions in the Catholic University of Leuven and Trinity College, Dublin. His research focus is on the economic performance of firms, households and individuals in various policy and institutional contexts. His recent publications are in *Industrial and Labor Relations Review, Journal of Agricultural Economics, Papers in Regional Science*, and *Economics and Human Biology*.

James Walker is Professor at Henley Business School, University of Reading. He has a PhD from the LSE and was a practitioner before becoming an academic. He has published in journals as diverse as *Journal of Applied Economics* and the *Journal of Economic History*, examining the spatial competition in product markets and between firms, varieties of capitalism, academic performance and pay, and attitudes to multinational enterprises. His overall research agenda is characterised by the application of empirical methods to solve real world problems and issues past and present.

1 Institutions and Firm Level HRM Practice

GEOFFREY WOOD, CHRIS BREWSTER AND
MICHAEL BROOKES

One of the most influential debates across business and management studies has been the relative impact of institutions on the fortunes of firms and of nations. However, what the specific defining features and consequences of institutions are is itself a matter of contestation. Moreover, a major limitation of the literature on comparative institutional analysis has been that, despite a central interest in firms and economic outcomes, analyses have drawn on a primary focus on societal features, rather than actual firm practices. There have been calls for more work on HRM that uses the institutional literature in general and the comparative capitalisms literature in particular as an analytical base (Delbridge et al. 2011). The Cranet surveys on firm level HRM practice have documented national and sectoral variations in how firms manage their people for many years. The purpose of this volume is to bring together recent trends in comparative institutional analysis with this rich body of firm level evidence, consolidating and extending more than a decade of research on this broad topic.

Understanding Institutions

Institutions may be conceptualized as structural societal features that mould social and economic conduct in a manner that goes beyond the doings of a single individual or collective. As such, they embody a certain continuity, even if, over time, they are in turn redefined through both agents and wider environmental circumstances. Whilst this very loose definition may be broadly acceptable to those operating from a range of different perspectives, there is, as will become apparent through this volume, much debate beyond this. Individual chapters will provide further insight into specific institutional features and questions, but this broad introduction serves to highlight schools of thought, and their relative applicability to understanding differences in HRM according to context. In this review, we focus primarily on different conceptualizations within the broad literature on political economy that accord specific attention to the role of the state and differences on national lines. Whilst we recognize that the more sociological approaches in the tradition of Powell and DiMaggio (1991) may have relevance in understanding how actors opt for familiarity in different settings, and how this may serve to reinforce any differences within and between settings, our focus in this book is on understanding national differences.

Institutions and Private Property Rights

A dominant approach within the economics and finance literature is one that prioritizes the role of institutions in the protection of private property rights. From a starting point that assumes that individuals and firms constitute rational actors, it is held that institutions are providers of incentives or disincentives to the latter (Goergen et al. 2009; Peters 2005); some institutional features may encourage optimal choices, and others sub-optimal ones. What is really important here is an underlying ideological assumption that the role of the state should be primarily one of a 'nightwatchman', a guardian of individual rights and, above all, the right to private property (Peters 2005; North 1990). Associated with this is the similarly ideologically-rooted assumption that nations with strong private property rights will perform better, in terms of generating wealth, than those without. Hence, in comparing national institutional features, the most important question is what aspects of institutions are most central in protecting private property, with subsidiary issues about the mechanisms through which this translates into stronger economic growth. In an influential account, North (1990) provided a broad foundation for subsequent comparative institutional analysis in this tradition, refining and loosely substantiating this general case.

However, it was left to Rafael La Porta and colleagues associated with Chicago to provide more detail on what precisely is the institutional foundation of property rights (1999). Quite simply, they suggest that it is the law and, more specifically, legal origin; common law systems are defined by a focus on case law, underpinned by basic assumptions as to the inalienability of core rights, above all, private property ones. In contrast, civil law systems are characterized by systematically weaker property rights, with the role of the legal system being defined by a desire to reconcile opposing interests. At firm level, this enables and encourages managers to engage and collude with employees, to the detriment of shareholders (see also Goergen et al. 2009).

Four broad conclusions are drawn from this. The first is that common law systems are bound to perform very much better than civil law ones (La Porta et al. 1999). In support of this argument, the authors provide some comparative economic evidence, although the conclusions they desire are greatly facilitated by the inclusion of the Francophone (civil law) West African states, who battle with severe physical, environmental and, indeed, historical legacies of brutal, externally led resource expropriation. Again, the time period covered by their review is rather selective, focusing on the latter 1980s and 1990s, which, together with the early 2000s, constituted the heyday of neo-liberalism. A comparative analysis conducted prior to or post this period would yield very different results.

A second conclusion is that institutional arrangements are hierarchical (see Boyer 2006). By this, it is meant that a single institutional feature over-codes all others. In practical terms, this means that the legal origin will, in turn, affect how all other institutions work, and any effects of the latter will be over-ridden by relative differences in property rights (Goergen et al. 2009). Again, this assumption could be contested. In many contexts, it is not just formal property rights under the law that matter, but how they may be exercised in practice. For example, in much of the Mediterranean world, worker rights are largely ignored by smaller and medium firms and not enforced there by the state. Conversely, the relative power of property owners may be stronger than a scrutiny of the countries' civil law origins and subsequent legislation might suggest; this would even encompass the relative proportion of profits paid back to the state in the form of taxation.

Third, these approaches assume that owner and worker rights are a zero-sum game (Goergen et al. 2009). In practical terms, it is assumed that in contexts where property owner rights are weaker, worker rights will be stronger, and vice versa (Botero et al. 2004). What this would suggest is that, at any particular time, organizational resources and external environmental conditions will lead to the generation of a finite amount of value which has to be, in some or other way, shared out, with inevitable losers and winners. A problem with this approach is that it assumes that labour in general, and human capabilities specifically, can be readily costed out, and can only be harnessed through clear incentives and disincentives, forcing individual employees to exert maximum effort for wages defined in external market terms. In reality, individuals and collectives may be motivated by a wide range of factors; and human capabilities are flexible and intangible (Aoki 2010). We do not deny that class conflict is a feature of capitalism but, by the same measure, as the regulation theorists remind us, compromises between classes and interest groupings are an essential feature of trajectories of accumulation (Lipietz 2001; Boyer 2006). In practical terms, this means that there is the possibility for compromise, synergies or complementarities, the latter being a situation where the outcomes are greater than a sum of the inputs would suggest (Crouch 2005). Indeed, much of the literature on HRM, since the early days (see for example Pfeffer 1996; Kochan and Osterman 1994; Osterman 1999), is precisely about understanding the circumstances under which such synergies may arise, and which HRM practices are most likely to unleash and sustain them.

The fourth conclusion that can be reached is that the legal origins approach is one that completely denies the possibility of diversity within national settings, whilst legal origin itself is seen as a coherent phenomenon. However, the reality is somewhat different. Within the UK, for example, whilst England may represent the epitome of common law, Scotland has a hybrid legal system incorporating civil law features (Deakin et al. 2007). This might explain the social democratic drift of Scotland in recent years, but would not explain the hard neo-liberalism imposed on that country during the Thatcher years or, indeed, changes in the fluctuations in union fortunes across the United Kingdom at large. Again, although La Porta et al. (1999) do recognize that some countries have weaker or more diluted forms of civil law than others, they discount the extent to which some aspects of law may be closer to the civil law model, and some to the common law model within a single country. A good example of this would be South Africa, which has a legal system somewhat akin to that of Scotland (Deakin et al. 2007; Deakin and Sarkar 2008). This has meant that the relative regulation of labour is in some areas closely defined according to explicit legislation, and in others left to case law.

Why, then, should we bother about La Porta et al. at all? One reason is that this approach has been undeniably influential and has impacted on the policy prescriptions of bodies such as the World Bank; its 'Doing Business Report' condemns countries with specific legal traditions and associated legislation as poor environments in which to do business (Cooney et al. 2010). Empirical evidence to the contrary may not shake ideological certainty, but does contribute to the development of effective counter-narratives. Second, the law may exert effects even if not on the lines suggested by La Porta et al. (Deakin and Sarkar 2008). Worker rights do matter, enforcement capabilities notwithstanding. In fundamentally disagreeing with the view that workers represent little more than greedy conspirators, seeking to extract more from property owners than is their due, it could be argued that worker rights will deter owners from the most exploitative short-termist strategies. In turn, this will encourage more intelligent utilization of labour, which will result in mutually beneficial long-term gains, even if the short-term costs would otherwise have made such an endeavour unattractive.

Another way of conceptualizing national differences in property rights is in terms of electoral systems. Pagano and Volpin (2005) argue that 'first-past-the-post' electoral systems are most effective in securing property rights. In such systems, political parties concentrate their attentions on ideologically uncommitted swing voters. The latter are unlikely to identify with the working class, and may be swayed by issues that leave fundamental questions surrounding property rights untouched. Furthermore, it could be argued that such voters are likely to be affected by expensive electoral campaigning and, hence, monied interests. In practical terms, most liberal market economies/Anglo-Saxon style economies do have first-past-the-post electoral systems, and most continental European countries have proportional ones. There is, at first glance, considerable evidence that can be marshalled in support of the consequences of electoral systems. Worker rights are indeed stronger in more proportional ones. Ireland's neo-corporatist experiments represented in part, a product of electoral realities. New Zealand's move to a more proportional system (in return, prompted by right wing governmental excess) has forced the main right wing party to adopt more moderate policies in government. That party's hostility to the MMP proportional system, and its failed attempt to scrap it, reflects the pressures towards coalition building embodied in such systems. However, this perspective does not explain why Ireland periodically undergoes periods of extreme neo-liberalism; again, the Quebec question forces Canadian governments onto more conciliatory paths than its first-past-the-post electoral system might suggest.

What does this mean for comparative HRM? In more proportional systems, neo-corporatist deals are more likely. In turn, this will lead to a more entrenched role for unions in such contexts, with inevitable pressures towards plant level co-determinist and supplemental bargaining structures. In contrast, in first-past-the-post systems, there will be less pressure on governments to engage in coalition building; hence, right wing governments will have a freer hand to impose their agendas in favour of the wealthy and the powerful. Left wing governments will be deterred from imposing worker-orientated agendas for fear of the uncommitted swing voter and in order to ensure adequate electoral finances to help sway those voters. Hence, moves to extend worker rights and restrain the hand of property owners will be muted. However, as can be seen from the above examples, electoral systems are neither immutable nor always exert consistent effects. At the same time, this would explain the importance of electoral reform, if the zero-sum assumptions of the rational–hierarchical property rights tradition are discounted. The more progressive HRM literature would suggest that compromises between workers, managers and owners are possible, and that this may lead to complementarities and, hence, more beneficial outcomes than if each party had pursued its own selfish interest.

In contrast to the above two approaches which focus on structural institutional features, Roe (2003a and 2003b) argues that it is political party ideologies and, more specifically, that of the ruling party, which really matter. Again, it is assumed that right wing parties, in their primary concern with property owner rights, will generate better economic outcomes, a point that can be contested on account of the vast structural contradictions such governments tend to engineer and the problems that these store up. Thatcher may have had the good fortune to have a North Sea windfall to fuel a boom in financial speculation, but this left the UK with all the adverse consequences of the resource curse, and, indeed, an uncontrollably voracious and often destructive financial services industry.

This is not to deny that politics matter. As Gourevitch and Shinn (2007) note, politics plays a central role in corporate governance. As Goergen et al. (2013) reveal, firms are more likely to lay off workers under right wing governments, than under left wing ones. However, in other areas of HRM practice, the effects of politics appear rather less pronounced. This may reflect the extent to which the espoused policies of political parties may vary from their actual practice. Indeed, as Streeck (2009) argues, much of the blame for the present crises can be placed at the door of the political classes at large and the failure of electoral politics. Hence, in concluding that political realities may mould work and employment relations (and firm conduct at large), a focus on formal ideologies of governments may discount structural political failures, and the extent to which politicians regardless of stated policy preferences may be co-opted to suit the interests of an emerging oligarchy.

Comparative Capitalism and HRM

The broad socio-economic literature on comparative capitalisms also embodies certain inherent (if, at times, implicit) assumptions as to the relative desirability of specific national growth trajectories. In a rather similar way to the legal theorists and the electoral systems theorists, and leading to some similar groupings, a key distinction is made between lightly regulated liberal markets and more coordinated alternatives. Although the highly influential Hall and Soskice (2001)

Varieties of Capitalism collection suggests that each of these two alternative models may be relatively viable, the bulk of work in this tradition suggests that a greater degree of coordination, or state mediation of market excess, is likely to lead to more stable growth, and secure skilled middle income jobs (c.f. Lincoln and Kalleberg 1990; Dore 2000; and see Chapter 9 here). In contrast, more liberal markets are likely to be associated with a greater volatility, and with more pronounced labour market segmentation between a generically skilled and well rewarded elite, and a large workforce confined to lower end work.

In practical terms, it is held that more coordinated markets will be associated with more developed industry-specific skills bases, stronger national labour movements, more developed plant and/or industry level bargaining, and workplace level structures for co-determination. In contrast, lightly regulated liberal markets are associated with a greater degree of individual contracting, lower levels of worker participation or involvement in work organization, weak vocational, but developed generic tertiary skills bases and weaker trade unions. However, the evidence supporting such assumptions has tended to post-date the original theoretical predictions; the mainstream Varieties of Capitalism literature has tended to rely on broad societal level indices supplemented with selective case study evidence.

The Cranet data, as subsequent chapters will illustrate, provides broad firm level evidence to support these assumptions. At the same time, it does highlight limitations of this approach. The liberal-coordinated market dichotomy does not encompass the Mediterranean world and Eastern Europe, yet the surveys confirm that these countries have very distinct features. Indeed, the surveys highlight much diversity within the coordinated market camp. In more recent extensions of the Varieties of Capitalism approach, other archetypes have been identified to cover the Mediterranean (Mixed Market Economies) and Eastern Europe (Emerging Market Economies) states (Hancke et al. 2007).

However, it is assumed firstly that all countries can be ranked along a polar scale with Coordinated Market Economies (CMEs) at one end and Liberal Market Economies (LMEs) at the other and second, that those in the middle, which fit neither stereotype, will have fewer inherent complementarities and hence will either have to evolve in the direction of one or the other or be doomed to underperform. Whilst there may be arguments that the MMEs and EMEs, for example, confirm that Hall and Soskice (2001) prediction, the same cannot be said of the Nordic or Social Democratic Economies. On some measures these have consistently outperformed the United States of America, for example, despite being clearly distinct from the LME or the CME ideal types.

In fact, again as borne out by the Cranet evidence, both these categories are themselves diverse, and appear to have strong tendencies to distinct development, rather than convergence. Countries can change according to their own trajectories without necessarily having to fit along a CME–LME polarity. Perhaps the most promising way forward here is literature that provides a closer exploration of the institutional features of the SDEs and of the patterns of change in Eastern and Central Europe that have come closer to one or other of the mature models (Slovenia, Slovakia, Estonia) (see Lane and Myant 2007; Frane et al. 2009). It is not just these transitional economies that are changing either: a study of successive waves of the Cranet data (see Mayrhofer et al. 2011, and here Chapter 8) suggests that firm level practices everywhere tend to change over time; national archetypes are not static, nor immune from rupture. In contrast, the mainstream Varieties of Capitalism literature suggests strong path dependence.

Business Systems Theory has often been conflated with the Varieties of Capitalism approach, but focuses much more on the state, and its role in facilitating societal trade-offs and, indeed, its potential in terms of neo-corporatist deals and active industrial policies (Hancke et al. 2007). As part of this relationship it pays more attention to the formal regulation of the employment relationship. Business Systems Theory proposes a wider range of archetypes, including the developed economies of the Far East, and regions within countries that have very distinct characteristics of their own, most notably northern Italy. A further strength of Business Systems Theory is the closer attention it gives to the case of MNCs, the latter being the subject of Chapter 10 in this volume. More specifically, Business Systems Theory suggests that some production regimes are more likely to exert a stronger modifying or localizing effect on MNCs than others, on account both of the specific advantages (e.g. skills and suppler networks) that may be accrued in adapting to fit in with them, and the extent to which this may help leverage access to specific markets (Whitley 2010). This suggests a mixed relationship between country of origin and domicile, a finding borne out by the empirical results presented in Chapter 10.

There are two major limitations to Business Systems Theory as a framework for comparative analysis here. First, it is assumed that the Nordic countries and continental Western Europe constitute a distinct category when, as can be seen from the evidence presented across this volume, these two regions are in many respects distinct. Such differences would include important variations in skills and in training systems (in the Nordic countries, vocational training is less developed, but there is often better access to lifelong learning in alternative skills sets), job tenure (which is generally weaker in the Nordic countries than in many of the western continental economies and especially so in the 'flexicurity' economy of Denmark) and relative union power (which is noticeably stronger in the Nordic countries). Second, as a result this approach has accorded little attention to the Nordic countries and even less to much of the Mediterranean (with the exception of northern Italy).

An alternative multi-archetype approach is that of Amable (2003), an approach that is rooted in the comparative capitalisms literature but draws heavily on regulationist thinking and historical institutionalism. Amable (2003) highlights five distinct archetypes. In addition to liberal markets, he argues the developed economies of the Far East and the Mediterranean constitute archetypes in their own rights. Crucially, he draws a distinction between the coordinated economies of continental Europe and the social democratic model (for which he uses the epithet 'Scandinavia' even though he includes Finland), on account of differences in a wide range of economic and societal features. As may be seen from subsequent chapters, it is this framework that comes closest to predicting what types of HRM practices may be encountered where.

Should we then have confined our analysis to Amable's categorizations? A limitation of the Amable groupings is that his country categorization is largely the result of a cluster analysis of broad economic and societal features. In comparing his categories with firm practices, it could be argued that one is simply comparing one set of empirical evidence (largely external to the firm) with another (in-firm practices) and that, perhaps, one could dispense with the theory altogether. Hence, we do not believe that Amable's account represents the definitive country classification. Indeed, certain firm level HRM practices (for example, redundancies) are more easily explained by other societal features – in this case, ideologies of ruling parties (Goergen et al. 2013). Again, Amable's account does not take account of the tendency towards greater diversity within some of his categories, and ignores central and eastern Europe altogether, when the evidence of successive waves of the surveys (and, indeed broader political and economic developments) would indicate that countries such as Slovenia, Estonia, Poland and Ukraine are all embarking on radically different paths. Finally, recent theoretical (Lane and Wood 2009; Wood and Lane 2012) and empirical evidence (Brewster et al. 2006; Brewster et al. 2013) have pointed to much diversity within national capitalist archetypes. What this literature suggests is that the diversity is not diffuse, but rather bounded, with specific sets of practices and clusters of practices being encountered within different locales and industries. Such diversity may reflect distinct historical experiences, differing sets of complementarities, industry and region specific intra-firm networks, and the uneven nature of systemic change (Crouch and Voelzkow 2004). Whilst national categorizations remain invaluable, further comparative analysis within and between archetypes may shed new light on all these phenomena.

Institutional effects are temporally and spatially specific (Boyer 2006). Moreover, at differing times, the same institutional feature may yield very different outcomes (Hollingsworth 2006). There is a wide range of possible causes of institutional change, ranging from technological advances, to changes in the political balance of power, to long term shifts in resource availability and costs. Here it is worth noting that, since the 1970s, energy inputs have become more volatile and costly, which in turn, has altered the relative competitiveness of specific industries, regions and nations (Wood and Lane 2012). In turn, this favours the interests of owners of highly fungible assets (rentiers, etc.) over those with less fungible ones (workers and more patient investors). Associated with this has been the global ecosystemic dominance of neo-liberalism (Jessop 2012). Does this mean that, at firm level, HRM practices are becoming uniformly more akin to those in the LMEs? The Cranet surveys do point to certain continuities throughout the crisis-ridden 2000s (organization-specific employee voice mechanisms remain stronger in more coordinated markets), but at the same time, there are some visible changes (for example, to greater numerical flexibility within firms).

Defining Features of HRM

To answer the question of how developments in market economy types impact HRM we first have to ask what constitutes the defining features of HRM? There are three broad approaches that might be adopted. The first would be simply to explore all the functional areas of people management in sequence, an approach somewhat akin to that adopted by most leading HRM textbooks. However, this does not encompass all dimensions of the operationalization of the employment contract, an example being different ways in which the working day may be configured, the subject here of Chapter 7. A second way might be to break up the different dimensions of work and employment relations. However, this may mean that one gets bogged down in comparing differences in wage rates versus relative costs of living, and in terms of subtle differences in the utilization of specific technologies. A third way, suggested by Whitley (1999), is to focus on two dimensions, interdependence between employer and employee, and the amount of delegation to the latter. The former concerns security of tenure and relative investment in people, whilst the latter concerns relative employee voice. Again, this distinction has considerable value, but it may not take full account of the complexities of national difference. For example, firms may spend a great deal on training in contexts characterized by high commitment, but broadly similar amounts when commitment is low and staff turnover high, necessitating significant spending on basic induction training (see Chapter 6). Hence, it is not just the resources that are devoted to training that matter, but the content and typical duration of that training. The relative utilization of temporary working may reflect a screening process, with most such workers moving on to highly secure jobs, or a structural addiction to insecure labour. In this volume, we explore a wide range of different approaches to comparing and contrasting people management, informed by these different starting points, highlighting the relative strengths and weaknesses of each in comparing and contrasting key dimensions of HRM.

Key Issues and Themes

In the subsequent chapters we return to these theoretical debates, comparing and contrasting HRM policies and practices within and between alternative capitalist archetypes. This first chapter and Chapter 2 which introduces the broad methodology of the Cranet surveys, Chapter 3 which covers recruitment and selection, and Chapter 11 on HRM outsourcing, are newly written for this book. The other chapters draw on material that has been published previously:

- Chapter 4 *Variations in Financial Participation in Comparative Context*, has been covered in articles drawing on Cranet data, by Pendleton, Poutsma, Brewster and van Ommeren (2002) but is mostly developed from Croucher, R., Brookes, M., Wood, G. and Brewster, C. (2010) 'Context, strategy and financial participation: A comparative analysis', *Human Relations* 63: 835–55 although it also uses more recent Cranet data. Further analysis on the topic is also available in Le, Demirbag, Wood and Brewster (2013).
- Chapter 5 *Is There Convergence Towards Individual Voice in Europe?* draws on Brewster, C., Brookes, M., Johnson, P. and Wood, G. (2013) 'Direct involvement, partnership and setting: A study in bounded diversity', *International Journal of Human Resource Management* (forthcoming, ISSN 0958-5192). Further analysis can be found in Brewster, Brookes, Croucher and Wood (2007) and Brewster, Wood, Croucher and Brookes (2007).

- Chapter 6 *Corporate Governance Systems and Investments in Human Capital* uses material from Goergen, M., Brewster, C., Wood, G.T. and Wilkinson, A. (2012) 'Varieties of capitalism and investments in human capital', *Industrial Relations* 51(2): 501–27 and from Goergen, M., Brewster, C. and Wood, G. (2009) 'Corporate governance and training'. *Journal of Industrial Relations* 51(4): 461–89 ISNN 0022-1856.
- Chapter 7 *Context and Working Time: Diversity in Practice* draws heavily on Richbell, S., Brookes, M., Brewster, C. and Wood, G. (2011) 'Non-standard working time: an international and comparative analysis', *International Journal of Human Resource Management* 22(4): 945–62.
- Chapter 8 *Diversity Between and Within Varieties of Capitalism* has been developed from Walker, J.T., Brewster, C. and Wood, G. 'Diversity between and within varieties of capitalism: Transnational survey evidence', *Industrial and Corporate Change* 23(2): 493–533.
- Chapter 9 *Institutions, Labour Management Practices and Firm Performance in Europe* uses the analysis in Rizov, R. and Croucher, R. (2009) 'Human resource management and performance in European firms', *Cambridge Journal of Economics* 33(2): 253–72 and has been largely written by Marian Rizov and Richard Croucher. Other papers applying the Cranet data to the HRM/performance debate include Apospori, Nikandrou, Brewster and Papalexandris (2008); Cunha, Cunha, Morgado and Brewster (2002); Stavrou, Brewster and Charalambous (2010) and Stavrou and Brewster (2005).
- Chapter 10 *What Role do MNCs Play in Different Market Economies?* has been developed from analyses in Farndale, Brewster and Poutsma (2008), but mainly from Brewster, C., Wood, G. and Brookes, M. (2008) 'Similarity, isomorphism or duality: recent survey evidence on the HRM policies of multinational corporations', *British Journal of Management* 19(4): 320–42.
- Chapter 11 *How Much Does Country Matter? A Cross-national Comparison of HRM Outsourcing Decisions* is written specifically for this book and draws on work by Michael Mol, who was instrumental in the writing of the chapter.

We have not been able to include in this book all the analyses of the Cranet that use the institutional framework. For those who are interested, other material is available in books edited by Lazarova, Morley and Tyson (2012) and by Parry, Stavrou and Lazarova (2013) and in Croucher, Wood, Brewster and Brookes (2012), Goergen, Brewster and Wood (2013), Johnson, Wood, Brewster and Brookes (2009), Mayrhofer, Brewster, Morley and Ledolter (2011), Stavrou, Brewster and Charalambous (2010), Vernon and Brewster (2012), Wood, Croucher, Brewster, Collings and Brooks (2009) and, indeed, in other texts (see the Cranet website www.cranet.org).

Conclusion

This chapter introduces the different ways in which variations in firm level practices according to national setting may be explained. As can be seen from the above, no single approach is without limitations or contradictions. At the same time, each has some merit in explaining the relative incidence of some or other dimension of firm level HRM practice in a particular locale. This would confirm the view that institutions are polyvalent, and that their effects vary not only according to setting, but also according to specific dimensions of human and organizational relations. The Cranet surveys point to both continuity and change; however, the empirical findings on which this book is based predate the 2008 economic crisis. It is likely that the effects of the latter may be towards greater experimentation in national settings, and, more generally, towards more insecure and contingent working. The extent to which conventional political processes have largely failed to generate viable electoral alternatives to parties broadly espousing neo-liberalism would suggest that, in the short term, espoused ideologies and electoral mechanisms will continue to exert a weak effect.

References

Amable, B. (2003) *The Diversity of Modern Capitalism*. Oxford: Oxford University Press.

Aoki, M. (2010) *Corporations in Evolving Diversity: Cognition, Governance and Institutions*. Oxford: Oxford University Press.

Apospori, E., Nikandrou, I., Brewster, C. and Papalexandris, N. (2008) 'HRM and organizational performance in northern and southern Europe', *International Journal of Human Resource Management* 19(7): 1187–1207.

Botero, J., Djankov, S., La Porta, R., Lopez-de-Silenes, S. and Shleifer, A. (2004) 'The regulation of labor', *Quarterly Journal of Economics* 119: 1339–82.

Boyer, R. (2006) 'How do institutions cohere and change', in G. Wood and P. James (eds) *Institutions and Working Life*. Oxford: Oxford University Press.

Brewster, C., Brookes, M. and Wood, G. (2006) 'Varieties of capitalism and varieties of firm', in G. Wood and P. James (eds) *Institutions, Production and Working Life*. Oxford: Oxford University Press.

Brewster, C., Brookes, M., Croucher, R. and Wood, G. (2007) 'Collective and individual voice: Convergence in Europe?', *International Journal of Human Resource Management* 18(7): 1246–62

Brewster, C., Brookes, M., Johnson, P. and Wood, G. (2013) 'Direct involvement, partnership and setting: A study in bounded diversity', *International Journal of Human Resource Management* (forthcoming, ISSN 0958-5192).

Brewster, C., Wood, G., Croucher, C. and Brookes, M. (2007) 'Are works councils and joint consultative committees a threat to trade unions? A comparative analysis', *Economic and Industrial Democracy* 28(1): 53–81.

Brewster, C., Wood, G. and Brookes, M. (2008) 'Similarity, isomorphism or duality: recent survey evidence on the HRM policies of multinational corporations', *British Journal of Management* 19(4): 320–42.

Cooney, S., Gahan, P. and Mitchell, R. (2010) 'Legal origins, labour law and the regulation of employment relations', in A. Wilkinson and M. Townshend (eds) *The Future of Employment Relations: New Paradigms, New Developments*. London: Palgrave Macmillan.

Crouch, C. (2005) 'Three meanings of complementarity', *Socio-Economic Review* 3, 2: 359–63.

Crouch, C. and Voelzkow, H. (2004) 'Introduction', in C. Crouch, P. Le Galès, C. Trigilia, and T.H. Voelzkow (eds) *Changing Governance of Local Economies*. Oxford: Oxford University Press.

Croucher, R., Brookes, M., Wood, G. and Brewster, C. (2010) 'Context, strategy and financial participation: A comparative analysis', *Human Relations* 63: 835–55

Croucher, R., Wood, G., Brewster, C. and Brookes, M. (2012) 'Employee turnover, HRM and institutional contexts', *Economic and Industrial Democracy* 33(4): 605–20.

Cunha, R.C., Cunha, M.P., Morgado, A. and Brewster, C. (2002) 'Market impacts on strategy, HRM practices and organizational performance: Toward a European model', *Management Research* 1(1): 79–91.

Deakin, S. and Sarkar, P. (2008) 'Assessing the long-run economic impact of labour law systems: A theoretical reappraisal and analysis of new time series data', *Industrial Relations Journal* 39: 453–87.

Deakin, S., Lele, P. and Siems, M. (2007) 'The evolution of labour law', *International Labour Review* 146(3–4): 133–62.

Delbridge, R., Hauptmeier, M. and Sengupta, S. (2011) Beyond the enterprise: Broadening the horizons of International HRM', *Human Relations* 64(4): 483–505.

Dore, R. (2000) *Stock Market Capitalism: Welfare Capitalism*. Cambridge: Cambridge University Press.

Farndale, E., Brewster, C. and Poutsma, E. (2008) 'Co-ordinated vs liberal market HRM: The impact of institutionalisation on multinational firms', *International Journal of Human Resource Management* 19(11): 2004–23.

Frane, A., Primoz, K. and Matevz, T. (2009) 'Varieties of Capitalism in Eastern Europe (with special emphasis on Estonia and Slovenia)', *Communist and Post-Communist Studies* 42(1): 65–81.

Goergen, M., Brewster, C., Wood, G.T. and Wilkinson, A. (2012) 'Varieties of capitalism and investments in human capital', *Industrial Relations* 51(2): 501–27.

Goergen, M., Brewster, C. and Wood, G. (2009) 'Corporate governance regimes and employment relations in Europe', *Industrial Relations/Relations Industrielles*, 64(6): 620–40.

Goergen, M., Brewster, C. and Wood, G.T. (2013) 'The effects of the national setting on employment practice: The case of downsizing', *International Business Review*. 22(6):1051–1068.

Gourevitch, P.A. and Shinn, J. 2007. *Political Power and Corporate Control: The New Global Politics of Corporate Governance*. Princeton, MA: Princeton University Press.

Hall, P. and Soskice, D. (2001) 'An introduction to the varieties of capitalism', in P. Hall and D. Soskice (eds) *Varieties of Capitalism: The Institutional Basis of Competitive Advantage*. Oxford: Oxford University Press.

Hancke, B., Rhodes, M. and Thatcher, M. (2007) 'Introduction'. In B. Hancke, M. Rhodes and M. Thatcher (eds) *Beyond Varieties of Capitalism: Conflict, Contradiction and Complementarities in the European Economy*. Oxford: Oxford University Press.

Hollingsworth, J. Rogers (2006) 'Advancing our understanding of capitalism with Niels Bohr's thinking about complementarity', in G. Wood and P. James (eds) *Institutions and Working Life*. Oxford: Oxford University Press.

Jessop, B. (2012) 'The world market, variegated capitalism and the crisis of European integration', in P. Nousios, H. Overbeek, and A. Tsolaskis (eds), *Globalisation and European Integration: Critical Approaches to Regional Order and International Relations*: 91–111. Abingdon: Routledge.

Johnson, P., Wood, G.T., Brewster, C. and Brookes, M. (2009) 'The rise of post-bureaucracy: Theorists' fancy or organizational praxis?', *International Sociology* 24(1): 37–61.

Kochan, T.A. and Osterman, P. (1994) *Mutual Gains Enterprise. Forging a Winning Partnership among Labor, Management and Government*. Cambridge, MA: Harvard Business School Press.

La Porta, R., Lopez-de-Silanes, F. and Shleifer, A. (1999) 'Corporate ownership around the world', *The Journal of Finance* 54(2): 471–517.

Lane, D. and Myant, M.R. (eds) (2007) *Varieties of Capitalism in Post-Communist Countries*. Basingstoke: Palgrave Macmillan.

Lane, C. and Wood, G. (2009) 'Diversity in capitalism and capitalist diversity', *Economy and Society*, 38(4): 531–51.

Lazarova, M.B., Morley, M.J. and Tyson, S. (eds) (2012) *International Human Resource Management: Policy and Practice.* Abingdon, Routledge.

Le, H., Demirbag, M., Wood, G. and Brewster, C. (2013) 'Management compensation In MNCs: Some empirical evidence', *Management International Review.* 53(5): 741–762.

Lincoln, J. and Kalleberg, A. (1990) *Culture, Control and Commitment: A Study of Work Organization in the United States and Japan.* Cambridge: Cambridge University Press.

Lipietz, A. (2001) 'The fortunes and misfortunes of post-Fordism', in R. Albritton, M. Itoh, R. Westra and A. Zuege (eds), *Phases of Capitalist Development, Booms, Crises and Globalizations.* Basingstoke: Palgrave.

Mayrhofer, W., Brewster, C., Morley, M. and Ledolter, J. (2011) 'Hearing a different drummer? Evidence of convergence in European HRM', *Human Resource Management Review* 21(1): 50–67.

North, D.C. (1990) *Institutions, Institutional Change and Economic Performance.* Cambridge: Cambridge University Press.

Osterman, P. (1999) 'Securing prosperity: new rules for a new economy', *Working USA. The Journal of Labor and Society* 3(4): 5–8.

Pagano, M. and Volpin, P. (2005) 'The political economy of corporate governance', *American Economic Review* 95: 1005–30.

Parry, E, Stavrou, E. and Lazarova, M.B. (eds) (2013) *Global Trends in Human Resource Management.* New York: Palgrave Macmillan.

Pendleton, A., Poutsma, E., Brewster, C. and van Ommeren, J. (2002) 'Employee share ownership and profit sharing in the European Union: Incidence, company characteristics and union representation', *Transfer* 8(1): 47–62.

Peters, G. (2005) *Institutional Theory in Political Science: The New Institutionalism.* London: Continuum.

Pfeffer, J. (1996) *Competitive Advantage through People: Unleashing the Power of the Work Force.* Cambridge, MA: Harvard Business School Press.

Powell, W. and DiMaggio, P. (1991) *The New Institutionalism in Organizational Analysis.* Chicago, IL: University of Chicago Press.

Richbell, S., Brookes, M., Brewster, C. and Wood, G. (2011) 'Non-standard working time: an international and comparative analysis', *International Journal of Human Resource Management* 22(4): 945–62.

Rizov, R. and Croucher, R. (2009) 'Human resource management and performance in European firms', *Cambridge Journal of Economics* 33(2): 253–72.

Roe, M. (2003a) *Political Determinants of Corporate Governance.* Oxford: Oxford University Press.

Roe, M. (2003b) 'Modern politics and ownership separation', in J. Gordon and M. Roe (eds), *Convergence and Persistence in Corporate Governance.* Cambridge: Cambridge University Press.

Stavrou, E.T. and Brewster, C. (2005) 'The configurational approach to linking strategic human resource management bundles with business performance: Myth or reality?', *Management Revue* 16(2): 186–201.

Stavrou, E., Brewster, C. and Charalambous, C. (2010) 'Human Resource Management and firm performance in Europe through the lens of business systems: Best fit, best practice or both?', *International Journal of Human Resource Management* 21(7): 933–62.

Streeck, W. (2009) *Reforming Capitalism: Institutional Change in the German Political Economy*, Oxford: Oxford University Press.

Vernon, G. and Brewster, C. (2012) 'Structural spoilers or structural supports? Unionism and the strategic integration of HR functions', *International Journal of Human Resource Management* 24(6): 1113–30.

Walker, J.T., Brewster, C. and Wood, G. 'Diversity between and within varieties of capitalism: Transnational survey evidence', *Industrial and Corporate Change* 23(2): 493–533.

Whitley, R. (1999) *Divergent Capitalisms: The Social Structuring and Change of Business Systems*. Oxford: Oxford University Press.

Whitley, R. (2010) 'The institutional construction of firms', in G. Morgan, J. Campbell, C. Crouch, O.K. Pederson and R. Whitley (eds) *The Oxford Handbook of Comparative Institutional Analysis*. Oxford: Oxford University Press.

Wood, G. and Lane, C. (2012) 'Institutions, change and diversity', in C. Lane and G. Wood (eds) *Capitalist Diversity and Diversity within Capitalism*. London: Routledge.

Wood, G.T., Croucher, C., Brewster, C., Collings, G.C. and Brookes, M. (2009) 'Varieties of firm: Complementarity and bounded diversity', *Journal of Economic Issues* 43(1): 241–60.

2 Researching Comparative Institutional Contexts

MICHAEL BROOKES, GEOFFREY WOOD,
CHRIS BREWSTER AND RICHARD CROUCHER

The purpose of this chapter is to enable the reader to achieve a clearer understanding of many of the empirical findings reached in the subsequent chapters. It focuses upon the data that is used as well as the empirical methods that are applied, explaining each in the necessary detail required in order to evaluate the findings and claims made in the later chapters.

As indicated in the first chapter, this book explores the institutional basis of business and management and particularly the relationships within the firm that Whitley (1999) and others have seen as indicative of the different forms that business within a society can adopt. These relationships are often studied by human resource management (HRM) specialists and therefore our text contributes both to a deeper understanding of the overall institutional bases of business within a society and to the way that human resources are managed in each society.

The need for comparative human resource management, the study of differences between societies in the way that they handle these issues, was flagged up in the earliest textbooks on the topic. Thus, the classic text by Beer et al. (1984) defined human resource management as having clear contextual elements, so that we should expect it to vary as the institutional background within which it was located varied. However, over the following years an almost obsessive concentration on 'strategic HRM' with a focus on what managements could do to improve their handling of HRM as a result of the research, meant that a universalistic view of the subject (Brewster, 1999) came to dominate the discourse, the journals and the teaching. In recent years however the growth of a more critical approach to HRM (see eg Delbridge et al., 2011; Thompson, 2011) and the increasing internationalisation of research have led to the development of comparative HRM as an academic topic (Brewster and Mayrhofer, 2012). The subject is now researched and taught on ever greater numbers of courses. Some of this research (see eg Budhwar and Sparrow, 2002; Easterby-Smith et al., 1995; Warner and Zhu, 2002) focuses on the cultural differences between societies. This book concentrates on the institutional differences. We hope therefore to provide part of the response to the call (Delbridge et al., 2011) to broaden the debate.

Most studies of HRM take place within a single national country and therefore have little or nothing to say about differences between countries (even if the commentaries on the research sometimes assume that any lessons drawn from such studies can be universally applied). In such studies the impact of contextual factors such as the size of the organisation or the sector (or sectors) in which it operates have been noted but national differences have, perforce, been ignored. It now seems increasingly obvious that to ignore such differences is to misunderstand the generalisability of the learning from such studies. In reality, in different nations there are differences in what HRM means, what criteria it is judged against and how it is practised. One authority has argued that given the differences in national context 'it seems unlikely that one set of HRM practices will work equally well no matter what the context' (Gerhart, 2005: 178).

In 1999 Clark et al. argued that after 20 years of research into international and comparative HRM the subject was 'running on the spot'. The problems they identified included limited coverage of various parts of the world and a lack of conceptual analysis. An extensive research project looking at peer-reviewed articles published in the years from 1990 to 2005 (Mayrhofer and Reichel, 2009) confirmed their analysis: the comparative HRM research was typically empirical rather than conceptual; focused on country, organisation or individual as the primary units of analysis; used cross-sectional 'snapshot' rather than longitudinal (i.e. panel or trend study) designs; and focused on comparison of one or more sets of HRM practices, such as recruitment, or described correlations between HRM and output measures such as satisfaction, performance or commitment. The research was indeed centred on a small number of mainly developed countries. This analysis is becoming increasingly outdated. Coverage of an ever wider range of countries has become a feature of even the English language journals now and, as we shall show later in this text, the institutional literature used over the past seven or eight years provides a solid conceptual basis even if it remains far from providing a consistent or complete analysis.

Comparative HRM is now a well-established field of enquiry (see eg the contributions on comparative HRM in overview works on HRM/international HRM such as Collings and Wood, 2009; Harzing and Pinnington, 2010; Sparrow, 2009). Comparative HRM studies are not easy. They have all the difficulties of studies of HRM in one country but magnified by the different requirements for data collection, data storage and analysis in each country. Understanding HRM in one country is difficult enough but to understand it in two, three or even many other countries is a severe challenge. One way around these issues – of data collection and analysis – is team-work: teams of researchers from different countries working together to collect and attempt to understand the evidence.

One such team is the Cranet network (for details see www.cranet.org). Having started in 1989 with a first survey of five countries, the network has expanded and spread. It now covers a wide group of different countries (see Table 2.1 below), though with a particular strength in Europe. Coordinated by Cranfield School of Management, Cranet consists of an academic partner in each of a number of countries. These partners meet regularly to design research questionnaires and to discuss findings. The partners are all self-funding and hence the network is not able to operate as a standard bureaucracy. Rather it works more like a club, in which members can join if the existing members agree but in which there are no penalties if they leave or allow their membership to become inactive (Mayrhofer, 1998). Partly in order to reduce the danger of ethnocentricity, the questionnaire is designed anew for each round of the survey with members from a variety of different countries in the design team. In practice, most of the questions remain the same, for reasons of comparability over time. The questionnaire is designed in English and then translated and back-translated (Brislin, 1976; Brislin et al., 1973) into the local language or languages for each country. Problems in ensuring that the selection and interpretation of topic areas are not biased by one country's approach, as well as problems related to the translation of concepts, are largely overcome by close collaboration between business schools located in each country (for a detailed description of the Cranet approach, see Brewster et al., 2004; Brewster et al., 2011; Mayrhofer, 1998). It is a substantial questionnaire and there are signs of reducing response rates, although the fact that the last round of the survey went out as the 2008 economic crisis was beginning to hit organisations across the world may have had something to do with that. Currently, there is a debate within the network about how to improve response rates.

The questionnaire was originally targeted at organisations with more than 200 employees, because that was what the literature said was the limit at which formal HRM departments (the intended recipients of the questionnaire) were to be found. However, it quickly became apparent that this threshold was too high and, particularly as a number of countries with generally smaller organisations joined the network, the threshold was reduced to organisations with 100 or more employees. In practice, there are always a number of organisations below that size that respond, and whilst these are often used in local analyses they are generally discounted for the comparative studies.

The survey is distributed to senior human resource management specialists in representative national samples of firms with more than 100 employees. Overall more than three quarters of the respondents fall firmly into this category and many of the others are either CEOs (of smaller businesses) or the only HRM person in the organisation.

The questionnaire attempts as far as possible to gather data that is factual; that is, it explores policies or practices by asking either yes/no questions or asking for numbers. Opinions are not sought. Small scale pilot surveys carried out by the Swiss partners found no statistically significant difference between the answers of the senior HRM specialist and those of the CEOs from the same firms, which is to be expected if they are reporting on the existence or non-existence or the percentages of visible practices. Similarly, there is evidence (Wall et al., 2004) that if sufficiently knowledgeable people are asked about, for example, firm performance measures, their responses will not be statistically different from an examination of reported measures (such as turnover or profits). Because measures such as profitability are subject to issues of exchange rates and fiscal systems which means that the 'raw' figures cannot be compared across national boundaries, perceptual measures are preferable for cross-national comparisons (Lahteenmaki, et al., 1998; Stavrou and Brewster 2005).

The survey covers public and private sector organisations, analysed according to the European Union's NACE categories of industries. It aims to be representative of the economy of each country (obviously above 100 employees), so that if the country has a larger public sector or a larger manufacturing sector, then so should the Cranet sample. The partners work hard to achieve this and broadly speaking are successful. In most countries the database for the survey is a full-population listing – every organisation with 100 or more employees. Although the response rate for the individual countries is relatively low, mostly between 10 and 20 per cent, compared to targeted research elsewhere, this is considerably above the response rates used for the vast majority of full population surveys. Analyses of earlier Cranet surveys suggest that its statistical representativeness is not impaired (Brewster et al., 1994).

As can be seen from the definitions above, Cranet is not a panel survey. It aims to ensure that the responses are broadly representative (above the size threshold) for each economy – as these change, so the survey changes. For example, the privatisation of public services in some countries has meant that recent surveys have a smaller percentage of public sector organisations in them. The alternative approach – panel surveys – was rejected for a number of reasons. First, our interest is in comparing policies and practices between countries; as panel surveys would not allow us to replicate the shape of each national economy as it changes and hence would become increasingly un-representative, it would be inappropriate. In the first Cranet surveys there were few high-tech IT companies because few existed then. It is obviously important, since we want to draw comparisons between countries, that the samples do broadly represent the changing nature of societies. Second, whilst panel surveys make sense for individuals they make a lot less sense for organisations, since organisations rarely remain the same for long. Thus, around a third of the organisations responding in each round report that they have been involved in major merger and acquisition or divestment activities. Apart from the fact that this would mean that our sample would decay dramatically over three rounds, it is clear that these 'same' organisations would in fact be very different beings.

Cranet is now an acknowledged leader in all aspects of international human resource management, both theoretical and practical, with a distinguished reputation worldwide and with a string of articles in the top ranked international journals. The Cranet data is a long-running and wide-ranging data set focusing upon HRM practices within a large number of institutions in, now, over 40 countries. Table 2.1 below records the number of responses from each country included in the survey for each of the available years.

Data

This book is heavily reliant upon data collected by the Cranet International Network and all the empirical chapters make use of the Cranet data.

Table 2.1 CRANET Responses per Country/Year

Country / Year	1989	1990/1	1992/3	1995/6	1999/2000	2004/5	2008/9
Australia	—	—	—	—	240	259	110
Austria	—	—	169	—	230	270	203
Belgium	—	—	—	393	282	230	240
Bulgaria	—	—	—	—	150	157	267
Canada	—	—	—	—	—	456	—
Cyprus	—	—	—	—	91	85	90
Czech Republic	—	—	170	—	188	72	54
Denmark	—	749	329	725	520	516	362
Estonia	—	—	—	—	218	118	74
Finland	—	—	225	322	290	293	136
France	1525	1185	651	514	400	140	157
BRD (West Germany)	516	1008	884	457	503	347	420
GDR (East Germany)	—	—	202	223	240	—	—
Greece	—	—	90	—	136	180	214
Hungary	—	—	—	—	—	59	139
Iceland	—	—	—	—	—	114	138
Ireland	—	—	140	359	446	—	103
Israel	—	—	—	—	194	175	114
Italy	—	203	—	108	79	117	157
Japan	—	—	—	—	847	—	389
Lithuania	—	—	—	—	—	—	119
Nepal	—	—	—	—	—	204	—
Netherlands	—	225	127	322	234	397	116
New Zealand	—	—	—	—	—	286	—
Northern Ireland	—	—	—	—	201	—	—
Norway	—	327	280	507	391	303	98
Philippines	—	—	—	—	—	56	33
Portugal	—	—	93	—	169	—	—
Russia	—	—	—	—	—	—	56
Serbia	—	—	—	—	—	—	50
Slovakia	—	—	—	—	—	259	225
Slovenia	—	—	—	—	205	161	219
South Africa	—	—	—	—	473	—	192
Spain	383	346	264	265	294	158	—
Sweden	334	368	322	367	352	383	282
Switzerland	—	299	—	249	168	311	99
Taiwan	—	—	—	—	373	—	229
Tunisia	—	—	—	—	64	189	—
Turkey	—	—	123	206	258	171	—
Turkish Cypriot community	—	—	—	—	61	87	60
UK	2591	1557	1248	1289	1091	1101	218
USA	—	—	—	—	—	260	1052
Total	**5349**	**6267**	**5317**	**6306**	**9388**	**7914**	**6415**

Source: Cranet 2012

Regression Modelling

The empirical analysis undertaken in the subsequent chapters makes use of a number of statistical techniques seeking to model the complex interactions that take place within organisations. The most commonly used approach to the empirical modelling is to apply a linear regression model. This estimates a particular measurable outcome as a linear function of those factors most likely to influence that outcome: the particular outcome under consideration being the dependent variable and those factors influencing the outcome being the independent or explanatory variables. Here, the empirical model is estimated, using ordinary least squares, with the dependent variable being a function of the explanatory variables. These functions are of the form;

$$W = \alpha + Z'_{i}, \beta + u_{i} \quad,$$

where; W = the dependent variable,
α = the intercept term,
Z'_{i} = a vector of explanatory variables,
β = a vector of coefficients on the explanatory variables,
and u_{i} = a disturbance or error term.

In statistics and mathematics, linear least squares is an approach to fitting a mathematical or statistical model to data in cases where the idealised value provided by the model for any data point is expressed as a linear function of the unknown parameters of the model. The resulting fitted model can be used to summarise the data, to predict unobserved values from the same system, and to understand the mechanisms that may underlie the system.

Probit/Logit Modelling

The linear regression models however are only applicable when the outcome under consideration can be measured on a continuous scale. Many of the topics explored in this book are dichotomous in their nature, i.e. a particular type of behaviour or action is observed or it isn't. In such cases these outcomes tend to be measured using a binary, rather than a continuous, variable and the empirical model is estimated using a logit or probit model. The principle is that for each set of circumstances, defined by the explanatory variables, the probability of each of the two outcomes is estimated and combined to create a probability density function. Some explanatory models of these key questions were estimated, as the dependent variable for most of these was binary, this is done using probit or logit modelling. The probit or logit model is estimated by maximum likelihood and has just two outcomes 0 and 1, representing, for example, no union recognition or union recognition. Based on the normal distribution the probit model is represented by;

$$\text{Prob}(Y=\text{recognition}) = \Phi \beta'x. \quad \text{(Greene 2003: 666)}$$

Where Φ is the standardised normal distribution, β' is the vector of estimated coefficients from the model and x is the vector of explanatory variables. Hence, in this example, the probability of each firm having union recognition is estimated as a non-linear function of the explanatory variables and their estimated coefficients. The logit model would estimate the model in a similar fashion, the only difference being that the model is based on the logistic distribution and hence the logit model is represented by;

$$\text{Prob}(Y = \text{recognition}) = \Lambda(\beta'x). \qquad \text{(Greene 2003: 667)}$$

Where Δ is the logistic distribution, β' is the vector of estimated coefficients from the model and x is the vector of explanatory variables.

Scaling

In addition, some of the empirical modelling makes use of scaling techniques, reflecting the complex nature of some of the relationships within HRM and borrowing ideas from psychology to represent certain types of behaviour or views as a summation of the responses to a number of key questions. Because of the complexity of the issues, any simplistic single measure will fail to capture its nature effectively, so a series of dichotomous variables indicating the extent of involvement are used. The scale is constructed using Mokken's non-parametric model for one-dimensional cumulative scaling (Sijtsma and Molenaar, 2002). This generates a scale ranging from 100 for those organisations recording 'yes' for all the included items, zero for those recording all 'no' answers and a position somewhere in between for the vast majority of organisations, with their relative position in the scale being determined by their number of positive responses and the relative scarcity of positive responses to each of those survey questions. The scale is then used as the dependent variable within an empirical model where the scale is regressed, using ordinary least squares, upon those variables deemed likely to promote or discourage that type of view or behaviour within the organisation. Within comparative HRM this follows the same approach as Gooderham et al. (1999) who calculated the extent of calculative HRM using a Mokken scale.

A Mokken scale builds on the idea of cumulativeness in Guttman's approach, but the probabilistic nature of Mokken's model allows for non-perfect response patterns. The probability of success (score '1') on a particular item depends on the subject's (organisation's) location on the latent trait, and is called its item response function (IRF). These functions may have the shape of a logistic curve. This is assumed in the parametric IRF models where the item responses for different items differ only in the parameters of the logistic curve. Mokken's model of monotone homogeneity poses no other restrictions than increasing IRFs and is designed to order subjects on the latent trait (Sijtsma and Molenaar, 2002). A Mokken scale is non-parametric in the sense that the IRF curve does not have to have a special form. This makes the model very flexible, but also implies that neither the subject (firm) parameters nor the item parameters may be estimated directly. However, the unweighted sum of item scores is monotonously related to the latent true score (Sijtsma and Molenaar, 2002: 15). This means that the Mokken model only provides estimates of scale scores at an ordinal level, whereas parametric IRF models allow for direct estimation of the true scores.

However, the strong assumptions of the latter models contribute to limiting their applicability.

The primary scaling criterion is Loevinger's H coefficient of homogeneity. This is defined as: $H_{ij} = 1 - (F_{ij} / E_{ij})$, where F_{ij} is the sum of observed errors according to the Guttman scale model (i.e., the observed number of respondents who give a negative response to the 'easier' item and a positive response to the more 'difficult' item), and E_{ij} is the expected number of errors assuming that the responses to the items are independent across persons and that the marginal distributions are fixed (Sijtsma and Molenaar, 2002). In the same way, the scalability of a single item with respect to the other items is defined by H_i, and the scalability of the total scale is measured by H. A set of items constitutes a scale if all $H_{ij} > 0$, and if every item coefficient of scalability, H_i, is larger than a constant c, set to at least 0.30. All H_i and the H should be significantly greater than zero according to a given level of significance.

Factor and Cluster Analysis

Factor analysis is also applied in a number of chapters, a technique that attempts to reduce a set of variables to a smaller number of hypothetical variables. The basic assumption is that there are some underlying factors (and, hence, an underlying social phenomenon) which are smaller in number than the number of observed variables, and which are responsible for the covariation among those observed variables.

In simple terms, factor analysis poses the question, how can we replace a large set of variables by a smaller set which best summarises the larger set? Principal component analysis presents this problem in a mathematical sense so that we look to reduce p variables to a set of m linear functions of those variables which best summarise the original p, therefore implying that m principal factors can best summarise the original data. The attendant problem is that the number of principal components (m) cannot be known in advance, hence some form of acceptance criterion needs to be adopted. For this analysis the commonly used Kaiser's rule which states that the number of principal components (m) is equal to the number of eigen values >1, is applied. The reasoning is that since an eigen value is the amount of variance explained by one more factor it makes little sense to add a factor that explains less variance than is contained in one variable.

Results from this type of analysis can be very difficult to interpret, since in many cases it is unclear which of the original variables relates to each factor. As a result factor analysis is generally refined using a technique known as rotation. In simple terms, this seeks to associate each original variable with one factor. In this analysis the commonly used Varimax rotation is applied, a technique that searches for a linear combination of the original factors so that the variance of the loadings is maximised, with the loadings being the correlations between the original variables and the components extracted by the process.

In summary factor analysis is a way of uncovering underlying dimensions within a set of data. It uses that data as a means of finding clusters of variables or factors by looking at shared variances, as well as enabling the factors explaining little variance to be discarded.

There is also one empirical chapter that makes use of cluster analysis and although this is not in any way derived from factor analysis the overall purpose is broadly the same. Undertaking cluster analysis is an attempt to group together objects that display similar features and generally large amounts of data can be reduced to a relatively small number of clusters in a similar fashion that would happen in factor analysis, the key difference being that in cluster analysis the similarities are based on the distance between the different outcomes, normally expressed using the standard deviation of the relevant variables, whilst within factor analysis it is based on the correlations between the variables.

Conclusion

Although there are many attempts to compare national institutional characteristics in terms of broad societal features, there have been far fewer systematic comparisons based on firm level practices. This chapter provides a detailed account of both the empirical basis of the comparisons in this volume and the principle analytical tools deployed. A distinguishing feature of the Cranet surveys is that they are designed by a multi-cultural team and conducted by an independent team of academics, the results are analysed in multi-cultural teams and experts from each country are available to explain the results. By obtaining credible data on policies and practices within the firm, we are able to address many of the institutional debates that have heretofore tended to rely on either (non-generalisable) case studies or (external) aggregate data about firm activities. The results, as you can see, provide both support for and challenges to the existing institutional analyses.

References

Beer M., Spector B., Lawrence P.R., Quinn Mills, D. and Walton R.E. (1984) *Human Resource Management*. New York: Free Press.

Brewster, C. (1999) 'Different paradigms in strategic HRM: Questions raised by comparative research', pp. 213–38 in P.M. Wright, L.D. Dyer, J.W. Boudreau and G.T. Milkovich (eds) *Strategic Human Resource Management Research in the Twenty First Century, Personnel and Human Resource Management*, Supplement 4. Stamford, CT: JAI Press.

Brewster, C., Hegewisch, A., Mayne, L. and Tregaskis, L. (1994) 'Methodology of the Price Waterhouse Cranfield project' in Brewster, C. and Hegewisch, A. (eds), *Policy and Practice in European Human Resource Management*. London: Routledge.

Brewster, C. and Mayrhofer, W. (eds.) (2012) *Handbook of Research on Comparative Human Resource Management*. Cheltenham, Glos: Edward Elgar.

Brewster C., Mayrhofer, W. and Morley, M. (eds) (2004) *Human Resource Management in Europe: Evidence of Convergence?* Oxford: Elsevier/Butterworth-Heinemann.

Brewster, C., Mayrhofer, W. and Reichel, A. (2011) 'Riding the tiger? Going along with

Cranet for two decades – a relational perspective', *Human Resource Management Review* 21(1): 5–15.

Brislin, R.W. (1976) *Translation: Applications and Research*. New York: John Wiley.

Brislin, R.W., Lonner, W. and Thorndike, R.M. (1973) *Cross-Cultural Research Methods*. London: Wiley Inter-science.

Budhwar, P. and Sparrow, P.R. (2002) 'An integrative framework for understanding cross-national human resource management practices', *Human Resource Management Review* 12(3): 377–403.

Clark T., Gospel, H. and Montgomery, J. (1999) 'Running on the spot? A review of twenty years of research on the management of human resource in comparative and international perspective', *International Journal of Human Resource Management* 10(3): 520–44.

Collings, D.C. and Wood, G.T. (2009) *Human Resource Management: A Critical Approach*. London: Routledge.

Delbridge, R., Hauptmeier, M. and Sengupta, S. (2011) 'Beyond the enterprise: Broadening the horizons of international HRM', *Human Relations* 64(4): 483–505.

Easterby-Smith, M., Malina, D. and Yuan, L. (1995) 'How culture-sensitive is HRM? A comparative analysis of practice in Chinese and UK companies', *International Journal of Human Resource Management* 6(1): 31–59.

Gerhart, B. (2005) 'Human resources and business performance: Findings, unanswered questions, and an alternative approach', *Management Revue* 16: 174–85.

Gooderham, P.N., Nordhaug, O. and Ringdal, K. (1999) 'Institutional and rational determinants of organizational practices: Human resource management in European firms', *Administrative Science Quarterly* 44: 507–31.

Greene, W.H. (2003) *Econometric Analysis (5th edn)*. New Jersey: Prentice Hall.

Harzing, A-W. and Pinnington, A.H. (2010) *International Human Resource Management*. London: Sage.

Lahteenmaki, S., Storey, J. and Vanhala, S. (1998) 'HRM and company performance: The use of measurement and the influence of economic cycles', *Human Resource Management Journal* 8(2): 51–65.

Mayrhofer, M. (1998) 'Between market, bureaucracy and clan: Coordination and control mechanisms in the Cranfield Network on European Human Resource Management (Cranet-E)', *Journal of Managerial Psychology* 13(3/4): 241–58.

Mayrhofer, M. and Reichel, A. (2009) 'Comparative analysis of HR', pp. 41–62 in P.R. Sparrow (ed.) *Handbook of International Human Resource Management: Integrating People, Process and Context*. Chichester: John Wiley.

Sijtsma, K. and Molenaar, I.W. (2002) *Introduction to Nonparametric Item ResponseTheory*. London: Sage.

Sparrow, P.R. (ed.) (2009) *Handbook of International Human Resource Management: Integrating People, Process and Context*. Chichester: John Wiley.

Stavrou, E.T. and Brewster, C. (2005) 'The configurational approach to linking strategic human resource management bundles with business performance: Myth or reality?', *Management Revue* 16(2): 186–201.

Thompson, P. (2011) 'The trouble with HRM', *Human Resource Management Journal* 21(4): 355–67.

Wall, T.D., Michie, J., Patterson, M., Wood, S.J., Sheehan, M., Clegg, C.W. and West, M. (2004) 'On the validity of subjective measures of company performance', *Personnel Psychology* 57(1): 95–119.

Warner, M. and Zhu, Y. (2002) 'Human resource management "with Chinese characteristics": A comparative study of the People's Republic of China and Taiwan', *Asia Pacific Business Review* 9(2): 21–42.

Whitley, R. (1999) *Divergent Capitalisms: The Social Structuring and Change of Business Systems*. Oxford: Oxford University Press.

3 Understanding Contextual Differences in Employee Resourcing

GEOFFREY WOOD, CHRIS BREWSTER,
MEHMET DEMIRBAG AND MICHAEL BROOKES

This chapter provides an overview of differences in the predominant ways of recruiting and selecting people in different national contexts. Recruitment can be defined as 'the different activities of attracting applicants to an organization'; the recruitment process seeks to draw in pools of suitable candidates who have the potential to make a meaningful contribution to the goals of the firm (Gold 2003: 226). Selection 'consists of sifting through the pool of applicants and making decisions about their appropriateness' (Bloisi 2007: 107); the aim is to match individuals within those pools to the job (Heraty and Morley 1998: 662). The process may be one aimed at choosing individuals for essentially probationary positions, or to fill vacancies for either short term needs or long term goals (Favell 2008: 141). Drawing on the Cranet dataset, this chapter concentrates on differences within and across Europe, according particular attention to variations in practice between continental/Rhineland Europe, the Nordic countries, Mediterranean Europe and the liberal market economies of the United Kingdom.

Recruitment and Selection: Key Issues in Practice

Recruitment and selection provides the basis not just for the written employment contract but also the unwritten set of rules and expectations that go with the job (Gold 2003: 222). Recruitment and selection has an intricate relationship with many other employment practices and human resource management policies and practices within the firm discussed in other chapters. The source of employees is closely connected to the type of relationship the individual wants with the firm and vice versa (Searle 2009: 151) and has a significant impact on employee retention, since certain pools of potential candidates will be likely to be more mobile than others. It will also impact training – do the employees come to the firm already well-trained or needing development? It will impact skills levels. There will be a symbiotic relationship between resourcing and reward packages and there may also be a relationship with propensity to join trade unions. Hence, recruitment and selection is not just the first element of the relationship between an oragnization and its employees, but in many senses a crucial one.

The key stages of the recruitment process as proposed didactically in the literature are depicted in Figure 3.1.

These texts propose a rather formalistic process that perhaps very few organizations follow in detail. However, they are a good guide to the analytic stages of the process. Here the first step is job analysis: a review of what the job involves (Gold 2003). This is followed by the drawing up of a formal job description, in other words, what the post-holder should do or achieve (Favell 2008: 143). The person specification outlines the capabilities and characteristics of an ideal incumbent (Favell 2008: 143). Recruitment strategies may range from the use of head-hunters and recruitment agencies, through advertisements in the press, at jobs fairs or on websites to the use of informal networks relying on the contacts amongst family and friends of existing employees. Each of these strategies has benefits and disadvantages: the more formal mechanisms will avoid discrimination, will attract top quality employees and will prevent the 'cloning' of existing employees, but they will cost a lot of money. The more informal mechanisms provide more background on the potential employees, who in turn know more

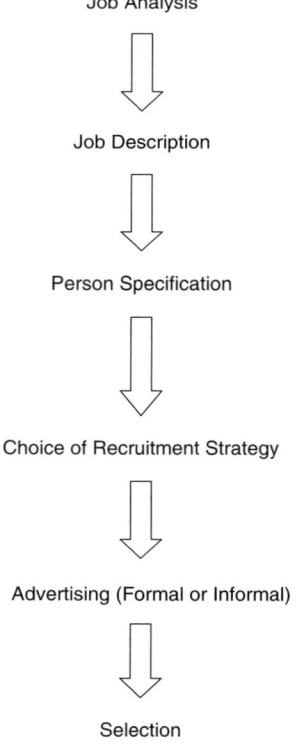

Job Analysis

Job Description

Person Specification

Choice of Recruitment Strategy

Advertising (Formal or Informal)

Selection

Figure 3.1 Stages of the Recruitment Process

about the firm and the staff appointed, have friends or relatives who are likely to closely scrutinize (and provide informal feedback) on the progress of their protégés so as not to jeopardize their own standing within the firm, and they are relatively cost-free and can be much quicker. However, they may reduce innovative thinking and they may risk discrimination (Russo et al. 1995: 6). Whether formal or informal, recruitment approaches may either aim to attract as broad a pool of applicants as possible or to narrowly target applicants more likely to be chosen as incumbents. Selecting those in a particularly poor bargaining position for 'McJobs' may be one way of cutting immediate wage costs, but is likely to be associated with high staff turnover rates.

In fact, the process delineated above is an ideal; in reality, many organizations will be a lot more ad hoc in their approach, and not proceed in such clear stages or may even skip stages altogether. And many firms do little to link recruitment and selection practice to overall organizational strategy (Heraty and Morley 1998).

Selection is different. As Russo et al. (1995: 8) note, there are two fundamental aspects to selection: individual and organizational. The former is about whether there is a fit between the personal attributes of the individual and the organization, whilst the latter is about skills and abilities, and the capacity for carrying out the job. There are many selection techniques: *inter alia* psychometric tests, assessment centres, the use of consultants, and interviews. Selection of the right applicant assumes that those doing the selection understand what the job is about (Heraty and Morley 1998: 664).

In a meta-analysis, Smith and Smith (2007) checked the validity of various selection techniques (whether they measure what they are supposed to) and found that none of them had a high return but that work samples, mental agility tests and structured interviews gave the best results. They also found that tests used incrementally gave better results than any single test. They found that interviews were poor predictors of subsequent performance (see also Gold 2003: 236).

The use of 'scientific' approaches such as psychometric tests and assessment centres (both of which Smith and Smith found had low validity) has varied over the years according to fad and fashion; recently, there seems to have been a return of interest in finding the right personal attributes (McCormack and Scholarios 2009: 73). Despite their scientific claims, the evidence to support the accuracy of psychometric tests is very mixed (Searle 2009: 161) and may fall into the category of pseudo-science rather than the real thing. A key problem is that managers do not really know what makes for success in a job. These tests are, as Gold (2003: 240) notes, based on the assumption that a narrow psychometric profile can tell the suitability of an individual for very complex jobs, whilst rendering the job applicant a passive provider of data. This may be why their popularity has been rhetorical rather than actual as far as the majority of organizations are concerned.

Organizations that take recruitment more seriously are likely to use more than one technique.

We expect that resourcing the right employees for organizations (their recruitment and selection) will vary with national context and will differ in different market economies.

Antecedents and Outcomes

What are the effects of context on the myriad of individual decisions that create an oragnization's approach to recruitment and selection? In general, employment legislation specifically tends to leave recruitment and selection largely unconstrained, though discrimination laws apply generally and in some countries there are limitations on the actions of recruitment agencies. It might therefore be argued that organizations have freedom to operate whatever recruitment and selection systems they wish. However, immediate legal provisions are not the only factors that may affect this particular area of human resource management. Do organizations use the full range of options they have or are they more likely in some settings to use a limited range? In other words, to what extent are their decisions constrained by the external antecedents of the decisions? We argue that the antecedents will include the legal system, the rather broader market economies and the use of flexible contractual policies by the organization. We also assume that there will be demographic features that will have an effect across these categories, particularly firm size, sector and industrial differences.

The Effect of the Legal System

Since much of the suggested effect of context on recruitment practices centres on the ability of organizations to correct 'mistakes' later by dismissals or radical redeployment, it implies that understanding differences in the law and legal traditions is of great importance. La Porta et al. (1999; 2002) argue that the principal distinction here is between common law and civil law legal traditions. In the former, a key strand has been the protection of private property rights, whilst in the latter it has been the use of the law to promote social solidarity or some broader socio-political agenda. As law within common law countries tends to be of the broad brushstroke variety, relying on the decisions of the courts to 'flesh out' the detailed meaning in specific circumstances (and with judges directed to follow the precedent of previous decisions in reaching their own) plaintiffs are more likely to have to resort to litigation to enforce – or even get a definitive interpretation on – their rights (Wood et al. 2004). Employers are more likely to have greater resources at their disposal and so be better equipped to fight legal action. Even if an individual employee is successful in her or his litigation, this is likely to prejudice the employment relationship, if, indeed, the individual chooses to stay in the job; there are many ways an employer may retaliate against a 'difficult' worker that are hard to prove. Botero et al. (2004) note that individual job protection under the law is generally weak in common law countries and stronger in civil law ones. La Porta et al. (1999) distinguish three legal sub-categories within the broad civil law compass: French civil law, German law and 'Scandinavian' law. In the former, property rights are likely to be weakest.

As employment protection is likely to impinge on the rights of owners to make use of their property in the manner they wish, La Porta et al. (1999) assume that in contexts where property rights are strong, employment protection is likely to be weak (Botero et al. 2004). This 'zero sum' view ignores the notion of complementarity: the argument that practices may work better than their component parts, allowing for mutually beneficial outcomes (c.f. Crouch 2005). Even negative consequences of specific institutional features may encourage complementarities in other areas. For example, good vocational skills bases afford German workers a good degree of marketability within industries, encouraging greater job mobility than would be suggested through a consideration of the degree of formal job protection afforded (Crouch 2005).

The La Porta et al. argument however leads us to our first proposition:

> *Proposition 1: Legal system is likely to help determine selection and recruitment practice: where job protection is stronger, firms are more likely to devote more resources to recruitment and selection, reflected in the usage of multiple methods.*

The Effect of Comparative Capitalisms

Law is only one way in which societies have been categorized. A more encompassing set of theories is covered by the rubric of comparative capitalism. There are, as indicated in Chapter 1, a number of different conceptions of the way that market economies may be differentiated. Hall and Soskice's (2001) approach is a dichotomous one; the main distinction drawn is between liberal and coordinated market economies. When considering employee resourcing – recruitment and selection (and careers generally) – a more detailed differentiation such as those in Whitley (1999) and Amable (2003) may be more useful.

In terms of recruitment and selection, in the Liberal Market Economies (LMEs) insecure contracting, weaker technical skills bases (meaning that the bulk of the labour force is in a relatively poor bargaining position) and a tendency of firms to rely on the external labour market mean that the hiring of labour is a relatively low risk process; candidates who prove to be 'unsuitable' can be more readily dispensed with (Hall and Soskice 2001; Thelen 2001; Marsden 1999). In the case of higher level jobs, a good generic tertiary skills base provides the foundation for high technology industry and services; industry specific skills are spread through high job mobility, with individuals rather than firms taking responsibility for their experiential development and marketability (Thelen 2001). Again, this would make the external labour market important; recruitment and selection will help winnow out those who have unsuitable skills and experience but, given relatively weak legal job protection, the risks of making a wrong decision are less than would otherwise be the case.

In the coordinated market economies (CMEs) employment rights are significantly stronger and, although it is certainly not impossible to push employees out of the organization, it is more difficult and more costly to get rid of them. Therefore, organizations are more likely to recruit carefully, perhaps using a wider range of methods, and more likely to emphasize those forms of recruitment and selection that research indicates are more likely to be effective or that managers have been persuaded are more 'sophisticated'. These might include selection techniques such as assessment centres and psychometric testing, but may also involve skills testing and initial recruitment to short term contracts so that managers can assess the individual in the workplace; in countries like Germany for example most people initially hired on short term contracts go on to obtain permanent employment contracts.

In the Nordic or Social Democratic Market Economies (SDEs) corporatist arrangements are both more dynamic and wider ranging (Harcourt and Wood 2003). Unemployment in these countries has been low over a number of decades, though of course with variations, but the pools of unconnected labour available for recruitment that exist in some other systems are limited. Those who are unemployed have some of the best social support from the state available anywhere in the world. Trade union membership is commonplace and the unions have broad general support. Education levels are high and in a meritocratic culture testing is widely accepted in many walks of life.

The Mediterranean or Mixed Market Economies (MMEs) have a high level of family ownership of even larger businesses and a more paternalistic management style. Over the decades these economies have had a variable record but generally unemployment has been a significant feature of the labour market, meaning unattached workers are readily available. Trade unions are weak, and education levels vary considerably within countries. It might be anticipated that personal networks and relationships will play a major role (Molina and Rhodes 2007).

The Emerging Market Economies (EMEs) of the ex-communist states in central and eastern Europe are becoming increasingly differentiated and have increasingly different labour markets. There has been a particular problem of unemployment in many of them. Trade unions in these states are weak, with the exception of Slovenia, but education levels have traditionally been high. The generic EME category may be breaking down as these states establish their own idiosyncratic trajectories (Babos 2010; Bandelj 2009; Brewster and Viegas Bennett 2010).

Based on Amable's (2003) categorization, it can be argued that the variety of capitalism will reflect recruitment practice.

> *Proposition 2: The variety of capitalism is likely to determine recruitment and selection practice: so that more care (a wider variety) of forms of recruitment and selection is likely to be more common in CMEs and SDEs, with less care (less variety) in MMEs and EMEs with least care (lowest variety) in LMEs.*

The effect of employment contract flexibility

If firms make greater use of temporary labour, then the risks associated with recruitment are likely to be less. Short-term employment gives managements a time period within which they can confirm whether the original hiring decision was a good one. If they decide it was, they can extend the contract, renew it or put the employee onto a permanent contract. Otherwise they can let the short term contract lapse.

> *Proposition 3: Greater usage of temporary and part time work means firms are less likely to devote more resources to recruitment and selection, reflected in the usage of multiple methods.*

The impact of recruitment and selection on employee turnover

As well as these antecedents, we were interested in the effect of recruitment and selection systems on employee turnover. The assumption here is that more attention to choosing the right candidate upfront is likely to reduce later turnover.

Proposition 4: When firms devote more resources to recruitment and selection, reflected in the usage of multiple methods, staff turnover is likely to be less.

Methods

This chapter focuses on organizations that can easily be categorized using Amable's (2003) classification for varieties of capitalism. The empirical analysis makes use of the Cranet survey 2008–09 data, which covers organizations with at least 100 staff in a total of 31 countries and focuses upon the 17 countries that unambiguously satisfy Amable's (2003) classifications. These being;

• Liberal Market Economies – USA, UK, Australia, Ireland, Israel
• Coordinated Market Economies – Austria, Germany, the Netherlands, Belgium
• Social Democratic Economies – Denmark, Sweden, Norway, Finland
• Emerging Market Economies – Hungary, Lithuania, Slovakia
• Mixed Market Economies – Greece.

The Cranet survey only enables quantitative measures of recruitment and selection to be explored, i.e. it only records the number of recruitment and selection methods used. There is no indication as to the quality of each of these methods within the individual firm. Hence there is a clear limitation to this particular analysis and an obvious target for future research. The data that is collected by the Cranet survey records the number of recruitment and selection methods that are used by the organization when appointing clerical staff. For each there are nine listed methods:

• Recruitment – Internal, Recruitment agencies/consultancies, Advertisement, Word of mouth, Vacancy page on company website, Vacancies on commercial job websites, Direct from educational institution, Speculative applications/walk-ins, Job centres/public recruitment agencies.
• Selection – Interview panel, One-to-one interviews, Application forms, Psychometric test, Assessment centre, Graphology, References, Ability tests, Technical tests.

As a quantitative measure for recruitment and selection each organization then has a score from 1 to 9, based on the number of methods they make use of, with this acting as a proxy for the amount of resources the firm puts into these two activities. To facilitate the empirical analysis the score from 1 to 9 is then reduced to a binary variable based upon whether the firm makes use of an above-average number of methods or not. Therefore each organization has two binary variables, one for recruitment and one for selection, which take the value of 1 if the number of methods used is above average and 0 if it is below average. These two variables are then used as the dependent variables in the empirical analysis, estimated using probit modelling and exploring the propositions outlined earlier in the chapter. Within these empirical models a number of controls are included as independent variables. First, size – measured by the total number of employees in the organization – is included since it is expected that larger firms are more likely to have dedicated HRM functions, hence it is expected that they will put relatively more resources into the recruitment and selection processes. Second, a dummy variable is included to separate public sector organizations from private sector ones; this controls for the possibility that the public sector has a different approach to recruitment and selection although no a priori expectations are assigned to this and it is simply a control. Third, 16 dummy variables are included representing the industry that each firm operates in and based upon the NACE industrial classification. It is expected that the different organization of production activities across industries, as well as the different demand and supply conditions present within each industrial labour market, is likely to lead to significantly different approaches to recruitment and selection. However, as with sector, no a priori expectations are assigned and they are merely included as a control.

In addition further variables are included to facilitate exploration of the various propositions outlined above. First, country dummies are included to highlight the impact of legal system upon recruitment and selection practice. Second, in a subsequent refinement to the model, the country dummies are reorganized by category to reflect the particular variety of capitalism and to enable the exploration of Proposition 2. Third, continuous variables are included reflecting the proportion of the workforce working part time or employed on a temporary or casual basis respectively, thus allowing Proposition 3 to be tested. Finally a further model is estimated, this time with average annual staff turnover as the dependent variable and estimated as a regression model using OLS, with recruitment and selection this time included as explanatory variables. Proposition 4 posits that putting greater resources into recruitment and selection is likely to lead to lower staff turnover and these models are able to test precisely these relationships.

Findings

For the first stage of the empirical analysis, regression models of the measures of recruitment and selection are estimated using the explanatory variables outlined in the previous section, and the results are recorded below in Table 3.1. First, in terms of the control variables, size is irrelevant to the recruitment process, but we can be fairly confident that larger firms tend to adopt a broader range of methods in the selection process. Furthermore, there is no significant difference between public and private sector firms in relation to the multiple methods applied to selection, however private sector firms tend to make greater usage of multiple methods in their approach to recruitment. Finally, in relation to industrial sector, there are a number of industries that differ significantly in terms of recruitment and/or selection in comparison to the metal manufacturing reference category.

Table 3.1 Regression Models by Legal System

Variable					
Constant	0.703***	7.15	0.481***	4.92	
Employment Conditions					
Total Employees (000s)	0.001	0.55	0.003*	1.91	2.754
Public Sector	−0.284***	−3.41	0.035	0.42	0.206
% Part-time Workers	0.001	0.47	0.002	0.71	10.970
% Temporary or Fixed-term	0.004**	2.26	0.002	1.00	11.594
Industry					
Agriculture, hunting, forestry, fishing	−0.714***	−2.93	−0.523**	−2.07	0.013
Energy and water	−0.023	−0.16	0.132	0.92	0.038
Chemical products	−0.120	−0.73	−0.017	−0.10	0.026
Other manufacturing	−0.190*	−1.90	−0.071	−0.69	0.110
Building and civil engineering	−0.177	−1.17	−0.218	−1.37	0.033
Retail and distribution; hotels; catering; repairs	−0.086	−0.73	−0.047	−0.39	0.071
Transport & communication	−0.018	−0.14	0.084	0.66	0.054
Banking; finance; insurance; business services	0.055	0.55	0.088	0.87	0.116
Personal, domestic, recreational services	0.163	0.60	0.548**	2.04	0.009
Health services	−0.149	−1.11	−0.103	−0.75	0.051
Other services	−0.012	−0.09	0.288**	2.04	0.040
Education	−0.265	−1.87	−0.250*	−1.71	0.051
Social services	−0.064	−0.32	−0.453**	−2.16	0.019
Public administration	−0.297**	−2.25	−0.202	−1.52	0.094
Other	−0.104	−1.07	−0.091	−0.91	0.136
Country					
Austria	0.198	1.51	−0.484***	−3.98	0.066
Australia	−0.285*	−1.73	−0.728***	−4.49	0.028
Denmark	−1.014***	−9.67	−1.353***	−12.28	0.105
UK	−0.120	−0.86	−0.032	−0.23	0.045
Ireland	−0.644***	−4.01	−0.411***	−2.59	0.029
Sweden	−1.609***	−12.64	−1.356***	−11.16	0.082
Israel	−0.664***	−2.68	−0.344	−1.38	0.010
Norway	−0.541***	−3.52	−1.329***	−7.65	0.031
Germany	−0.812***	−7.87	−1.298***	−12.15	0.132
Netherlands	−0.659***	−3.99	−1.731***	−8.47	0.028
Finland	−0.247*	−1.73	−0.440***	−3.14	0.041
Hungary	−0.775***	−5.29	−0.917***	−6.20	0.036
Belgium	−0.719***	−5.96	−0.435***	−3.63	0.069
Lithuania	−1.064***	−6.91	−0.945***	−6.14	0.035
Greece	−0.693***	−5.73	−0.727***	−6.01	0.064
Slovakia	−0.695***	−5.90	−0.921***	−7.72	0.073

Dependent Variable	Recruitment	Selection
Mean	0.492	0.387
Model Type	Probit	Probit
Observations	2851	2851
Log likelihood function	−1780.9	−1683.5
Restricted log likelihood	−1975.7	−1902.1
Chi-squared (35)	389.7	437.1

***, ** and * indicate significance at the 1%, 5% and 10% levels respectively.

Turning to the formal propositions, in Table 3.1 the country dummies are ordered based upon the Botero et al. (2004) categorization of employment regulation, hence the first country has the lowest level of employment protection and the last country the highest. In relation to the reference category of the USA, Austria is the only country with less employment protection than the USA, therefore all of the remaining countries have more protection, ranging from Australia which is only marginally higher, to Slovakia with the highest level of employment protection amongst these countries. The upshot of this is that in terms of the regression results, if Proposition 1 holds, there should be a clear relationship where for both recruitment and selection, as you get further away from the USA benchmark, the size and significance of the coefficients should increase and, in all cases excepting Austria, should be positive. Looking closely at the results indicates that Proposition 1 can be rejected on all levels as there is no clear relationship between employment protection and recruitment and selection.

To explore Proposition 2 the models are estimated again but on this occasion re-coding the country dummies into their varieties of capital categories, with the results recorded below in Table 3.2. These results indicate that although there is strong evidence of clear differences across the various types of economy the widest range of methods used for both recruitment and selection is clearly within the LME economies. This is the opposite of what the theory would predict and as a consequence Proposition 2 is also rejected.

Proposition 3 implies that there is a negative relationship between the use of part time and/or temporary workers and the amount of resources being devoted to recruitment and selection. In most cases, in terms of the number of methods used, the percentage of part time and temporary workers has no significant impact. However firms using a higher proportion of temporary or fixed term employees do have significantly higher usage of multiple methods, which is the opposite of what is predicted, hence it is impossible to accept Proposition 3 based on these results.

Finally, Proposition 4 suggests that there should be an inverse relationship between recruitment and selection and employee turnover, i.e. if greater resources are focused upon recruitment and selection, staff turnover rates should be lower. To explore this regression models are now estimated using staff turnover as the dependent variable and recruitment and selection as explanatory variables, with the results reported in Table 3.3. Recruitment has no discernible impact upon

Table 3.2 Regression Models by Variety of Capitalism

Variable	Coeff.	t-ratio	Coeff.	t-ratio	Mean
Constant	0.506***	6.49	0.333***	4.24	
Employment Conditions					
Total Employees (000s)	0.001	0.59	0.003*	1.94	2.399
Public Sector	−0.261***	−3.58	0.027	0.36	0.212
% Part-time Workers	0.001	0.42	0.002	0.87	9.812
% Temporary or Fixed-term	0.003**	2.23	0.000	0.04	11.321
Industry					
Agriculture, hunting, forestry, fishing	−0.744***	−3.98	−0.504***	−2.67	0.020
Energy and water	−0.014	−0.11	−0.053	−0.41	0.039
Chemical products	−0.108	−0.74	−0.065	−0.44	0.027
Other manufacturing	−0.186**	−2.09	−0.102	−1.11	0.115
Building and civil engineering	−0.330***	−2.63	−0.485***	−3.55	0.041
Retail and distribution; hotels; catering; repairs	−0.059	−0.59	−0.086	−0.83	0.080
Transport & communication	−0.057	−0.51	0.048	0.42	0.054
Banking; finance; insurance; business services	0.077	0.84	0.101	1.09	0.105
Personal, domestic, recreational services	0.372	1.47	0.700***	2.78	0.008
Health services	−0.136	−1.12	−0.106	−0.85	0.049
Other services	−0.030	−0.23	0.170	1.28	0.035
Education	−0.222*	−1.78	−0.215*	−1.68	0.052
Social services	0.197	1.11	−0.314*	−1.70	0.019
Public administration	−0.135	−1.17	−0.058	−0.49	0.093
Other	−0.072	−0.82	−0.055	−0.61	0.125
Economy type					
Continental European	−0.411***	−6.27	−0.748***	−11.37	0.309
Nordic	−0.822***	−11.78	−1.019***	−14.27	0.219
Mediterranean	−0.726***	−9.83	−0.764***	−10.31	0.193
Transitional	−0.605***	−6.36	−0.654***	−6.83	0.077
Dependent variable	Recruitment		Selection		
Mean	0.469		0.369		
Model type	Probit		Probit		
Observations	3369		3369		
Log likelihood function	−2195.9		−2069.3		
Restricted log likelihood	−2328.5		−2219.2		
Chi-squared (23)	265.7		299.8		

***, ** and * indicate significance at the 1%, 5% and 10% levels respectively.

Table 3.3 Regression Models of Annual Average Staff Turnover

Variable	Coeff.	t-ratio	Coeff.	t-ratio	Mean
Constant	10.778***	15.63	11.542***	16.94	
Employment Conditions					
Total Employees (000s)	0.044***	3.27	0.046***	3.39	2.064
Public Sector	−2.105***	−3.47	−2.148***	−3.55	0.205
% Part-time Workers	0.059***	3.62	0.059***	3.66	9.620
% Temporary or Fixed Term	0.076***	5.86	0.077***	5.89	10.803
Industry					
Agriculture, hunting, forestry, fishing	−2.745*	−1.96	−2.978**	−2.13	0.021
Energy and water	−2.389**	−2.31	−2.383**	−2.30	0.041
Chemical products	−0.806	−0.65	−0.850	−0.69	0.026
Other manufacturing	1.869***	2.54	1.817***	2.47	0.114
Building and civil engineering	3.444***	3.37	3.280***	3.20	0.042
Retail and distribution; hotels; catering; repairs	5.682***	6.75	5.652***	6.72	0.078
Transport & communication	1.108	1.20	1.111	1.20	0.056
Banking; finance; insurance; business services	1.753**	2.32	1.805**	2.38	0.106
Personal, domestic, recreational services	1.233	0.58	1.468	0.69	0.008
Health services	1.087	1.06	1.047	1.02	0.046
Other services	2.776***	2.49	2.806***	2.52	0.033
Education	−0.779	−0.75	−0.853	−0.82	0.049
Social services	1.082	0.73	1.064	0.72	0.018
Public administration	−0.477	−0.50	−0.509	−0.54	0.090
Other	1.985***	2.75	1.972***	2.73	0.127
Economy Type					
Continental European	−6.463***	−12.02	−6.729***	−12.34	0.317
Nordic	−2.691***	−4.59	−3.081***	−5.20	0.206
Mediterranean	−0.074	−0.12	−0.416	−0.68	0.194
Transitional	−6.738***	−8.47	−7.015***	−8.81	0.076
Recruitment/Selection					
Recruitment	0.516	1.36			0.474
Selection			−0.659*	−1.67	0.376
Dependent variable	Turnover		Turnover		
Mean	10.162		10.162		
Standard deviation	10.508		10.508		
Model type	OLS		OLS		
Observations	2873		2873		
R-squared	0.134		0.135		

***, ** and * indicate significance at the 1%, 5% and 10% levels respectively.

turnover but selection does have an effect upon staff turnover that is significant at the 10% level, therefore Proposition 4 can be at least partially accepted.

Conclusions

First, and as noted above, there is the issue of convention and expectation. Even if job protection is slight, in some contexts individuals and firms have greater expectations of security than in others; such expectations lower transaction costs and form part of the unwritten dimension of the employment contract (Marsden 1999). Second, whilst employment protection is likely to encourage firms and individuals to promote organization-specific human capital development (Harcourt and Wood 2007), other dimensions of the recruitment and selection process include the effects of the operation of social networks. This may contribute to the persistence of, for example, discriminatory practices even if they are formally outlawed.

Our measures of recruitment and selection practices may not be strong, in the sense that, first, we have no measures of the quality of the practices, only of their extent, and second, that the number of practices being used is a fairly crude measure of sophistication. It is clear that interview alone has little validity as a means of selection (Smith and Smith 2007), for example, and that since interviews are used by close to all organizations, adding other forms will improve validity. The value of the other forms, however, may depend on which other options are used. Nevertheless, the results show a clear distinction between types of legal system and different types of market economy in their use of recruitment and selection practices.

How do we explain the fact that the results generally seem to indicate that the differences are the opposite of the predictions? It may be that in the area of recruitment and selection, which is one of the more lightly regulated areas of HRM in all market economies, organizations feel less pressure to conform to any national recipe. In this area of HRM, firms have more autonomy than they have in others. There is therefore a tendency to accept the tried and trusted methods that are typical of that economy type. It is not unexpected, for example, to find that in the mainly family controlled MMEs, recruitment through family and friends plays a larger role and that therefore less attention is paid to other forms of recruitment.

What all the above points to is neither uniformity nor 'diffuse diversity' in recruitment and selection practices. However, the diversity is neither likely to be dichotomous (simply between liberal and coordinated markets) nor simply represent an inverse product of property rights under specific legal tradition. Bounded diversity there may well be, but it can be argued that sub-categories of nations within specific camps (e.g. civil law/coordinated market) may exhibit very distinct features, indeed so much so as to render very simplistic categorizations of little value.

References

Amable, B. 2003. *The Diversity of Modern Capitalism*. Oxford: Oxford University Press.

Babos, P. 2010. 'Varieties of capitalism in central and eastern Europe: measuring the co-ordination index of a national economy', *SEER Journal for Labour and Social Affairs in Eastern Europe*, 13(4): 439–58.

Bandelj, Nina. 2009. 'The global economy as instituted process: the case of Central and Eastern Europe', *American Sociological Review*, 74(1): 128–49.

Bloisi, W. 2007. *An Introduction to Human Resource Management*. Maidenhead: McGraw-Hill.

Botero, J., Djankov, S., La Porta, R. and Lopez-de-Silanes, F. 2004. 'The regulation of labor', *The Quarterly Journal of Economics*, 119: 1339–82.

Brewster, C. and Viegas Bennett, C. 2010. 'Perceptions of business cultures in Eastern Europe and their implications for international HRM', *Human Resource Management Journal*, 21(4): 2568–87.

Crouch, C. 2005. 'Three meanings of complementarity', *Socio-Economic Review*, 3 (2): 359–63.

Favell, I. 2008. 'Recruitment'. In M. Muller-Camen, R. Croucher and S. Leigh, *Human Resource Management: A Case Study Approach*. London: CIPD.

Gold, J. 2003. 'Recruitment and Selection'. In J. Bratton and J. Gold, *Human Resource Management: Theory and Practice*. London: Palgrave.

Hall, P. and Soskice, D. 2001. 'Introducing varieties of capitalism'. In P. Hall and D. Soskice, *Varieties of Capitalism*. Oxford: Oxford University Press.

Harcourt, M. and Wood, G. 2003. 'Under what circumstances do social accords work?', *Journal of Economic Issues*, 37(3): 747–67.

Harcourt, M. and Wood, G. 2007. 'The importance of employment protection for skill development in coordinated market economies', *European Journal of Industrial Relations*, 13(2): 141–59.

Heraty, N. and Morley, M. 1998. 'In search of good fit: policy and practice in recruitment and selection in Ireland', *Journal of Management Development*, 17(9): 662–85.

La Porta, R., Lopez-de-Silanes, F. and Shleifer, A. 1999. 'Corporate ownership around the world', *The Journal of Finance*, 54(2): 471–517.

La Porta, R., Lopez-de-Silanes, F., Shleifer, A. and Vishny, R. 2002. 'Investor protection and corporate faluation', *The Journal of Finance*, 57(3): 1147–70.

Marsden, D. 1999. *A Theory of Employment Systems: Microfoundations of Societal Diversity*. Oxford: Oxford University Press.

McCormack, A. and Scholarios, D. 2009. 'Recruitment'. In T. Redman and A. Wilkinson, *Contemporary Human Resource Management*. London: FT/Prentice Hall.

Molina, O. and Rhodes, M. 2007. 'The political economy of adjustment in mixed market economies: a study of Spain and Italy', pp 223–52 in B. Hancké, M. Rhodes and M. Thatcher (eds), *Beyond Varieties of Capitalism: Conflict, Contradictions and Complementarities in the European Economy*. Oxford: Oxford University Press.

Russo, G., Rietveld, P., Nijkamp, C. and Gorter, C. 1995. 'Issues in recruitment strategies: an economic perspective', *The International Journal of Career Management*, 7(3): 3–13.

Searle, R. 2009. 'Recruitment and selection'. In D. Collings and G. Wood, *Human Resource Management: A Critical Approach*. London: Routledge.

Smith, M.J. and Smith, P. 2007. *Testing People at Work: Competencies in Psychometric Testing*. Oxford: British Psychological Society/Blackwell.

Thelen, K. 2001. 'Varieties of labor politics in the developed democracies'. In P. Hall, and D. Soskice (eds), *Varieties of Capitalism: The Institutional Basis of Competitive Advantage*. Oxford: Oxford University Press.

Whitley, R. 1999. *Divergent Capitalisms: The Social Structuring and Change of Business Systems*. Oxford: Oxford University Press.

Wood, G., Harcourt, M. and Harcourt, S. 2004. 'The effects of age discrimination legislation on workplace practice', *Industrial Relations Journal*, 35(4): 359–71.

4 Variations in Financial Participation in Comparative Context

MICHAEL BROOKES, GEOFFREY WOOD AND
CHRIS BREWSTER

It is perhaps significant that whilst much of the comparative institutional literature focuses on contextual features exterior to the firm, some of the most extensive comparative theoretical accounts that focus on work and employment relations within the organization (see Whitley 1999; Dore 2000) neglect a key feature
of the employment contract: the amount of reward accruing to the employee and
the nature of how this is delivered. Yet, whilst other factors are important, central
to work in the modern economy is the nature and extent of financial reward. In
this chapter, we focus on differences in a particular aspect of financial reward
– financial participation – and how it varies according to context. We discuss the
rationales for financial participation, the forms it may take and then consider the
antecedents that may make financial participation more or less likely.

Rationale for Financial Participation

Financial participation represents the means by which employees have a stake
either in the physical ownership of the organization or its overall performance
(Kessler 2010: 338). As such it may provide employees with a direct reward in
the performance of the firm and, in providing the basis for broader staff engagement, with issues likely to impact on performance. Financial participation is
fundamentally different to voice based participation. The latter may be relatively
weak or strong, but in the end is a dynamic process, whose outcome directly
depends on the conscientious and immediate choices of employees. In contrast,
financial participation is rather less direct.

Although employees may choose to enhance their returns through working
harder, in many cases, any effect of financial participation is remote and indirect.
The outcome of some forms of employee participation may have no relationship
at all to individual effort. For example, in the case of share ownership schemes,

the shares may be held in trust, giving employees no say at AGMs nor the opportunity to readily and immediately trade them in. Moreover, the share price may have little do to with employees' efforts; it may, for example, be boosted through artificial measures such as share buy-backs which at least temporarily disengage stock market valuation from the real capabilities of the organization. Hence, as Wilkinson et al. (2010: 17) note, their effect on the employment relationship may be negligible or totally absent. Key issues encompass the relative liquidity of the payment (cash, shares, and whether or not the latter are held in trust), timescale (current or future benefits), closeness of the link between effort and outcome (direct or indirect), and perspective (past or projected future performance) (Kessler 2010: 340).

Although financial participation may form part and parcel of broader pressures towards greater contingency linking pay to effort, there are other reasons firms might make use of such systems. First, during historical moments where capital is particularly advantaged vis-à-vis labour, there are likely to be great crises of legitimation which, in turn, may force the type of concessions that allow for, at the least, some modest reallocation of resources and the appearance of equity. At a micro-level, employee share options have often been used as a device to make privatization more acceptable and re-nationalization more difficult. Second, employee financial participation may be on altruistic grounds, as part and parcel of a broader commitment to social fairness and as a contribution to a more just social order. What this means in practice is that depending on the type and underlying rationales, financial participation might be a feature of hard HRM and, indeed, either simply a more sophisticated variation of classic Taylorism, or an overly complex system designed to obscure the real allocation of value generated within the enterprise. Alternatively, it may be part and parcel of a more stakeholder orientated order that gives employees a real say in the enterprise and a fair proportion of profits.

Key Issues in Financial Participation: Trends to Contingency

A central theme of this book is that national differences in firm level practice persist as systems change. However, it is important to recognize that whilst institutions might mediate supranational forces, there are certain objective pressures which can, indeed, be seen to be features of the global ecosystem (Jessop 2012). This is not to assume that there is a globalization process which is coherent and unifying. Rather, structural changes in input costs and the entry of new physical goods and capital exporting nations has fundamentally altered the fortunes of entire states and regions and made for a greater precariousness. In turn, this has favoured investors with shorter time frames, and owners with more fungible assets (Lane and Wood 2012). In contrast, more patient investors and those with human capital tied up in the fortunes of specific firms and industries – above all, workers – have found themselves in a weaker position. Hence, there have been structural pressures towards more contingency in employment and in reward systems. Such pressures will continue to vary from system to system, and the persistence of higher levels of employee voice and countervailing collective power might adjust these pressures to bring about very different configurations of reward systems than in less informally and formally regulated environments. Again, and with regard to formal regulation, national variations in work and employment law may direct pressures towards or away from more contingency and in a direction that is more or less collective, transparent and equitable.

Alternative Forms of Financial Participation in Practice

There is a broad body of literature on work and employment relations that emphasizes the role of implicit mutual understanding and trust (Marsden 1999). Management may seek to develop such relations and influence the manner in which employees view the firm (MacInnes et al. 1985). Alternatively, they may deploy such tools to enhance control, firmly directing worker interests towards the managerial agenda (Baddon et al. 1989: 856). Often, this reflects part and parcel of a broader ideology, whereby workers – and managers – are seen as agents of shareholders (Pendleton 2006: 754). Such an approach suggests that the employees are selfish, individual profit maximizing actors, who will seek to capture the property of shareholders and the latter's just rewards through 'conspiring' with their peers to restrict output, and/or to waste organizational resources. Such individuals may only be reined in by direct incentives that appeal to their own selfishness. The latter, in turn, will result not only in individuals exerting maximum effort, but also policing their peers to control shirkers (Gollan et al. 2006: 501). Such devices are likely to be encountered as part and parcel of a broader palette of individualistic and contingent HRM practices or 'hard' HRM (Storey 2001). In practical terms, more risk is offloaded onto employees but, in return, they have a potential to gain more materially in return for exceptional effort (Kato and Morishima 2002: 488).

Whatever the grounds, there is a range of ways in which financial participation may manifest itself. Under profit sharing, individuals gain immediate cash or deferred rewards based on firm profits (Kato and Morishima 2002: 488). In contrast, share ownership schemes involve the award of equity through some mixture of employer and individual contributions, or one or the other exclusively (Poutsma and de Nijs 2003: 866). A key difference between profit sharing and share ownership is that the former is typically closely related to the employment contract, and the latter rather to the ownership of the firm (D'Art and Turner 2004: 336). Indeed, Poutsma and de Nijs (2003: 865) argue that it is rare for a share ownership scheme to be formally incorporated into the employment contract. In some cases, this may reflect a fundamental incompatibility with collective bargaining. Profit sharing really seeks to reward immediate performance. In theory, share ownership – especially where the shares are not immediately saleable – should reward longer term contributions to the organization's well-being (Cin et al. 2002: 922). However, in reality, share prices may, through one or other form of financial engineering, become quite divorced from actual organizational capabilities and real profits. Indeed, it may encourage employee complicity in strategies which may bilk more patient investors and those in the wider community that have some or other stake in the organization's well-being. Given these competing pressures, it is perhaps hardly surprising that when different types of share ownership scheme are operational within the same organization, the results are often sub-optimal (McNabb and Whitfield 1998: 184).

So far, we have seen that certain forms of financial participation may constitute part and parcel of broader moves towards more contingent terms and conditions of employment and an overall weakening of the terms and conditions of employment. Despite this, there is some research evidence to suggest that, in practice, more instrumentalist approaches to financial participation are less likely to succeed than softer, more collective and equitable ones (Jones 1997). Specifically, there is some evidence to suggest that financial participation schemes yield more optimal results when working hand in hand with other structures and mechanisms for employee voice (Kato and Morishima 2002; Pendleton 2006).

This would suggest that financial participation is not a universal panacea and only certain types of it, in certain institutional settings, are likely to prove effective. Indeed, there is considerable evidence to suggest that the overall track record for financial participation is, at best, mixed (D'Art and Turner 2004: 338; Nykodym et al. 1994: 48; c.f. McNabb and Whitfield 1998: 171).

The case of employee share ownership plans is particularly contentious. Jones and Kato (1993) argue that they are likely to be more efficacious in contexts where the recent organizational track record has been poor and when labour is cheap. Blasi et al. (1996) suggest that such schemes are more likely to be successful in smaller firms, perhaps because in such instances there may be strong pressures towards greater transparency; it is not so easy for employers to veil what is really going on in the firm and its overall performance behind overtly complex financial procedures. As the firm gets larger, the linkage between actual employee effort and overall share value is likely to become increasingly remote. In other words, the linkages between day to day work and overall organizational gains may appear arbitrary (Nykodym et al. 1994: 50). There is also some evidence that they may work better in new economy firms (Sesil et al. 2002). Often new high tech start-ups will use such schemes as a form of deferred pay, encouraging employees to stay with emerging organizations whose overall position is precarious and where present resources are limited. There may also be some link between the success of such schemes and employee skills and education; share ownership schemes are complex and, hence, incomprehensible to many employees (Bakan et al. 2004).

So whilst there is some evidence to suggest that financial participation may work better when combined with other forms of employee participation (McNabb and Whitfield 1998; Applebaum et al. 2000), it is quite distinct from other forms of participation and, indeed, may be part and parcel of managerial strategies to weaken collective representation. Above all, it does not impact on real managerial power, or managers' ability to make autonomous decisions (Appelbaum et al. 2000: 48). Indeed, Strauss (2006: 779) suggests that financial participation is often not participation at all: workers are given no greater role in the running of the firm and the relationship between effort and reward becomes dislocated.

Share ownership schemes often deny workers the full range of shareholder rights, with managers acting as the legal trustee and proxy voter of employee shares. Those with most to gain from short term rises in shareholder value may be the type of investors who see the firm as little more than a debt vehicle and a stock of accumulated assets to be liquidated (Straus 2006: 790).

On this basis the chapter explores five potential antecedents of the existence and extent of financial participation: alternative (voice) forms of participation; hard or calculative HRM; legal origin; the wider differences in market economies, and then the situation (size and sector) of the firm.

Financial Participation and Voice

As noted earlier, financial participation and employee voice may be complementary (Conyon and Freeman 2001), although this is by no means always the case (Dell'Aringa et al. 2007). Yates (2006: 709) asserts that employee share ownership is not intrinsically undermining of the position of unions and, indeed, Black and Lynch (2004: 113) argue that unionization may contribute to higher job security, allowing workers more room to take the risk of trusting management in implementing performance based pay and some means to rein the latter in should the scheme have adverse effects for their position. It could be argued that works councils or joint consultative committees (JCCs) mean that workers are better informed as to what goes on in the firm, making it difficult for managers to implement opaque schemes that hold little benefit for workers.

Alternatively, financial participation may be deployed as a means of undermining unionization or helping to facilitate radical changes of ownership (such as privatization) that are likely to be detrimental to the long term position of workers. And management may promote such schemes from a paternalistic starting point (Gollan et al. 2006: 501) that is both antithetical to unions and likely to prompt hostility from the latter (D'Art and Turner 2004).

This leads us to our first set of alternative hypotheses.

> *Hypothesis 1a: The presence of collective bargaining, works councils and JCCs makes financial participation more likely.*

> *Hypothesis 1b: Financial participation is more likely when collective bargaining, works councils and JCCs are absent.*

Financial Participation and Hard HRM

Some commentators have construed financial participation as part of a bundle of hard HRM practices. Hence, Gooderham et al. (2006: 1500) argue that it represents part of a broader *calculative* paradigm, associated with individual appraisal and active and direct monitoring of the outcomes of any investment in the capabilities of people. There is some evidence from the WERS survey that share ownership plans may coincide with a broader commitment to more contingent terms and conditions of service (Pendleton 2006: 772). Kochan and Osterman (1994) suggest that flexible pay is often part and parcel of contingent and insecure working. Against this, it can be argued that financial participation, particularly perhaps profit sharing, may represent a step towards fairness in the allocation of value generated by the firm. Hence, it could be argued that it is less likely to be encountered together with HRM practices that might objectively be construed of as calculative.

So our next two alterative hypotheses are:

> *Hypothesis 2a: Organizations practising calculative HRM are more likely to use financial participation.*

> *Hypothesis 2b: Organizations practising calculative HRM are less likely to use financial participation.*

Legal Origin and Financial Participation

Since, as we noted above, there may be a linkage between shareholder primacy and the relative propensity of firms to make use of financial participation, we need to consider the role of the law in making such schemes more or less likely. We know, for example, that in France profit sharing is required by law for many larger firms. This brings us to perhaps the most influential attempt to categorize countries according to shareholder primacy, the legal origins approach of La Porta and colleagues (1998; 2000). They argue that shareholder rights are strongest in common law systems, and significantly weaker in civil law ones. Hence, in categorizing countries, the most important indicator is whether they are closest to the civil law or common law ideal types (La Porta et al. 1998; Djankov et al. 2003). If employee share ownership is a reflection of developed stock markets and the primacy of an agenda centring on shareholder value, then this form of financial participation is most likely to be encountered in settings where owner rights are strongest (c.f. Botero et al. 2004: Djankov et al. 2003).

> *Hypothesis 3: Financial participation is more likely to be more widely encountered in common law than civil law systems.*

Financial Participation and Comparative Capitalism

The extent to which shareholder rights are paramount may of course be mediated by the rights of other stakeholders. As may be seen from other chapters of this volume, using this wider view there are many different ways of categorizing national institutional orders. Here, we return to the original dichotomy of the early literature on varieties of capitalism (Lincoln and Kalleberg 1990; Dore 2000; Hall and Soskice 2001) because the importance of share-holding is a key factor in this way of categorizing the most advanced developed societies, the set of countries that constitute the focus of our research. The shareholder dominant countries of the Liberal Market Economies (LMEs) and the stakeholder orientated Coordinated Market Economies (CMEs) show some crucial differences in relevant aspects of the stock market. Within LMEs, not only are shareholder rights paramount, but stock markets are more developed and investors less patient/more activist and more short term orientated (Dore 2000). All this makes for adversarial competition, with workers being clearly subordinated to the maximization of shareholder value (Hall and Soskice 2001). In contrast, within CMEs, there is less emphasis on finance from the stock market, and ownership structures are interlocked (indeed, some of the most successful large German firms are controlled by trusts with agendas orientated towards the wider stakeholder community). Shareholder rights are also restrained by traditions of neo-corporatism and centralized bargaining. In turn, this is likely to impact on employee participation within the firm (Szabo 2006: 277). In LMEs, employee voice is likely to be weaker and jobs and reward more contingent. In contrast, in CMEs, employees are more likely to enjoy access to a range of entrenched voice mechanisms and, hence, the power of employers to adjust terms and conditions of service unilaterally or in an opaque and unaccountable manner is more likely to be circumscribed (Brewster et al. 2007).

Given the stronger emphasis on stock market finance and share price performance as an indicator of organizational well-being, it can be argued that employee share ownership schemes will be more common in LMEs. Such schemes are likely to come with 'junior' shareholder rights, however, and the overall proportion of shares held by employees will be limited (Poutsma and de Nijs 2003: 868). Employee share ownership may, as noted above, be deployed as a vehicle to legitimize and accelerate privatization and make it difficult to reverse (Ogden 1995). When held in trust, employee share ownership may also be deployed as a mechanism to protect the interests of specific shareholders and make hostile takeovers more difficult: even if not held in trust, employees may be reluctant to sell their shares to an outsider with a poor reputation for husbanding the long term well-being of the firm (Davidson and Worrell 1994).

In contrast, profit sharing schemes may readily be agreed upon as part of a collective agreement (Poutsma and de Nijs 2003). However, Kochan and Osterman (1994) argue that it is still about bringing about greater flexibility in pay rates and, therefore, may be viewed with hostility by unions; at the same time, this may impart some flexibility between collective bargaining rounds. Again, they are mandated by the law in some CMEs, given that they conform to the principle that employees are entitled to a just share of value generated.

Alternatively, it could be argued that national institutional setting might have little impact on the actual nature and extent of financial participation. For example, Cin et al. (2002: 940) argue that it may reflect differences in public policy or tax arrangements – that may, for example, simply reflect the ideology of serving governments rather than structural institutional orders (Cin et al. 2002: 940). Or it could be argued that the process of Europeanization may have encouraged the firms to adopt financial participation on a continent wide basis (McNabb and Whitfield 2007: 1008). This, and/or general pressures towards liberalization might have made for a broad diffusion of such schemes (Lane 2003; Jessop 2012). Indeed, Kalmi et al. (2005: 65) found little link between national European contexts and the nature of employee involvement or participation in the development of financial participation schemes.

This leads us to alternative hypotheses to hypothesis 3.

Hypothesis 4a: Financial participation is more common in LMEs.

Hypothesis 4b: There is little link between variety of capitalism and the incidence of financial participation in firms.

Financial Participation and the Situation of the Firm

It is likely that, in addition to the factors noted so far, the sector in which the firm operates and the firm's size will have an impact on their likelihood of having financial participation schemes. If financial participation reflects a broader move towards more uncertainty and contingency in work and employment relations, then it could be argued that profit sharing may be more likely in contexts where workers have lower skills and when the business environment is more uncertain: in such context, employers are more likely to wish to offload some of the risks of running the firm back on employees and be more able to do so (Robinson and Wilkinson 2006). Similarly, it is possible that firms doing poorly may be more likely to experiment with share ownership (Jones and Kato 1993). Once more, it serves as a way of offloading risk and may serve as a substitute for overdue wage increases. Alternatively, it could be argued that, as share ownership may encourage workers to trade off lower pay for greater long term prosperity, it may be encountered in contexts where workers have a higher level of skill. Indeed, it could be argued that such schemes encourage workers with highly sought-after generic skills to stay with one employer as opposed to job hopping (Poutsma and de Nijs 2003: 884). Once more, the performance of more skilled workers may be harder to measure (piecework is unlikely in such settings), making financial participation more likely (Pendleton 2006: 754).

Thus, we have two more alternative hypotheses:

Hypothesis 5a: The incidence of financial participation is likely to vary according to sector: it will be less likely in sunset industries in developed economies, such as some areas of traditional manufacturing.

Hypothesis 5b: Financial participation is more likely in sectors making use of highly skilled workers.

Finally, firm size may impact on the propensity of firms to make use of financial participation. In smaller firms, it is easier to identify shirkers who might benefit from broad based forms of financial participation (c.f. Whitfield and Poole 1996). Indeed, Blasi et al. (1996) found that employee share option plans worked better in small firms. However, this may not only reflect the easier resolution of free-riding issues but also be because, as noted above, employees may accept share options as a deferred form of reward in start-ups with promise.

So our final hypothesis is that:

Hypothesis 6: Financial participation is more common in smaller firms.

Method

Chapter 2 provides a general overview of the survey methods. In comparing the presence of different manifestations of financial participation, we constructed a Mokken scale comprised of dichotomous variables, each reflecting the presence or absence of a particular financial participatory practice. These variables comprised the presence or absence of share schemes, stock options and profit sharing, each for four different categories of employee (managerial, professional/technical, clerical, manual). Mokken's non-parametric model for cumulative one-dimensional scaling was deployed (Sijtsma and Molenaar 2002). Firms recording positive responses for all 12 items generate a ranking of 100, zero for negative responses for all items, and some type of intermediate ranking for firms giving an answer in-between. Final position on the scale in respect of the latter depends on the number of responses, and the relative scarcity of positive responses as a whole to each questionnaire item; a positive response to an item having fewer positive answers as a whole will impact more strongly on the scale than those more common positive answers. The combined scale then constituted the dependent variable, within an OLS (ordinal least squares model). In order to take account of the extent to which factors influencing the three broad types of financial participation might differ (share ownership, stock options, profit sharing) the scale was disaggregated into its three components, each being then used as a dependent variable regressed against the same potential explanatory variables identified. The latter would encompass the nature of employment relations, the extent of calculative HRM, capitalist archetype, size and sector. In terms of employment relations, dummy variables were added for those responding firms where a JCC or a works council was present and/or where there was collective bargaining. The scale for calculative HRM was again a Mokken one, replicating the items of the Gooderham et al. (1999) scale. The LME/common law UK was the base group for the dummy on capitalist archetype and legal model. Metal manufacturing was used as reference category for sector, the latter being controlled by the 16 NACE industry sector dummies. Firm size was defined in terms of workplace size. We recognized that that it was possible for the explanatory and dependent variables to have a relationship that was not the same across all countries, and this was controlled for by including the interaction terms that reflect the interactions between size, capitalist archetype and overall HRM paradigm. We then re-categorized the countries, replacing capitalist archetype with legal origin. The UK remained the base group in terms of Botero et al's (2004) employment law index. We did also look at the possibility that specific causal variables might have a stronger effect on financial participation aimed at one level of employees against another, and that particular differences might be encountered between those aimed at the rank and file (manual and clerical workers) versus those in more senior positions. This is the same distinction between narrow and broad based schemes made by Poutsma et al. (2005) but we separate out managers and technical specialists from other employees. Hence, we constructed dichotomous variables reflecting the presence or absence of profit sharing, share ownership and stock options aimed at manual and/or clerical workers. These binary variables were then deployed as the dependent variables and estimated against the same potential explanatory variables, but this time using logit models (as there was no longer a scale, but a limited dependent variable in each instance).

Findings

The Mokken scale of financial participation is presented in Table 4.1.

We then went on to establish the scale's validity; more specifically, we examined the reliability and scaleability of the data and the resultant scale. First, we used Loevinger's H-coefficient of homogeneity (H_{wgt}) which is recorded for each item and the scale as a whole. All the individual items and the scale as a whole meet the minimum acceptable criterion for an H-value of at least 0.3. We moved on to test for the reliability of the indicators, with a Cronbach's alpha value of 0.79 exceeding the minimum of 0.7. We did the same thing for the calculative HRM scale, which again satisfied both conditions.

We then deployed the financial participation scale as the dependent variable. Table 4.2 presents the descriptive statistics for the entire set of variables used in the analysis. As noted above, we used OLS; Table 4.3 depicts the results, as well as the subsequent models where the dependent variables were each of the three elements (share ownership scheme, stock options, profit sharing) disaggregated from the overall index.

With regard to Table 4.3, it is apparent that the r-squared is low, with the independent variables only explaining some 11% of variation in financial participation. It is therefore evident that further unidentified variables are impacting on the decision to make use of financial participation.

Hypothesis 1a broadly suggests that financial participation is more likely when employee collective voice is stronger, and 1b the converse. In fact, we found

Table 4.1 Mokken Scale of Financial Participation

		Mean	**H_{wgt}**	**Corr.**
Scale	Overall calculative scale, 12 items (Cronbach's alpha = 0.79)		0.36	0.33
Item 1	Employee share scheme – management	0.27	0.38	0.52
Item 2	Employee share scheme – professional	0.21	0.39	0.55
Item 3	Employee share scheme – clerical	0.19	0.40	0.56
Item 4	Employee share scheme – manual	0.16	0.34	0.44
Item 5	Profit sharing – management	0.37	0.36	0.39
Item 6	Profit sharing – professional	0.28	0.36	0.48
Item 7	Profit sharing – clerical	0.23	0.35	0.49
Item 8	Profit sharing – manual	0.17	0.33	0.43
Item 9	Stock options – management	0.23	0.30	0.39
Item 10	Stock options – professional	0.09	0.36	0.36
Item 11	Stock options – clerical	0.05	0.36	0.27
Item 12	Stock options – manual	0.03	0.39	0.22

Table 4.2 Descriptive Statistics

Variable	Mean	St. Dev	Min.	Max.	Obs.
Financial Participation Scale	18.023	20.07	0	100	1640
Share Ownership Scale	20.964	36.19	0	100	1640
Profit Sharing Scale	25.897	37.87	0	100	1640
Stock Option Scale	8.981	20.40	0	100	1640
Broad Based Share Ownership	0.218	0.41	0	1	1640
Broad Based Profit Sharing	0.245	0.43	0	1	1640
Broad Based Stock Option	0.047	0.21	0	1	1640
Total no. of employees (000's)	1982.538	10709.31	6	211063	1640
Agriculture	0.010	0.10	0	1	1640
Energy & water	0.026	0.16	0	1	1640
Chemical products	0.038	0.19	0	1	1640
Metal Manufacturing	0.222	0.42	0	1	1640
Other manufacturing	0.207	0.41	0	1	1640
Building & civil engineering	0.038	0.19	0	1	1640
Retail & distribution	0.117	0.32	0	1	1640
Transport & communication	0.052	0.22	0	1	1640
Banking, finance & insurance	0.123	0.33	0	1	1640
Personal & domestic services	0.009	0.09	0	1	1640
Health services	0.018	0.13	0	1	1640
Other services	0.023	0.15	0	1	1640
Education	0.007	0.08	0	1	1640
Social Services	0.003	0.06	0	1	1640
Public Administration	0.019	0.14	0	1	1640
Other	0.088	0.28	0	1	1640
Coordinated market economy	0.570	0.50	0	1	1640
Liberal market economy	0.430	0.50	0	1	1640
JCC/WC present	0.666	0.47	0	1	1640
Collective bargaining	0.741	0.44	0	1	1640
Calculative HRM scale	39.395	28.36	0	100	1640
Size * VOC	906.646	6009.98	0	210000	1640
Calculative HRM * VOC	21.937	29.41	0	100	1640
Denmark, Austria	0.288	0.45	0	1	1640
Germany, Sweden	0.282	0.45	0	1	1640

insufficient evidence to support either hypothesis. As can be seen from Table 4.3, in each of the four models, collective voice was irrelevant. There are two reasons why this might be the case. First, there may be a difference between the physical presence of a union and the latter's actual strength (see Flynn et al. 2004). Indeed, a union may play a residual role, reflecting past union power, with managers retaining formal structures of engagement out of convention or because they are compelled to do so by the law, and the union trading on formal rights and agreements rather than its actual power on the ground.

When it came to JCCs/works councils (JCC/WCs), we found some evidence of causality. Although, according to the first model, using all forms of financial

Table 4.3 Empirical Models of Financial Participation

Variable	Financial Part.		Share Ownership		Profit Sharing		Stock Options		Mean
	Coefficient	t-ratio	Coefficient	t-ratio	Coefficient	t-ratio	Coefficient	t-ratio	
Constant	15.775***	8.76	17.822***	5.43	22.205***	6.47	8.703***	4.65	
Employee relations									
JCC/WC present	0.874	0.76	1.900	0.91	4.615**	2.11	−3.095***	−2.59	0.67
Collective bargaining	−0.267	−0.24	−1.303	−0.64	1.188	0.56	−0.547	−0.47	0.74
Calculative HRM									
Calculative HRM scale	0.116***	4.19	0.175***	3.46	0.088*	1.66	0.088***	3.06	39.4
VOC									
Coordinated market economy	−5.016***	−2.84	−13.822***	−4.30	0.839	0.25	−2.060	−1.12	0.57
Size									
Total no. of employees (000's)	0.298***	5.50	0.414***	4.19	0.252***	2.44	0.234***	4.15	1.983
Industry									
Agriculture	−0.380	−0.08	1.653	0.19	−2.825	−0.31	−0.167	−0.03	0.01
Energy & water	6.381**	2.04	11.683**	2.05	2.688	0.45	4.739	1.46	0.03
Chemical products	3.841	1.45	11.013**	2.28	−6.097	−1.21	5.670**	2.06	0.04
Other manufacturing	−2.078	−1.43	2.915	1.10	−8.168***	−2.95	−1.484	−0.98	0.21
Building & civil engineering	−0.638	−0.24	6.491	1.35	−3.611	−0.72	−4.479*	−1.64	0.04
Retail & distribution	−6.767***	−3.87	−0.082	−0.03	−18.899***	−5.68	−2.712	−1.49	0.12
Transport & communication	−1.366	−0.59	8.913**	2.11	−13.863***	−3.13	−0.176	−0.07	0.05
Banking, finance & insurance	−0.546	−0.32	4.303	1.38	−8.800***	−2.70	1.947	1.10	0.12
Personal & domestic services	−9.830*	−1.88	−8.864	−0.93	−14.594	−1.46	−6.777	−1.25	0.01
Health services	−3.487	−0.96	1.575	0.24	−20.719***	−2.98	6.176*	1.63	0.02
Other services	−1.253	−0.38	4.602	0.77	−14.219**	−2.28	4.215	1.24	0.02
Education	−13.026**	−2.22	−13.921	−1.30	−19.988*	−1.79	−6.532	−1.07	0.01
Social Services	−13.212	−1.53	−8.757	−0.56	−29.091*	−1.77	−4.122	−0.46	0.003

	Fin. Part Scale	Share Ownership	Profit Sharing	Stock Options	
Public Administration	-4.175	2.802	-13.486*	-2.689	0.02
	-1.15	0.42	-1.95	-0.71	0.09
Other	1.138	7.122**	-9.760***	4.800***	
	0.60	2.05	-2.68	2.41	
Interactions					
Size * VOC	-0.175*	-0.527***	0.160	-0.140	906.6
	-1.81	-2.99	0.87	-1.39	21.9
Calculative HRM * VOC	0.049	0.014	0.154**	-0.005	
	1.41	0.23	2.30	-0.15	
Model	OLS	OLS	OLS	OLS	
Dependent Variable	Fin. Part Scale	Share Ownership	Profit Sharing	Stock Options	
Mean	18.02	20.96	25.89	8.98	
Observations	1640	1640	1640	1640	
R-squared	0.11	0.09	0.09	0.06	

*, ** and *** denote significance at the 10, 5 and 1% levels respectively

participation as the dependent variable, the presence or absence of a JCC/WC had no significant impact, when we unpacked things, a rather different picture emerged. We found that the presence of a JCC/WC had a positive and significant effect on profit sharing. Against that, stock options were less likely when JCCs/WCs were present. Why do these bodies apparently favour one type of financial participation and not another? As noted earlier, there may be little connection between share price and the well-being of an organization and its employees. And, share ownership schemes may be opaque and constrain the rights of employees to trade in shares or vote at annual general meetings. In contrast, profit sharing is more transparent than many share ownership schemes, and allows for immediate rewards.

We then went on to explore the relationship between calculative HRM and financial participation. Hypothesis 2a suggests that firms using calculative HRM policies are more likely to make use of financial participation; and 2b the converse. Our results strongly confirmed hypothesis 2a and disproved hypothesis 2b. In other words, financial participation was more likely in firms practising calculative HRM. Here, a caveat is in order: such firms are particularly likely to practise those forms of financial participation centring on share ownership.

We found that there was a significant link between legal origin and the nature and extent of financial participation. Share based financial participation was generally less common under civil than common law legal origin. However, whilst hypothesis 3 is broadly confirmed, the situation is in fact, more complex than suggested by Botero et al. (2004). A closer look at the results revealed much diversity within the civil law camp. This could reflect the gradual encroachment of the common law model into other countries, or the fact that all national economies have some diversity, or simply that, in some contexts, the role of share ownership schemes and, indeed, the manner in which they operate, may serve very different purposes according to setting. Once more, this would highlight the limitations of categorizing countries simply according to common law legal origin, or not, and the need to take account of considerable differences within and between different civil law countries.

Given the previous findings, it is perhaps hardly surprising that hypothesis 4a was confirmed, and hypothesis 4b disproved. In other words, financial participation is more likely in LMEs than CMEs. Again, we encountered much diversity in the civil law camp, most probably for very similar reasons to those outlined in the preceding paragraph. Once more, however, it is worth noting that when financial participation is unpacked, it is clear that this is really only the case with share ownership schemes. In contrast, there was no difference between profit sharing and variety of capitalism. Again, this would highlight the ambiguous nature of many share ownership schemes, and the extent to which they do not always deliver in rewarding workers fairly for effort, or indeed, link reward to the real performance – and sustainability – of the firm.

We then went on to look at the relationship between sector and financial participation. Here, we found that financial participation was less likely in manufacturing, the relative importance of which has declined in many developed economies. This would seem to confirm hypothesis 5a, which suggests that industries undergoing long declines may be less likely to make use of financial participation. This would on first glance disprove hypothesis 5b that suggests that given manufacturing's relatively high skills base in many European economies, this might encourage financial participation. A closer examination again revealed a more complex picture. The only sectors that strongly differed from the manufacturing base group were utilities (electricity and water), an area where share options have been used to make privatizations more palatable (see Ogden 1995).

In looking at the relationship between size and financial participation, we disproved hypothesis 6. Maybe larger firms have greater resources to devote to developing more sophisticated HRM systems and maybe most small and medium firms do not represent ambitious start-ups, with a clear anticipation of growth, but rather either stable mature players or more recent entrants locked into a relative low level of activity.

We went on to estimate logit models, using as the dependent variables firms deploying broad based financial participation and not.

Whilst this broadly confirmed our findings, it emphasizes that calculative HRM policies were again primarily associated with share options.

Conclusion

This chapter has revealed some important relationships between context, firm size, sector, and financial participation but, at the same time, indicates a complex picture. Interestingly, we encountered no relationship between the existence or absence of collective bargaining and the usage of financial participation. Whilst it may be self-evident that unions would not encourage the use of financial participation (preferring standardized and predictable reward systems set by collective bargaining), it is perhaps surprising that they have not been more effective in preventing it. This could reflect either union weakness or simply that, as long as core terms and conditions are agreed to, unions see the existence or absence of additional financial incentives as less of a concern or priority (Hyman et al. 1989). In contrast, we found that the presence of a works council or JCC appeared to deter the use of share ownership schemes: this may be due to the fact that in such cases workers are likely to be better informed as to the broad production processes and strategies and, hence, better equipped to spot gross disparities between share performance and real output. Our findings on the relationship with HRM policies show some linkages but may also challenge the simplistic notions inherent in the categorizations of such policies. In practice, firms often mix and match HRM policies, adopting seemingly hardline HRM policies in some areas and pluralist ones in others. Whilst clearly there is a link between the incidence of some calculative HRM policies and share options, this does not mean that the HRM practices of such firms are universally calculative and, our analysis found, often policies in those firms will also encompass some pluralist features.

This would be confirmed by the complex relationship between financial participation and context. Whilst financial participation – and more specifically share

Table 4.4 Logit Models of Broad-Based Financial Participation

Variable	Share Ownership Coefficient	t-ratio	Profit Sharing Coefficient	t-ratio	Stock Options Coefficient	t-ratio	Mean
Constant	-1.776***	7.57	-1.301***	-5.60	-2.665***	-6.13	
Employee relations							
JCC/WC present	0.199	1.34	0.182	1.20	-1.090***	-3.86	0.67
Collective bargaining	-0.058	-0.41	-0.021	-0.15	-0.008	-0.03	0.74
Calculative HRM							
Calculative HRM scale	0.007**	2.08	0.004	0.99	0.001	0.17	39.40
VOC							
Coordinated market economy	-1.048***	-4.28	-0.063	-0.27	0.186	0.41	0.57
Size							
Total no. of employees (000's)	0.078***	3.03	0.019***	2.55	0.010	1.12	1.983
Industry							
Agriculture	0.046	0.06	-0.236	-0.40	0.189	0.18	0.01
Energy & water	0.936***	2.43	0.155	0.44	0.928	1.57	0.03
Chemical products	0.8567***	2.59	-0.096	-0.32	0.511	0.87	0.04
Other manufacturing	0.514***	2.58	-0.441***	-2.49	-0.706	-1.52	0.21
Building & civil engineering	0.791**	2.37	-0.357	-1.10	-1.245	-1.19	0.04
Retail & distribution	0.176	0.70	-1.395***	-5.10	-0.434	-0.91	0.12
Transport & communication	0.644**	2.10	-0.560*	-1.90	-0.756	-0.97	0.05
Banking, finance & insurance	0.636***	2.82	-0.197	-0.98	0.380	1.00	0.12
Personal & domestic services	n/a		-0.445	-0.66	n/a		0.01
Health services	0.372	0.71	-1.533***	-2.44	0.389	0.18	0.02
Other services	0.600	1.38	-0.528	-1.26	0.074	0.10	0.02
Education	n/a		-1.217	-1.15	n/a		0.01
Social Services	n/a		n/a		n/a		0.003
Public Administration	0.469	1.07	-0.744	-1.42	-0.513	-0.48	0.02
Other	0.814***	3.32	-0.297	-1.28	0.725*	1.88	0.09

Interactions

	Share Ownership	Profit Sharing	Stock Options
Size * VOC	-0.162***	-3.24	0.056**	2.23	-0.003	-0.18
Calculative HRM * VOC	0.009*	1.95	0.009**	2.05	0.004	0.49
Model	Logit		Logit		Logit	
Dependent Variable	Share Ownership		Profit Sharing		Stock Options	
Mean	0.218		0.245		0.047	
Observations	1640		1640		1640	
Iterations	7		6		8	
Log-likelihood	-792.3		-850.0		-290.2	
Restricted Log-likelihood	-859.3		-912.2		-310.7	
Chi-squared	133.9		124.3		41.1	
Degrees of freedom	19		21		19	

*, ** and *** denote significance at the 10, 5 and 1% levels respectively

options – was more common in a liberal market setting, there were considerable differences in the coordinated market camp; financial participation was very much more likely in some coordinated markets. This might reflect either the uneven diffusion of liberalization or that seemingly similar HRM policies might serve different purposes according to setting.

References

Appelbaum, E., Baily, T., Berg, P. and Kalleberg. A.L. (2000) *Manufacturing Advantage: Why High Performance Work Systems Pay Off.* Ithaca, NY: ILR Press.

Baddon, L., Hunter, L., Hyman, J., Leopold, J. and Ramsay, H. (1989) *People's Capitalism?: A Critical Analysis of Profit-Sharing and Employee Share Ownership.* New York: Routledge.

Bakan, I., Suseno, Y., Pinnington, A. and Money, A. (2004) 'The influence of financial participation and participation in decision making on employee job attitudes', *International Journal of Human Resource Management* 15(3): 587–616.

Black, S. and Lynch, L. (2004) 'What's driving the new economy? The benefits of workplace innovation', *Economic Journal* 114(493): F97–116.

Blasi, S., Konte, M. and Kruse, D. (1996) 'Employee stock ownership and corporate performance among public companies', *Industrial and Labor Relations Review* 50(1): 60–79.

Botero, J., Djankov, S., La Porta, R., Lopez-de-Silanes, S. and Shleifer, A. (2004) 'The regulation of labor', *Quarterly Journal of Economics* 119: 1339–82.

Brewster, C., Wood, G., Croucher, R. and Brookes, M. (2007) 'Collective and individual voice: Convergence in Europe?', *International Journal of Human Resource Management* 18(7): 1246–62.

Cin, B., Han, T. and Smith, S. (2002) 'A tale of two tigers: Employee financial participation in Taiwan and Korea', *International Journal of Human Resource Management* 14(6): 920–41.

Conyon, M.J. and Freeman, R.B. (2001) 'Shared modes of compensation and firm performance: UK evidence', NBER Working Paper 8448.

D'Art, D. and Turner, T. (2004) 'Profit sharing, firm performance and union influence in selected European countries', *Personnel Review* 33(3): 335–50.

Davidson, W. and Worrell, D. (1994) 'ESOP's Fables: The influence of Employee Stock Ownership Plans on corporate stock prices and subsequent operating performance', *Human Resource Planning* 17: 69–85.

Dell'Aringa, C., Ghinetti, P. and Lucifora, C. (2007) 'High performance work systems, industrial relations and pay setting in Europe'. Instituto di Economia dell'Impresa e del Lavoro, Università Cattolica del S. Cuore, Milan, Italy. Downloaded 10 March 2008.

Djankov, S., Glaeser, E., La Porta, R., Lopez-de-Silnes, F. and Shleifer, A. (2003) 'The new comparative economics', *Journal of Comparative Economics* 31: 595–619.

Dore, R. (2000) *Stock Market Capitalism: Welfare Capitalism.* Cambridge: Cambridge University Press.

Flynn, M., Smith, R., Rigby, M. and Brewster, C. (2004) 'Trade union democracy: Issues and contestations' in M. Harcourt and G. Wood (eds) *Trade Unions and Democracy: Strategies and Perspectives.* Manchester: Manchester University Press.

Gollan, P., Poutsma, E. and Veersma, U. (2006) 'Editors' introduction: New roads in organisational participation?', *Industrial Relations* 45(4): 499–512.

Gooderham, P., Nordhaug, O. and Ringdal, K. (1999) 'Institutional and rational determinants of organizational practices: Human resource management in European firms', *Administrative Science Quarterly* 44: 507–31.

Gooderham, P., Nordhaug, O. and Ringdal, K. (2006) 'National embeddedness and calculative human resource management in US subsidiaries in Europe and Australia', *Human Relations* 59(11): 1491–1513.

Hall, P. and Soskice, D. (2001) 'An introduction to the varieties of capitalism', in P. Hall and D. Soskice (eds) *Varieties of Capitalism: The Institutional Basis of Competitive Advantage*. Oxford: Oxford University Press.

Hyman, J., Ramsay, H., Leopold, J., Baddon, L. and Hunter, L. (1989) 'The impact of employee share ownership', *Employee Relations* 11(4): 9–16.

Jessop, B. (2012) 'Rethinking the diversity and variability of capitalism: on variegated capitalism in the world market', in C. Lane and G. Wood (eds), *Institutions, Internal Diversity and Change*. London: Routledge.

Jones, D. (1997) 'Employees as stakeholders', *Business Strategy Review* 8(2): 21–24.

Jones, D. and Kato, T. (1993) 'The scope, nature, and effects of employee stock ownership plans in Japan', *Industrial and Labor Relations Review*, 46(2): 352–67.

Kalmi, P., Pendleton, A. and Poutsma, E. (2005) 'Financial participation and performance in Europe', *Human Resource Management Journal* 15(4): 54–67.

Kato, T. and Morishima, M. (2002) 'The productivity effects of participatory employment practices', *Industrial Relations Journal* 41(4): 487–520.

Kessler, I. (2010) 'Financial participation', in A. Wilkinson, P. Gollan, M. Marchington, and D. Lewin, (eds), *The Oxford Handbook of Participation in Organizations*. Oxford: Oxford University Press.

Kochan, T. and Osterman, P. (1994) *The Mutual Gains Enterprise*. Boston: Harvard Business School Press.

Lane, C. (2003) 'Changes in corporate governance of German corporations: Convergence to the Anglo–American model?', *Competition and Change* 7(2–3): 79–100.

Lane, C. and Wood, G. (2012) *Capitalist Diversity, Work & Employment Relations*. Sheffield Political Economy Research Institute, Paper No. 2.

La Porta, R., Lopez-de-Silanes, F., Shleifer, A. and Vishny, R. (1998) 'Law and finance', *Journal of Political Economy* 106: 1113–55.

La Porta, R., Lopez-de-Silanes, F., Shleifer, A. and Vishny, R. (2000) 'Investor protection and corporate governance', *Journal of Financial Economics* 58: 3–27.

Lincoln, J., and Kalleberg, A. (1990) *Culture, Control and Commitment: A Study of Work Organization in the United States and Japan*. Cambridge: Cambridge University Press.

MacInnes, J., Cressey, P. and Eldridge, J. (1985) *Just Managing: Authority and Democracy in Industry*. Milton Keynes: Open University Press.

Marsden, D. (1999) *A Theory of Employment Systems*. Oxford: Oxford University Press.

McNabb, R. and Whitfield, K. (1998) 'The impact of employee financial participation and employee involvement on firm level performance', *Scottish Journal of Political Economy*, 45(2): 171–87.

McNabb, R. and Whitfield, K. (2007) 'The impact of varying types of performance related pay and employee participation on earnings', *International Journal of Human Resource Management* 18(6): 1004–25.

Nykodym, N., Symonetti, J., Nielson, W. and Welling, B. (1994) 'Employee empowerment', *Participation in Organisations* 2(3): 45–55.

Ogden, S. (1995) 'Profit sharing and the construction of employee commitment in the newly privatised water industry', *Accounting, Auditing and Accountability Journal* 8(4): 34–48.

Pendleton, A. (2006) 'Incentives, monitoring, and employee stock ownership plans: New evidence and interpretations', *Industrial Relations* 45(4): 753–77.

Poutsma, E. and de Nijs, W. (2003) 'Broad based employee financial participation in Europe', *International Journal of Human Resource Management*, 14(6): 863–92.

Poutsma, E., Ligthart, P.E.M. and Schouteten, R. (2005) 'Employee share schemes in Europe, a case of Anglo-Saxonisation', *Management Revue*, 16(1): 99–122.

Robinson, A. and Wilkinson, N. (2006) 'Employee financial participation and productivity: An empirical reappraisal', *British Journal of Industrial Relations* 44(1): 31–50.

Sesil, J., Kroumova, M., Blasi, J. and Kruse, D. (2002) 'Broad-based employee stock options in US "New Economy" firms', *British Journal of Industrial Relations* 40(2): 273–94.

Storey, J. (2001) 'Human resource management today: An assessment', in J. Storey (ed.) *Human Resource Management: A Critical Text*. London: Thompson.

Strauss, G. (2006) 'Worker participation–some under-considered issues', *Industrial Relations: a journal of economy and society*, 45(4): 778–803.

Szabo, E. (2006) 'Meaning and context of participation in five European countries', *Management Decision* 44(2): 279–89.

Whitfield, K. and Poole, M. (1996) 'The distribution of financial participation schemes in British workplaces', *Management Research News* 4/5: 54–55.

Whitley, R. (1999) *The Diversity of Modern Capitalism*. Oxford: Oxford University Press.

Wilkinson, A., Gollan, P., Marchington, M. and Lewin, D. (2010) 'Conceptualizing employee participation in organizations', in A. Wilkinson, P. Gollan, M. Marchington and D. Lewin (eds) *The Oxford Handbook of Participation in Organizations*. Oxford: Oxford University Press.

Yates, D. (2006) 'Unions and employee ownership: A road to economic democracy?', *Industrial Relations* 45(4): 709–33.

Is There Convergence Towards Individual Voice in Europe?

RICHARD CROUCHER, MICHAEL BROOKES,
GEOFFREY WOOD AND CHRIS BREWSTER

Introduction

This chapter examines whether, as often suggested, there has been a convergence towards individual forms of employee voice in Britain, Germany and Sweden. It contributes to debates about the nature and extent of convergence in HRM practices within European organisations. The three countries are generally categorised within different 'varieties of capitalism' (Hall and Soskice, 2001) or 'business systems' (Whitley, 1999). Britain is widely viewed as an archetypical liberal market economy; although Germany and Sweden are conversely seen as exemplifying more European or collaborative economies, Sweden shows a particularly strong social aspect. Sweden recorded a strong macro-economic performance in the 1990s and early twenty-first century, which may have favoured those resistant to pressures seeking to change their system in a more liberal market direction.

The chapter is structured in the following way. Initially, we advance reasons for the importance of employee voice; subsequently we review competing views on the utility of different types of employee voice and how they are manifested within different varieties of capitalism. We discuss the vexed topics of 'convergence' and 'divergence', hypothesising a trend away from collective and towards individual voice mechanisms. Cranet data is then deployed to test our hypothesis. Since we find very little evidence for the hypothesis, we discuss our findings' theoretical implications.

The Significance of Voice

Why is voice, as Hirschman (1970) first defined it, important in organisations? In the industrial relations literature, employee participation and involvement were conceived of in *equity* terms, while involvement was envisaged as promoting fairness (Flanders, 1980; Fox, 1980; Woodall and Winstanley, 2001). Alternatively, within the human relations tradition (e.g. Mayo, 1945), arguments were more likely to be advanced on *efficiency* grounds; involvement was viewed in motivational terms (Adams, 2005). The human relations themes were picked up in HRM literature that also saw participation and involvement as efficiency-promoting, but the previous tradition's humanist conceptions were marginalised (Woodall and Winstanley, 2001). HRM arguments were underpinned by neo-liberal economic assumptions that unions distorted labour markets by inflating wages above their 'natural' market levels (Woodall and Winstanley, 2001). Consequently, the best case was a trade-off between increased wage costs on the one hand and potential transactional benefits on the other. The worst case was that unions were viewed as prejudicial to competitiveness, and welfare reducing in that they tended to raise levels of unemployment (Freeman and Medoff, 1984). The assumptions of this efficiency or 'business case' viewpoint are currently less relevant because the union wage premium has declined in Europe. It has been found that the union membership wage premium disappeared in Britain in the last decade of the twentieth century (Forth and Millward, 2000). It has been shown that it persists there, though at lower levels than previously (Bryson, 2002). The most recent population data for the USA showed its persistence there at a comparable historic point (Budd and Na, 2000).

The neo-classical viewpoint has several theoretical limitations, as Kaufman (2004) adumbrates. First, rationality is bounded – decision making is influenced by limited cognition, incomplete information and emotional considerations. Effective voice mechanisms have the potential to increase the efficiency of exchange relations. Second, the costs of exit are very high for employees with high or rare skills, making voice mechanisms more significant. Third, no contract can be complete; voice mechanisms can therefore assist in identifying and tackling complex and unforeseen difficulties.

Recent research has proposed the central role of voice not only in promoting fairness in workplaces, but as an essential fundament of democratic societies; in its most advanced forms, it provides workers with effective expression of their interests (Martens, 1992; Budd, 2004). Budd suggests that this effect should be distinguished from both efficiency and equity considerations. Voice may impact efficiency and equity, yet it also reflects a moral imperative (Budd, 2004; Adams, 2005).

Voice, Participation and Involvement

We define collective voice to encompass all mechanisms founded on employee collectives. In this definition it includes trade unions and joint consultative committees (JCCs) or works councils but also includes other forms. Individual voice also takes various forms: briefing groups, problem solving teams, regular meetings between management and the workforce, newsletters and notice boards, electronic communication including intranet and emails (including email-administered employee surveys) and suggestion schemes (Bryson, 2004). Whilst the latter may be categorised as either union or management friendly forms (Colvin, 2004), some practices are harder to allocate to simple categories without considering power relations contexts. However, practices may be grouped by *dimension* (i.e. whether they are founded on collective or individual constituencies) and *depth* (i.e. how far a specific practice appears likely to influence management).

At the lowest level, involvement entails consultation, i.e. soliciting opinions that may be rejected (Wood, 1998). By contrast, participation gives workers a genuine (clearly delineated) input into how firms are governed, even if the input is likely to be limited. Employee involvement may therefore include briefings or meetings where information is communicated by managers and responses are requested. Whilst the latter constitute channels for individual voice, consultation can assume a collective dimension. We summarise the situation in Figure 5.1.

For its advocates, individual voice allows firms to comprehend the diverse needs of contemporary workforces (Bryson, 2004). Some accounts propose that it permits closer and more direct communication between managers and employees, without interference by unions or other interests (Reddish, 1980: 298–301). On the other hand, collective voice allows workers to raise concerns with reduced fear of victimisation (Harcourt et al., 2004). It may promote productivity by reducing turnover; given the greater depth of collective voice, employees have less need to express concerns by quitting (Kaufman, 2004). It provides a valuable mechanism for resolving collective and individual problems arising from flexible working (Singe and Croucher, 2003). Management may restrict the depth of individual voice to reduce the possibilities of it assuming a collective dimension; in unionised enterprises, managers may already be reconciled to this possibility, and have therefore modified their approach (Kaufman, 2004). Finally, collective voice mechanisms also have potential to raise productivity by direct means (see Brewster et al., 2007). Thus, efficiencies may be maximised through collective voice. All of these arrangements are most likely to be effective where the context is favourable to them; participation will lack credibility if job security is low, and/or wage costs minimised (Kochan and Osterman, 2000).

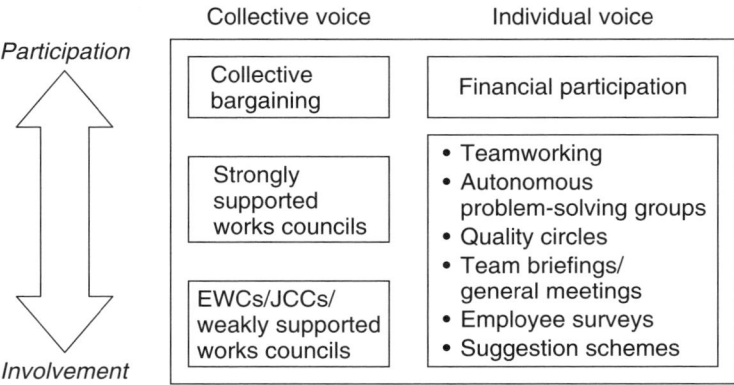

Figure 5.1 Forms of Voice, Participation and Involvement.

Unions and works councils are specific vehicles for collective voice. Voice is *externalised* through unions; generally (although a few national exceptions may be noted) employees opt for a multi-workplace body to bargain on their behalf. In contrast, elected delegates to works councils or joint consultative committees are responsible only to the workers in that workplace who form their constituency. It may be argued that this latter form of voice will be more effective as representatives are directly answerable to their constituents. Yet precisely this indirectness may generate greater strength. Union officers not employed by firms are clearly less open to victimisation by them (Harcourt et al., 2004) Moreover, they can utilise union resources to formulate well researched negotiating positions, and are well equipped to draw comparisons with other firms' practices. Therefore, it may be that *internal representational voice* represents a distinct and also inferior (because more limited) form to voice that is *externalised* to the union (ibid; c.f. Millward et al. 2000). Potentially, these internal options may be favoured by employers as a way of weakening collective bargaining.

The relationship between JCCs, works councils and collective bargaining is discussed elsewhere by the authors. We note there that JCCs *and* statutory works councils were associated with trade union presence in both liberal market and collaborative economies (Brewster et al., 2006). Viewed longitudinally, no evidence was found that workplaces with JCCs were associated with lower union presence. As findings from the British Workplace Employment Relations Study (WERS) demonstrate, JCCs are often to be found alongside collective bargaining (Kersley et al., 2005). We therefore focus here on associations between individual and collective voice, possible shifts from one to the other, and whether trans-national convergence to particular configurations of voice mechanisms is in evidence.

Institutions, Complementarity and Voice

Hyman (2004) argues that voice is an aspect of wider regulation of employment issues. Thus, the relative effectiveness and sustainability of any specific voice mechanism is linked to other systemic social and economic features. How governance is structured within and beyond companies is a key feature of national business systems. In some systems, mutually reinforcing forms of voice are found together, optimising workers' remuneration and working conditions, as well as productivity and organisational performance (Hubler and Jirjahn, 2003). In other systems, there may be tensions between different forms of voice, with considerable pressures towards the adoption of individual forms (Bryson, 2004). Hopner (2005) notes that countries such as Germany and Sweden, characterised by strong labour market institutions, also have highly organised systems of governance inside the firm; these systems have been denominated *stakeholder orientated* or *cooperative* varieties of capitalism, as opposed to the *shareholder oriented* varieties to be found in Anglo-Saxon countries (Hall and Soskice, 2001; Dore, 2000). These researchers argue that employers and employees may vary the extent to which they invest in the firm; labour may vary its investment in its skills and its organisational commitment, whilst management may vary the degrees of reinvestment and how far it seeks to develop cooperative arrangements. This encompasses the extent to which employers and employees become mutually dependent through formal rights and obligations, and the presence and nature of mechanisms designed to build employee participation (Whitley, 1999; Dore, 2000). A key difference between different varieties of capitalism in terms of labour management is the *nature and degree of employer–employee interdependence* (Whitley 1999). Firms which operate in cooperative national environments will likely make use of *collective* and *representational* forms of participation, while different types of representative participation are frequently complementary (Thelen 2001).

The position is summarized in Figure 5.2 below.

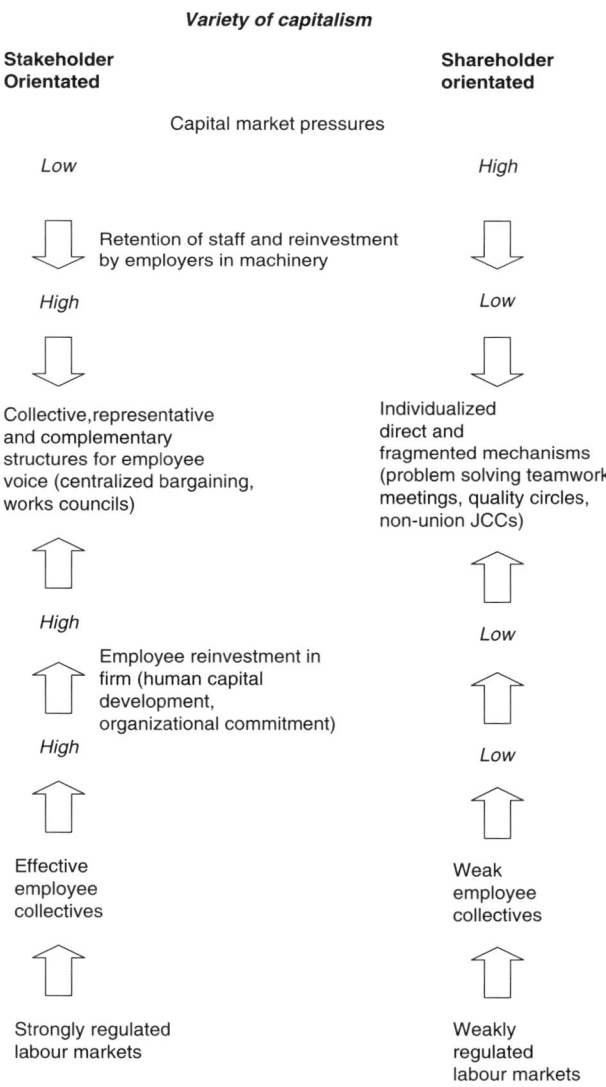

Figure 5.2 Institutional Complementarity in Different Settings.

In Germany, despite contrary pressures, powerful legal support for the institutions of co-determination remains, tending to support employee commitment and unions' positions. Unions retain a central position in the polity, partly due to strong institutional mediation and mobilisation capacity (Turner, 2004:6); this is also the case in Sweden (Lindeberg et al., 2004). However, external liberalising pressures render such institutional support vulnerable (Lindeberg et al., 2004: 282; 2004: 7; Lane, 2000). Indeed, German union density declined from the late 1980s onwards, although this in part was due to German reunification; actual membership increased (Behrens et al., 2004:19). Public discussion of labour market reform has increasingly focused on a supposed need to remove 'rigidities'. Employers press for works councils to be permitted to conclude agreements without union approval (Lane, 2000; Singe and Croucher, 2005), thereby seeking to disarticulate central elements of the IR system (ibid.). Lindeberg et al. (2004: 282) argue that in Sweden, the employers' confederation SAF has established the terms of public discussion with similar arguments since the 1990s. In brief, both Germany and Sweden have seen liberal viewpoints deployed to question long-standing arrangements without these having brought significant state interventions to change systemic essentials.

In the UK, unions lost strength during the Thatcher years, reflected in a loss of overall membership and declining union density (Turner, 2004: 6). Unions' position improved marginally under New Labour – union density briefly stabilised at around 30% – but gains were limited, fragile, and vulnerable to recently renewed governmental attacks (Turner, 2004: 7). The Labour government enacted three significant statutes – the Employment Relations Acts of 1999 and 2002 and the Employment Act 2002 in a re-ordering of employment law which has been judged to 'not unduly constrain managerial prerogative' (Smith and Morton, 2004: 1). Similarly, the Information and Consultation of Employees Regulations 2004 were passed, a relatively weak piece of pro-consultation legislation (Hall, 2005). Thus, wider institutional support for unions in the country remain restricted, and therefore union-based collective voice remains vulnerable under the Coalition government.

A trend towards convergence?

A growing literature has explored whether HRM practices within firms are losing their national distinctiveness (c.f. Weber et al., 1998). Some have suggested that inevitable global pressures militate in the direction of weak regulation, low commitment and low levels of organisational citizenship (Duysters and Hagedoorn, 2001). The global diffusion of the US model is posited as occurring albeit in an uneven manner (c.f. Locke et al., 1995). Convergence theorists recognise that variations persist, but suggest that their salience is likely to diminish.

These theories suggest that differences in management systems linked with different national historic paths have already been superseded by the logic of technology and markets, which are argued to demand the adoption of universally applicable management techniques (Kidger, 1991). They tend to assume that management practices are largely driven by a desire to maximise technological or economic efficiency and relatively little attention is paid to specific socio-political contexts (c.f. Kerr, 1983). In the early 1990s it was suggested that convergence in the EU towards a European alternative to the US model was likely (Due et al., 1991). However, considerable diversity continues to be apparent within Europe. Yet a lack of evidence for convergence potentially suggests either stasis or divergence. Both of these possibilities underline the embeddedness of national institutions (Poole, 1986; Hollingsworth and Boyer, 1997).

The US HRM model overthrew the previous settlement forged in the 1930s and 1940s. It includes weakening of the collective basis of employee voice and a systematic move towards individual voice, geared towards enhancing productivity through individual motivation, turning away from conceptions based on workplace democracy (Weinstein and Kochan, 1995). The US economy's relatively strong performance in the 1990s and early 2000s fuelled international interest in American practices. Encouraged by the international financial institutions, moves by many national governments towards labour market deregulation, the global decline of organised labour and the widespread diffusion of neo-liberal ideology all suggest that the environment favours diffusion of the US model, leading to the gradual replacement of collective voice mechanisms by individual ones. However, in Europe forms of collective and representative voice are often entrenched by norms as well as by law: most notably in the Netherlands, Denmark and Germany, firms are legally required to have two-tier management boards, with employees having the right to representation on senior supervisory boards (Slomp, 1998). These laws reflect widely held norms. The EU has remained committed to promoting the role of 'social partners', albeit in ways that also reflect its participation agenda. This commitment is reflected in its promulgation of European works councils, the Information and Consultation Directive and the European Companies Statute.

Divergence Theories

Institutional divergence theorists have long argued that national contexts are insulated from the hypothetical imperatives of technology, the market or essentially permissive legislation from supra-national bodies, reflecting the embeddedness of institutions (DiMaggio and Powell, 1983: Meyer and Rowan, 1983; Oliver, 1991; Hollingsworth and Boyer, 1997). MNCs, for whom legitimacy in host countries is a key concern, help to maintain this situation. Surveys show that US companies are highly observant of German industrial relations law (Singe and Croucher, 2005).

The complexity and wide range of forces in operation underscores the different theoretical ways in which convergence or divergence may take place. Convergence may be towards a new bundle of common practices, or alternatively may be towards a specific set of practices within a particular country. There may be evidence of a trend in a particular direction, or the final convergence of practices among the majority of firms. Therefore, one may refer to *directional convergence* as distinct from *final convergence*. The latter is the type of convergence most commonly assumed to be taking place in the literature, although it is often confused or conflated with other types. This may be either cause or effect, or both, of a limited incidence of longitudinal studies. Similarly, divergence may merely reflect the persistence of difference – this may be *stasis* – or, alternatively, centrifugal tendencies.

Hypothesis

In summary, the varieties of capitalism literature suggest that within cooperative systems, employee voice mechanisms will include centralised bargaining, and that this will coexist with and reinforce other forms of representative voice, such as works councils. In liberal market systems on the other hand, collective bargaining is *less* likely to coexist with other voice mechanisms, which tend to be 'direct' and individually orientated. It appears clear that overall, the variety of voice mechanisms has increased; however, the tendency towards convergence (of whatever variety) is less clear, although it has been widely argued that the predominant trend is towards the liberal market model (see Streeck, 1995; O'Hagan, 2002). Our hypothesis is therefore:

> *There has been a general trend away from collective and towards individual voice mechanisms, reflecting the predominant trajectory of managerial practices towards convergence with the liberal market model.*

Method

Data

The data used here are drawn from the repeating Cranet survey, described in Chapter 2. The dataset used is from the UK, Germany and Sweden and covers all four waves of the Cranet survey, i.e. 1991, 1995, 1999 and 2003, collectively giving a total sample size of 8,844 firms.

Mean company sizes in the three countries are as follows: for Britain 3,532; for Germany 5,774 and for Sweden 2,272 employees. Companies both recognising a union for collective bargaining purposes and reporting the presence of at least some union members amounted to 71% of the companies operating in the UK, 84% in Germany and 95% in Sweden. These rates of unionisation are clearly higher than those generally reported for the entirety of these economies; the dataset contains a high proportion of large, unionised companies. It is therefore suitable for testing our hypothesis since collective voice is widely present though not exclusively so.

The Model

The basic propositions are that a trend away from collective and towards individual voice mechanisms has occurred, with countries converging in voice mechanism terms. Employees communicating with management through trade unions or JCC/WCs is employed as an indicator of collective voice. Communication by means of workforce meetings, team briefings, suggestion schemes and attitude surveys is used as an indicator of individual voice. The decision to use collective and/or individual voice mechanisms likely reflects the firm's operating environment as well as the nature of its operations. The voice mechanism used is likely to be dependent upon two central factors. The first of these is firm size, as larger organisations may tend to opt for more formalised forms of voice (e.g. collective bargaining, works councils) than informal voice forms (e.g. general meetings). Smaller firms are likely to choose less formal methods. This is not to imply that all forms of direct and individual voice are informal; workforce surveys administered by e-mail may in fact be highly structured and formal. However, collective voice mechanisms are likely to be relatively formal and in many case governed by norms and even legislation. Many agreements are in some sense binding, negotiations are often complex, representatives are generally accountable to their constituents. These approaches may therefore be more common in larger firms. The second factor dictating use of voice mechanism is industrial sector, since the typical mode of operation in each industry may vary in the degree to which it is conducive to individual voice.

Therefore, in order to test our two basic propositions, we estimate two empirical models. These use the presence of communication through unions or JCC/WCs on the one hand and workforce meetings, team briefings, suggestion schemes and attitude surveys on the other, separately as the dependent variables, using size and industrial sector as the explanatory variables.

For each country a series of binomial logit models are estimated of the form;

$$\text{Prob}(y_i = 1) = \frac{\exp(\beta' x_i)}{1 + \exp(\beta' x_i)} \ .$$

where y_i is the use of communication through first trade unions or WC/JCCs and second through the alternative methods (1 = yes and 0 = no), x_i is the vector of explanatory variables, in this case size measured by number of employees and a set of dummies to identify fifteen different industrial sectors, and β' their estimated coefficients.

The hypothesis' first dimension, *that there has been a trend away from collective and towards individual voice*, is tested by pooling the four waves of data, then estimating the probability of communicating through collective and individual means for each country. The hypothesis suggests that individual voice should be less in evidence, and more collective voice in the first wave. More individual and less collective voice should be apparent, in the last wave, in all the countries under review. We therefore apply a likelihood ratio test to assess whether these relationships are as expected.

The second dimension of the hypothesis proposes that the predominant trajectory of change has been towards the liberal market/Anglo Saxon model, with the individualisation of practices becoming widespread through the 1990s and 2000s. This requires that the data for all three countries are pooled. Then, separately for

1991 and 2003, the empirical models are estimated, but on this occasion a set of dummies is included for each country with the UK as the reference category. If the convergence hypothesis is correct, the differences between the countries should reduce across time, while the coefficients on the country dummies should be smaller in the latter wave as the countries converge.

Findings

Communicating with management through a trade union or JCC/WC is used as the indicator of collective voice, and team briefings, workforce meetings, suggestion schemes or attitude surveys are used as indicators of individual voice. Table 5.1 below gives raw figures for each of these measures. The hypothesis suggests a reduction in collective voice and a rise in the use of individual. Yet a reduction in collective voice only appears to have occurred in the UK whilst there is also evidence of increased use of individual voice particularly through attitude surveys and suggestion schemes.

The hypothesis also suggests that the three countries are converging towards the liberal market/Anglo-Saxon model. Figure 5.3 maps the use of collective voice

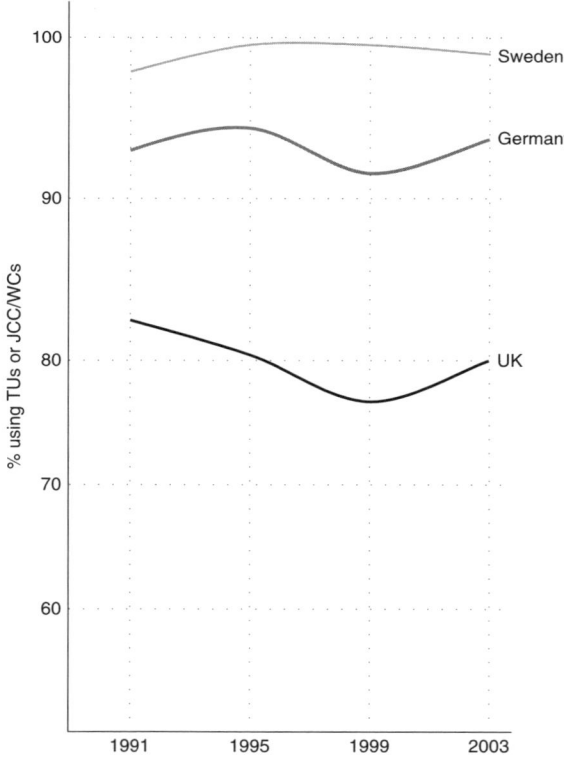

Figure 5.3 Changes in the Use of Collective Voice, 1991–2003

Table 5.1 Use of Voice Mechanisms, 1991–2003

	UK				Germany				Sweden			
	1991	1995	1999	2003	1991	1995	1999	2003	1991	1995	1999	2003
% Using TUs or JCCs/WCs	82	78	71	77	90	94	93	92	95	99	99	98
% Using Workforce Meetings	69	80	81	83	79	94	92	94	n/a	99	99	99
% Using Team Briefings	n/a	86	89	93	n/a	74	76	75	n/a	96	99	98
% Using Suggestion Schemes	47	58	52	54	67	73	70	72	57	92	84	75
% Using Attitude Surveys	44	59	53	64	36	54	59	65	55	71	79	84
Observations	1483	1204	981	895	906	638	526	301	289	285	317	331

through JCC/WCs or trade unions across the period considered. It reveals that there has been no real convergence. Sweden has maintained a high level of collective voice throughout. The UK and Germany both initially moved away from collective voice, but in more recent survey waves both countries have returned to levels similar to those shown in the initial survey. In sum, the use of voice method is not moving in a simple convergent direction but rather is subject to contingencies that, in terms of method (other than team briefings), Germany and the UK appear to share but Sweden does not.

Figure 5.4 maps the use of individual voice through the incidence of workforce meetings. In this case it suggests a certain amount of convergence. Sweden maintained almost total coverage throughout the period, whilst the UK and Germany both display large increases in its prevalence.

Figure 5.5 maps the use of team briefings. Use has remained high in Germany and Sweden, and has increased markedly in the UK. Use in Germany peaked in 1999 but declined again in the 2003 survey. Thus, there is no support for the

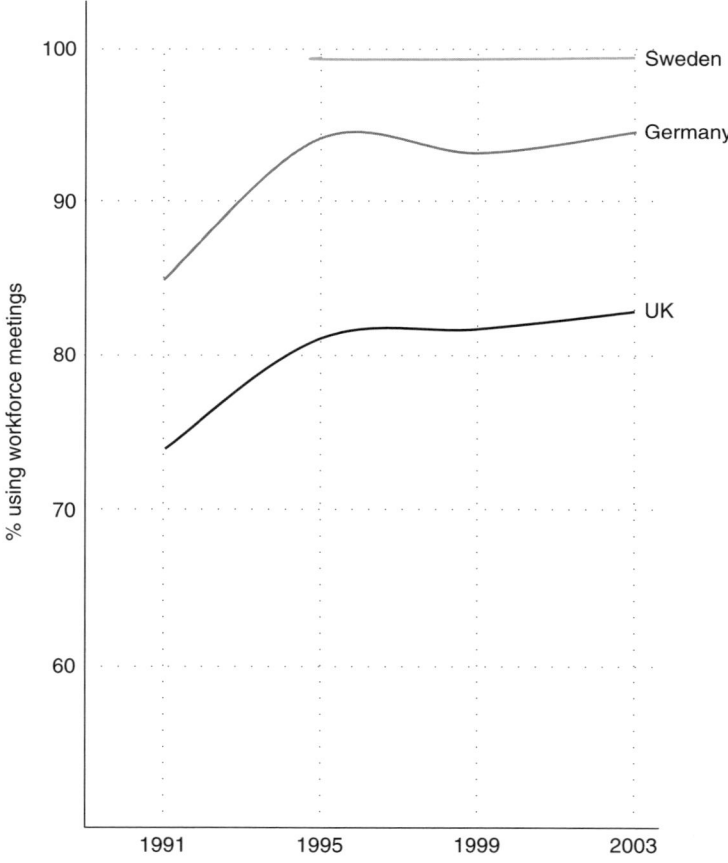

Figure 5.4 Changes in the Use of Workforce Meetings, 1991–2003

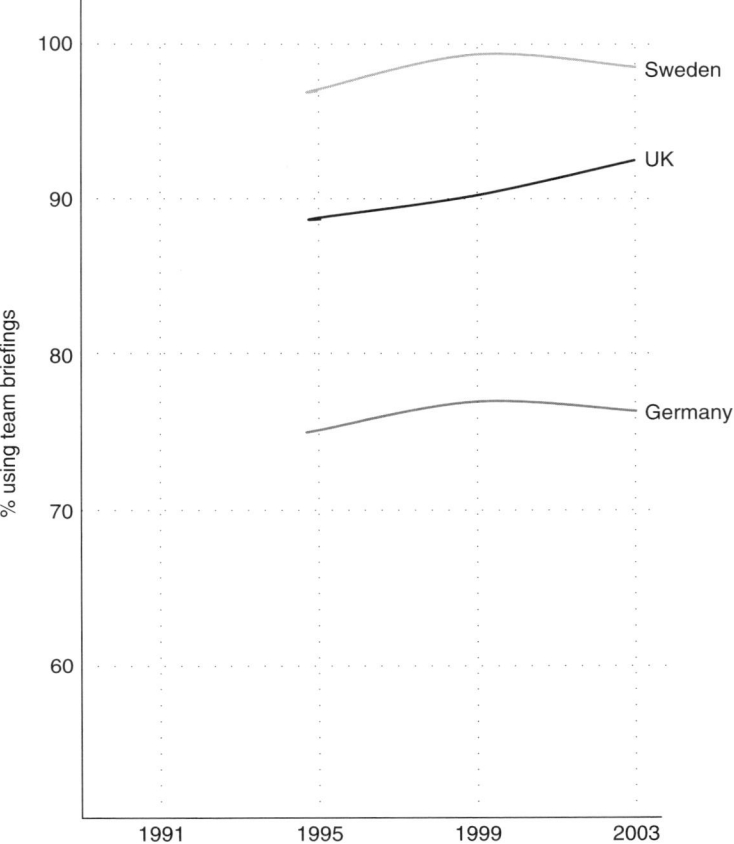

Figure 5.5 Use of Team Briefings, 1991–2003

hypothesis that Germany and Sweden have converged towards the Anglo-Saxon/liberal market model.

Some differences are likely to result from disparities in company characteristics and their environments. In this case the disparities are between their organisational sizes and the industrial sectors in which they operate. Consequently, we next estimate the likelihood of voice occurring through collective or individual means as a function of size and industrial sector. We estimate a series of logit models with communication through trade unions or JCC/WCs, workforce meetings and team briefings as the dependent variables.

In order to test the first sub-hypothesis, the models are estimated separately for each country using all of the years available in the survey. A likelihood ratio test is then applied. This simply tests whether the model's structure is the same in the earliest year as in the latest year. The hypothesis suggests greater use of individual voice mechanisms, and less use of collective, longitudinally. If that were the case, the null hypothesis of the model being the same in both periods should be rejected in all cases. The results are summarised in Table 5.2.

Table 5.2 The Prevalence of Different Forms of Voice

Category	Country	Structural Test	LR Test Stat.	Outcome
Communication	UK	1991 vs. 1995–2003	19	Accept
through	UK	2003 vs.1991–99	33.6	Reject at 1%
TU or JCC/WC	Germany	1991 vs. 1995–2003	10	Accept
	Germany	2003 vs. 1991–99	4.4	Accept
	Sweden	1991 vs. 1995–2003	3.6	Accept
	Sweden	2003 vs. 1991–99	8.8	Accept
Communication	UK	1991 vs. 1995–2003	135.6	Reject at 1%
through	UK	2003 vs. 1991–99	49	Reject at 1%
Workforce	Germany	1991 vs. 1995–2003	112	Reject at 1%
Meetings	Germany	2003 vs. 1991–99	25.6	Reject at 1%
	Sweden	1995 vs. 1999–2003	12.4	Accept
	Sweden	2003 vs. 1995–99	8	Accept
Communication	UK	1995 vs. 1999–2003	24	Reject at 5%
through Team	UK	2003 vs. 1995–99	19.4	Accept
Briefings	Germany	1995 vs. 1999–2003	19.8	Accept
	Germany	2003 vs. 1995–99	9	Accept
	Sweden	1995 vs. 1999–2003	18.8	Accept
	Sweden	2003 vs. 1995–99	12	Accept

Applying the likelihood ratio tests provides a different picture in each country. First, Sweden displays high levels of coverage for most of the modes of communication; this remained consistent throughout the entire period. However our evidence also indicates a significant increase in the incidence of suggestion schemes and attitude surveys. Second, the UK followed the hypothesis' implication fairly closely, since it shows a decrease in collective voice, although it has revived to a degree in the most recent survey. In addition, there is strong evidence of an increase in workforce meetings, suggestion schemes and attitude surveys together with some evidence of an increase in team briefings in the UK. Finally, Germany shows clear evidence of an increase in the use of workforce meetings, suggestion schemes and attitude surveys but no other significant changes.

Testing the second sub-hypothesis requires estimating the models with all the countries' data included and adding country dummies to control for cross-country differences. The models are estimated for the first available year and then re-estimated using our 2003 data. In all cases the UK is used as the base country. Confirmation of our hypothesis would exist if the impact of the German and Swedish dummies on the model fell over the period considered. The results are summarised in Table 5.3.

Table 5.3 records the marginal effects of the country dummies on the model. Thus, for example once controls were used for differences in size and industrial sector, firms in Germany were 11.4% more likely in 1991 to use union or JCC/WC channels than their UK counterparts. The equivalent measure fell to 5.3% by 2003. This lends support to the second sub-hypothesis, since it indicates that

Table 5.3 Marginal Effects of Country Dummies

Category	Year	Marg. Effects – Germany	Marg. Effects – Sweden
Communication through TU or JCC/WC	1991	.1141 (.0165)	.1463 (.0326)
	2003	.0529 (.0141)	.1454 (.0262)
Communication through Workforce Meetings	1995	.1078 (.0179)	.2755 (.0329)
	2003	.0651 (.0175)	.2170 (.0232)
Communication through Team Briefings	1995	−.1302 (.0188)	.1184 (.0313)
	2003	−.1156 (.0156)	.1043 (.0255)
Communication through Suggestion Scheme	1991	.1212 (.0208)	.0470 (.0293)
	2003	.1510 (.0345)	.1951 (.0339)
Communication through Attitude Surveys	1991	−.0114 (.0210)	.0337 (.0318)
	2003	−.0393 (.0274)	.1497 (.0309)

firms in the two countries are in this sense becoming increasingly similar over time. However, beyond this very little support exists for the sub-hypothesis. None of the other changes, apart from German use of workforce meetings, reaches any level of significance. Therefore the second sub-hypothesis cannot be simply confirmed or rejected outright. There is little evidence of a general trend towards convergence by Sweden and Germany, but it does appear that the latter may be adopting some aspects of the liberal market model. However it could be argued that there is simply a different picture in each of the three countries. Sweden continues on its path, making broad and comprehensive use of all of the communication methods, whilst Germany and the UK are indeed converging.

Conclusions

We analysed how far there has been a trend within organisations operating in Britain, Germany and Sweden towards use of individual rather than collective voice practices between 1991 and 2003. Our analysis gives the convergence argument some limited support since German organisations, controlling for differences in size and sector, showed a decreasing tendency to use their works councils in the period. The finding is significant since the German model has considerable wider importance for the European model. However, the data provide little overall support for the argument that convergence has occurred in a general sense, despite increasingly vociferous calls by neo-liberals for the greater individualisation of employment relations in Western Europe. The direction of change has certainly not been linear. The UK and Germany appear to have been moving away from collective voice in the 1990s, but have since returned to levels similar to those observed in 1991. This seems to demonstrate a return to the use of collective voice by managers in both countries. This *de facto* return to these channels sits uneasily with much contemporaneous managerial rhetoric in both countries, as well as with a good deal of academic work. However, collective voice is a broad term that goes well beyond trade unionism and encompasses many different representational forms, processes and outcomes. Dundon et al. (2004) argue that voice represents a contested process shaped by both external regulatory pressures and internal managerial choice. These researchers suggest that it is essential to examine how well such mechanisms are embedded within organisations (ibid.: 1167). It may be that the return to collective voice obscures a shift in the content of voice processes towards more managerially driven forms. Examining the possibility would require case study work.

We argued at the outset of this article that efficiencies are likely to be maximised through collective voice, and on this argument the results are positive. Our central finding about a lack of directional convergence between countries should be placed in the context of the apparently more robust performance of liberal market economies in the early 2000s, and any demonstration effects at the organisational level that this might suggest. It appears clear that collective channels remain significant in larger organisations, a finding encouraging both to trade unions and proponents of other forms of collective voice such as works councils.

The findings have two key theoretical implications. The first is that researchers from the 'regulation school' (such as Boyer, 2004), who have argued that national systems continue to evolve according to a 'path dependent' logic specific to each country, appear to be largely correct. The second is that 'universalist' US paradigms of HRM centring on the elimination of conventional collective voice mechanisms have not made much headway in Western Europe.

However, as we noted above, evidence exists that the German system has been subject to some individualisation of voice and in particular to increased diffusion of direct forms of communication, especially in the form of general meetings. This provides support for more pessimistic assessments of the current state of the German system of co-determination (Hassel, 2002). It is also raises wider concerns for the fate of the 'European model' of voice arrangements as propagated by the EU. Effective extension of the model to other countries, and not only within the EU but more widely, may appear problematic if that form is in Germany itself in retreat not only on the political but also on the organisational level.

References

Adams, R. (2005) 'Efficiency, equity and voice as moral imperatives', *Employee Responsibilities and Rights Journal* 17(2): 111–17.

Behrens, M., Hamann, K. and Hurd, R. (2004) 'Conceptualizing labour union revitalization', in C. Frege, and J. Kelly (eds) *Varieties of Unionism*. Oxford: Oxford University Press.

Boyer, R. (2004) 'New growth regimes, but still institutional diversity', *Socio–Economic Review* 2(1): 1–32.

Brewster, C., Brookes, M., Croucher, R. and Wood, G. (2007) 'Collective and individual voice: Convergence in Europe?', *International Journal of Human Resource Management* 18(7): 1246–62.

Brewster, C., Wood, G., Croucher, R. and Brookes, M. (2007), 'Are works councils and JCCs a threat to trade unions?', *Economic and Industrial Democracy* 28(1): 49–77.

Bryson, A. (2002) 'The Union membership Wage Premium: an Analysis Using Propensity Score Matching' Centre for Economic Performance, London.

Bryson, A. (2004) 'Managerial responsiveness to union and nonunion worker voice in Britain', *Industrial Relations* 43(1): 213–41.

Budd, J. (2004) *Employment with a Human Face: Balancing Efficiency, Equity and Voice*. Ithaca: Cornell University Press.

Budd, J.W. and Na, I-G. (2000) 'The union membership wage premium for employees covered by collective bargaining agreements', *Journal of Labor Economics* 18(4): 783–807.

Colvin, A. (2004) 'The relationship between employee involvement and workplace dispute resolution', *Relations Industrielles–Industrial Relations* 59(4): 681–701.

DiMaggio, P. and Powell, W. (1983) 'The iron cage revisited', *American Sociological Review* 48: 147–60.

Dore, R. (2000) *Stock Market Capitalism: Welfare Capitalism*. Cambridge: Cambridge University Press.

Due, J., Madsen, J. and Jensen, C. (1991) 'The social dimension', *Industrial Relations Journal* 22(2): 85–102.

Dundon, T., Wilkinson, A., Marchington, M. and Ackers, P. (2004) 'The meanings and purpose of employee voice', *International Journal of Human Resource Management* 16(4): 1149–70.

Duysters, G. and Hagedoorn, J. (2001) 'Do company strategies and structures converge in global markets? Evidence from the computer industry', *Journal of International Business Studies* 32(2): 347–56.

Flanders, A. (1980) 'Industrial relations: What is wrong with the system?', in B. Barrett, E. Rhodes and J. Beishon (eds) *Industrial Relations and the Wider Society: Aspects of Intepretation*. London: Collier Macmillan.

Forth, J. and Millward, N. (2000) 'The determinants of pay levels and fringe benefit provision in Britain', Discussion Paper 171. London: NIESR.

Fox, A. (1980) 'Industrial relations: A social critique of pluralist ideology', in M.B. Barrett, E. Rhodes and J. Beishon (eds) *Industrial Relations and the Wider Society: Aspects of Interpretation*. London: Collier Macmillan.

Freeman, R. and Medoff, J. (1984) *What Do Unions Do?* New York: Basic Books.

Hall, M. (2005) 'Assessing the information and consultation of employees regulations', *Industrial Law Journal* 34(2): 103–26.

Hall, P. and Soskice, D. (eds) (2001) *Varieties of Capitalism: The Institutional Foundations of Competitive Advantage*. Oxford: Oxford University Press.

Harcourt, M., Wood, G. and Harcourt, S. (2004) 'Do unions affect employer compliance with the law?', *British Journal of Industrial Relations* 42(3): 527–41.

Hassel, A. (2002) 'The erosion continues: a reply to Klikauer', *British Journal of Industrial Relations* 40(2): 309–17.

Hirschman, A.O. (1970) *Exit, Voice and Loyalty*. Cambridge, MA: Harvard University Press.

Hollingsworth, R. and Boyer, R. (1997) 'Coordination of economic actors and social systems of production', in R. Hollingsworth and R. Boyer (eds) *Contemporary Capitalism: The Embeddedness of Institutions*. Cambridge: Cambridge University Press.

Hopner, M. (2005) 'What connects industrial relations and corporate governance?', *Socio-Economic Review* 3(2): 331–58.

Hubler, O. and Jirjahn, U. (2003) 'Works councils and collective bargaining in Germany: The impact on productivity and wages', *Scottish Journal of Political Economy* 50(4): 471–92.

Hyman, R. (2004) 'Where next for partnership?', in M. Stuart and M. Martinez Lucio (eds) *Partnership and Modernization in Employment Relations*. London: Routledge.

Kaufman, B. (2004) 'What do unions do: Insights from economic theory', *Journal of Labor Research* 25(3): 351–82.

Kerr, C. (1983) *The Future of Industrial Societies: Convergence or Continuing Diversity?* Cambridge, MA: Harvard University Press.

Kersley, B., Alpin, C., Forth, J., Dix, G., Bryson, A. and Bewley, H. (2005) *Inside the Workplace. First Findings from the 2004 Employment Relations Survey.* London: Routledge.

Kidger, P. (1991) 'The emergence of international human resource management', *International Journal of Human Resource Management* 2(2): 149–63.

Kochan, T. and Osterman, P. (2000) 'The mutual gains enterprise', in C. Mabey, G. Salaman and J. Storey (eds) *Strategic Human Resource Management.* London: Sage.

Lane, C. (2000) 'Globalization and the German model of capitalism', *British Journal of Sociology* 51(2): 207–34.

Lincoln, J. and Kalleberg, A. (1990) *Culture, Control and Commitment: A Study of Work Organization in the United States and Japan.* Cambridge: Cambridge University Press.

Lindeberg, T., Månson, B. and Vanhala, S. (2004) 'Sweden and Finland: small countries with large companies', pp. 279–312 in C. Brewster, W. Mayrhofer and M. Morley (eds) *Human Resource Management in Europe.* Amsterdam: Elsevier.

Locke, R., Kochan, T. and Piore, M. (eds) (1995) *Employment Relations in a Changing World Economy.* Cambridge, MA: MIT Press.

Martens, H. (1992) *Gewerkschaftspolitik und Gewerkschaftssoziologie, Gewerkschaftsforschung am Landesinstitut Sozialforschungsstelle.* Dortmund: Montania.

Mayo, E. (1945) *The Social Problems of an Industrial Civilization.* New Hampshire: Ayer.

Meyer, J. and Rowan, B. (1983) 'The structure of educational organizations', in J. Meyer and W. Scott (eds) *Organization Environments.* Beverly Hills, CA: Sage.

Millward, A., Bryson, J. and Forth, J. (2000) *All Change at Work: British Employment Relations 1980–1998 as Portrayed by the Workplace Industrial Relations Survey Series.* London: Routledge.

O'Hagan, E. (2002) *Employee Relations in the Periphery of Europe: The Unfolding of the European Social Model.* London: Palgrave.

Oliver, C. (1991) 'Strategic responses to institutional processes', *Academy of Management Review* 16(1): 145–79.

Poole, M. (1986) *Industrial Relations – Origins and Patterns of National Diversity.* London: RKP.

Reddish, S. (1980) 'Written memorandum of evidence to the Royal Commission on Trade Unions and Employer Associations', in M.B. Barrett, E. Rhodes and J. Beishon (eds) *Industrial Relations and Wider Society.* London: Collier Macmillan.

Singe, I. and Croucher, R. (2003) 'The management of trust-based working time in Germany', *Personnel Review* 32(4): 492–509.

Singe, I. and Croucher, R. (2005) 'US multi-nationals and the German industrial relations system', *Management Revue* 16(1): 123–37.

Slomp, H. (1998) *Between bargaining and politics.* London: Praeger.

Smith, P. and Morton, G. (2004) 'Seven years New Labour: The Third Way, management prerogative and workers' rights'. Working paper, University of Keele Department of HRM.

Streeck, W. (1995) 'Neo-voluntarism: A new European social policy regime', *European Law Journal* 1(1): 31–59.

Thelen, K. (2001) 'Varieties of labor policies in developed democracies', in P. Hall and D. Soskice (eds) *Varieties of Capitalism: The Institutional Foundations of Competitive Advantage.* Oxford: Oxford University Press.

Turner, L. (2004) 'Why revitalize? Labour's urgent mission in a contested global economy', in C. Frege and J. Kelly (eds) *Varieties of Unionism.* Oxford: Oxford University Press.

Weber, W., Käbst, R. and Gramley, C. (1998) 'Does the Common Market imply common human resource management policies?' Proceedings of the 6th Conference on International Human Resource Management, Paderborn, Germany.

Weinstein, M. and Kochan, T. (1995) 'The limits of diffusion', in R. Locke, T. Kochan and M. Piore (eds) *Employment Relations in a Changing World Economy*. Cambridge, MA: MIT Press.

Whitley, R. (1999) *Divergent Capitalisms.* Oxford: Oxford University Press.

Wood, G. (1998) *Trade Union Recognition: Cornerstone of the New South African Employment Relations*. Johannesburg: Thompson International.

Woodall, J. and Winstanley, D. (2001) 'The place of ethics in HRM', in J. Storey (ed.) *Human Resource Management: A Critical Text*. London: Thomson Learning.

6 Corporate Governance Systems and Investments in Human Capital

MARC GOERGEN, GEOFFREY WOOD,
CHRIS BREWSTER AND MICHAEL BROOKES

Introduction

First attempts at developing taxonomies of corporate governance systems, such as Hicks (1969) and Chandler (1977, 1984), focused on differences in the financing of industrial enterprise and differences in corporate control and ownership. More recent taxonomies take into account employee protection legislation as well as other ways firms relate with their workforce. The latter include the amount of training as well as the nature of the training that firms are willing and able to provide for their employees. The taxonomy of corporate governance systems that has been the most prescriptive in terms of cross-national differences in investments in human capital is the varieties of capitalism (VOC) literature (see e.g. Dore 2000; Hall and Soskice 2001; Lincoln and Kalleberg 1990). In what follows, we seek to investigate whether extensive cross-country survey data confirm the predictions of the VOC literature as to the trans-national differences in the provision of government education as well as firm-level training for employees.

The main research question of this chapter is to undertake a simple test to determine which of the VOC approaches, the dichotomous approach or approaches that involve more than two varieties of capitalism (Whitley 1999, Amable 2003) fits with training patterns.

Taxonomies of Corporate Governance Systems and Investments in Human Capital

This section starts by reviewing the so called 'law and finance' literature which started with the seminal paper of La Porta et al. (1997). This literature considers the rights conferred on investors as the paramount driver of financial development and economic performance. While labour may be an important production factor, this literature argues that it takes second place relative to capital, given the sunk nature of the latter. In contrast, the VOC literature, which will be reviewed in the remainder of this section, argues that capital and labour are equally important inputs into the production process.

The Law and Finance Literature

As Chapter 1 indicates, there are now several well known theories in the finance, law and management literature proposing classifications of corporate govern-ance systems based on the importance of investors, i.e. shareholders, relative to other stakeholders, mainly employees. Most of these theories tend to distinguish between two main and fairly broad systems of corporate governance. For exam-ple, La Porta et al. (1997, 1998) distinguish between common law and civil law, which differ in terms of the protection they confer to shareholders. Roe's (2003) theory is also of a dichotomous nature. According to Roe it is politics rather than law that is the main driving force behind corporate governance. He argues that left-wing governments favour employees over investors and they devise laws that strengthen the power of employees within corporations. However, Pagano and Volpin (2005) predict that the type of electoral system is the main determinant of the corporate governance setting, in particular the distribution of power between shareholders and workers. They argue that proportional voting systems favour strong employee rights as political parties will need to obtain the support of the large homogeneous social group of the workers and managers to win elections, whilst majoritarian or first-past-the-post systems will favour strong property rights for owners.

What all of the above theories have in common is that strong investor rights are a necessary and sufficient condition for strong economic growth while strong employment protection hinders economic growth and efficiency. In contrast, the varieties of capitalism literature, reviewed next, accords similar roles to capital and labour in fostering economic growth. Crucially, it does not share the premise that strong shareholder rights cannot coexist alongside strong worker rights.

The Varieties of Capitalism Literature

The varieties of capitalism (VOC) literature is the body of literature that says the most about the role of workers and human resource management (HRM) prac-tices across corporate governance systems. Similar to the above three theories from the law and finance literature, its simplest form distinguishes between just two broad systems of corporate governance: liberal market economies (LMEs) and collaborative market economies (CMEs) (Dore 2000; Hall and Soskice 2001; Lincoln and Kalleberg 1990). In LMEs political power is concentrated in the executive and the economy is coordinated via strong market forces (Hall and Sos-kice 2001). In CMEs the economy is coordinated via non-market mechanisms, given that CMEs are less antagonistic and more collaborative in nature, it makes sense for employers to provide industry-specific and/or firm-specific training. Indeed, given that labour markets are highly regulated and hence relatively rigid, employees are less likely to change jobs and more likely to be loyal to their current employer. In addition, powerful employer associations police entire industries ensuring that corporations do not free-ride on their competitors' efforts to train their employees by poaching them once the training has been completed. Hence, firms can spread the costs of training over an extended period of time, with the confidence that any spend will provide a long term contribution to organisational capabilities (Goergen et al. 2012).

While most of the VOC literature adopts the dichotomous approach, there have also been attempts to distinguish between more than two types of corporate governance regimes (Amable, 2003, Whitley 1999). Whitley does explore the cases of central European countries that have undergone transitions from state socialism, examining the issues of continuities at organisational level in relation to changes in external environments (Whitley, 1999: 240). It is argued that these countries also face pressure to conform to international standards in terms of their training provisions and their regulation of labour and capital markets.

Table 6.1 highlights the key differences and similarities in company level approaches to training and development that have been identified by – or suggested in – the literature. These include relative sectoral strengths of the different varieties of capitalism, summarising the above issues and trends. The underlying causes of these differences are explored in more detail below.

Differences in national competitive advantages are mirrored by national training systems. LMEs have generally weak vocational training systems, but good tertiary and generic educational systems. Hence, a poorly skilled and paid labour force is complemented by one that has good generic skills valuable in both finance and IT (Thelen, 2001). In contrast, most CMEs have training systems that are more vocationally orientated. The state also plays a more active role by sustaining the competitiveness of incrementally innovative manufacturing. As to the transitional and Mediterranean economies, the provision of training and education is likely to be mixed as traditional state institutions face major challenges both from private sector providers and in coping with changing market needs, (Patiniotis and Stavroulakis 1997).

On paper at least, shareholders and owners play a paramount role in determining company policy in LMEs while in practice executives frequently have great discretion. In CMEs, key decisions are likely to be moulded by a range of associations, including both unions and employer associations. Mediterranean-based firms would tend to the former, whilst in transitional economies pressures to converge with the LME paradigm are likely to be mitigated by a desire by managers to favour incremental development in the interests of familiarity and continuity (Whitley 1999: 240).

Stronger security of tenure in CMEs forces firms to take continuous skills development seriously; in contrast, weaker tenure in LMEs means that firms have to invest more in induction training to cope with high staff turnover rates, (Harcourt and Wood 2007). Finally, it can be argued that a more active state role in providing training and skills development in CMEs compared to LMEs – and a declining one in transitional economies and Mediterranean ones – will mould firm policies towards the use of external training providers.

Table 6.1 Varieties of Capitalism and the Practice of Training at Firm Level – Some Predictions

		CME	LME	Mediterranean	Transitional
Days training	Managerial employees	Average to high, given the focus on technical rather than generic managerial skills	Low, given good tertiary education in generic management skills	High, given the relatively weak tertiary education	High, given the relatively weak tertiary education
	Clerical employees	Average, given the system's focus on vocational training	Average, to fill gaps in a system orientated to tertiary level generic education	Average to high, reflecting gaps in educational system. The high staff turnover in the highly important SME sector calls for more condensed, intensive training. However, SMEs face funding constraints in terms of the training they can provide	Average to high, reflecting gaps in educational system. The higher staff turnover implies that training is more condensed and intensive
	Technical and professional employees	Average as there is need for top up training in firm-specific skills to complement good industry-specific skills. This need for training is offset by low staff turnover rates	Average, reflecting the long term decline in manufacturing which is gradually reducing the need for technical skills. This is somewhat offset by increased needs for professional skills	Average to high, reflecting gaps in educational system. The high staff turnover in the highly important SME sector calls for more condensed, intensive training. However, SMEs face funding constraints in terms of the training they can provide	Average to high, reflecting gaps in educational system. The higher staff turnover implies that training is more condensed and intensive
	Manual employees	Average to low, given the relatively low staff turnover. However, there is a need for top up training to put workers up to speed with technological advances. This top up training typically builds on good industry-relevant vocational training	Average to high. The high staff turnover creates a need for basic induction training	Intermediate. Gaps in state provision necessitate firm-specific training. However, SMEs face funding constraints in terms of the training they can provide	Average to high, reflecting gaps in educational system. The higher staff turnover implies that training is more condensed and intensive

Percentage of salaries and wages devoted to training	Conventional CME – low to average. Manual employees are likely to enter the organisation with good foundation in industry specific skills Flexicurity model CME – high, given need to ensure continuous employability of individuals in the external labour market A minority of CMEs have weak vocational training: here the cost of in-firm training is likely to be higher Lower staff turnover means that training costs can be spread over many years	Mixed. The need for induction training due to high staff turnover in the lower job bands is offset by organisational reluctance to invest in skills	Relatively low given the duration of training. Many reflect the widespread use of informal and cost-effective on the job training	Mixed as percentage varies from context to context, given gaps in national training systems, and increasing staff turnover rates in many instances
Use of external training providers	Low in most CMEs Average in Flexicurity CMEs, reflecting state labour market training provisions	Relatively high, reflecting shortages of industry-specific (as opposed to generic) skills	Variable, reflecting high restrictions on the operation of private training institutions in some Mediterranean countries	Variable, demand for providers not always matched by capacity
Defining training needs	Role of the individual only prominent in Flexicurity CMEs and those with weak vocational training systems	Role of the individual more prominent than in other contexts	Relatively prominent role for HR departments, probably in response to organisational transformations	Relatively prominent role for HR departments, probably in response to organisational transformations

Implementing training needs	Prominent role for management may be mitigated by constraints imposed by neo-corporatism	Managerial autonomy	Managerial autonomy	Managerial autonomy

Sources: Goergen et al. (2012); Goergen et al. (2009); Harcourt and Wood (2007); Amable (2003); Hall and Soskice (2001); Thelen (2001); Papelexandris and Chalikias (2002).

Method

This chapter brings together the findings of four consecutive waves of the Cranet survey which were carried out in 1991, 1995, 1999–2000 and 2004–05. The survey waves provide evidence on the practice of strategic HRM in organisations in a large cross-section of countries. We focus on the above four waves of the Cranet survey rather than just one for two reasons. First, focusing on a single wave may lead to erroneous conclusions as there are clear instances in the data where a given country behaves significantly different from its typical pattern in a single wave of the survey. Second, although this is not the focus of this chapter, analysing consecutive waves will shed further light on whether the varieties of capitalism across Europe are in the process of converging.

Whilst the Cranet survey has always encompassed a core of major economies (such as the UK, Germany, the Netherlands and Sweden), over the years, other countries have been added to the sample, most notably transitional economies in Eastern Europe, and a number of developing non-European countries that are also undergoing economic modernisation. This means that continuous analysis is only possible for a limited number of countries. However, including countries that were covered in later waves of the survey provides a more thorough view of the relationship between types of corporate governance and training and development practices. At the same time, given changes in the composition of the panel of the countries, advanced quantitative tools are inappropriate. As a purely descriptive exercise, it is difficult scientifically to examine the precise strength of changes over time. However, from graphical presentation of the findings, a number of clear differences are readily visible. These would include clear distinctions in HRM practices within different varieties and sub-categories of capitalism, and continued diversity despite supposed pressures towards a global convergence in corporate governance regimes and practices. We also perform a factor analysis which provides evidence of a multivariate nature in addition to the univariate evidence provided by the descriptive analysis.

While the Cranet survey covers organisations both from the public and private sectors, here we focus on private sector firms only. The variables that will be analysed are as follows. We will first analyse the average days of training spent per year for the four categories of managerial, professional/technical, clerical and manual employees. The second variable is the percentage of salaries and wages spent on training. The third variable is the use of external providers for training and development (as well as recent changes in that use). Other variables include annual staff turnover, the main influence on defining training needs and the main influence on designing training activities.

Findings

We start with a descriptive, univariate analysis of the four waves of the Cranet survey, followed by a factor analysis.

Univariate Analysis

Figure 6.1 compares days of training spent in a cross-section of countries and job bands in 1991, the first wave of the survey covered by this chapter. Amongst managerial employees, the highest spend is in Spain, an example of Mediterranean capitalism, and the lowest in the United Kingdom, a liberal market economy.[1] Amongst collaborative markets, there appears some variation, ranging between a relatively low spend in France (often only seen as a marginal

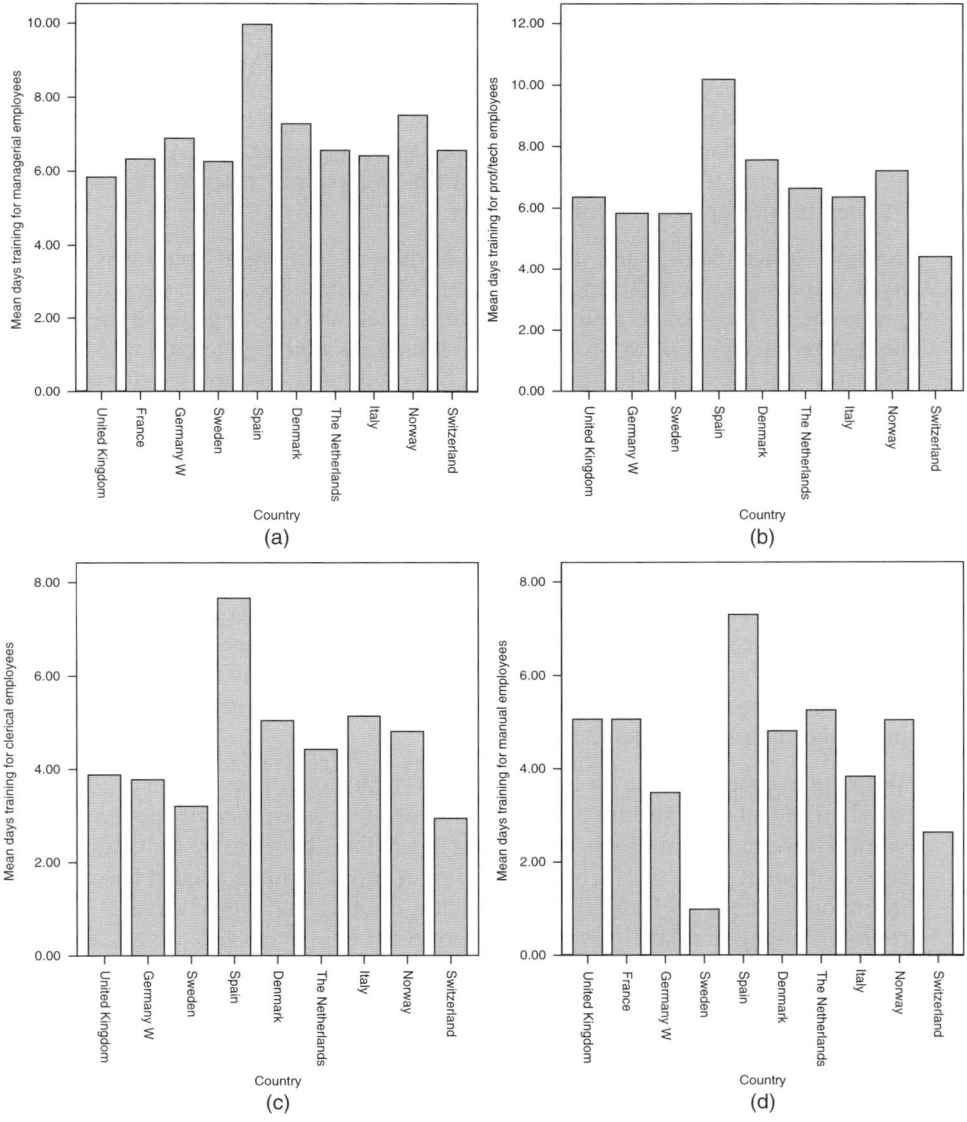

Figure 6.1 Average Days of Training in 1991

member of the CME category on account of it becoming increasingly integrated into Anglo-Saxon model capital markets [Hancke 2001, 307]), to relatively high spends in the case of Denmark.

These national differences can be accounted for in terms of national training systems, and fit the predictions of the existing literature and, hence, Table 6.1. As Thelen (2001) notes, training should be viewed in the context of specific national corporate governance regimes, associated with complementary sets of practices. The shareholder-value paramount model found in liberal markets has proved conducive both to areas of high technology and to low value added service sector activity. Underpinning growth in the former has been a strong generic tertiary-level skills base. At managerial level, this has provided a class of managers with good general managerial and cross-functional skills, skills which may also be of value in terms of running service sector enterprises. Within CMEs, a stronger emphasis on vocational and industry specific skills may provide a good relevant skills base for managers in established industries; however, industry specific skills may be of less value in emerging areas of economic activity, or within conglomerates that span different industries.

Among clerical employees, the number of days of training in Spain was also high. Otherwise, the differences between CMEs and LMEs were also not very pronounced. This would reflect the fact that such work does generally rely on neither tertiary generic skills (which are relatively well developed in LMEs) nor industry specific skills (CMEs). Hence, both types of economy would be likely to devote roughly similar amounts to these activities. A roughly similar pattern appears regarding professional and technical employees. Within CMEs, this could reflect the relative match between specific national vocational provisions and company specific skills needs; any mismatches would have to be plugged at company level.

It is worth noting that, within the United Kingdom, an LME, training provision in terms of days per professional or technical employee is higher than that to managerial employees. This would reflect the greater utility of generic tertiary level skills to the practice of management than to professional and technical work: such skills may require top up training to make them more relevant to the needs of a particular industry (Thelen 2001).

With the exception of the Swedish anomaly (which only prevails for 1991 as we shall see later), a similar pattern was observable when it came to manual work. However, an emphasis on training in LMEs is likely to be for different reasons than in the case of CMEs. The former provide much needed basic skills in important areas such as the service sector, training that would have to be often repeated owing to relatively high staff turnover rates. In contrast, in CMEs, spending on employees in this area is likely to be aimed at promoting long term, organisation specific skills – high security of tenure is likely to make for lower staff turnover rates, resulting in organisations being able to invest in organisation specific skills on a cost effective basis. Such a system is underpinned by the close relations firms have with their employees via unions: collective regulation imparts a greater stability and predictability into the employment relationship.

Figure 6.2 looks at variations in firm level orientations towards training for 1995. New countries were added to the survey for this year, including an emerging market, Turkey; the average time devoted to training employees for Turkey was relatively high, probably reflecting skills shortfalls in this area given structural changes in the national economy, (see Daylan 2004).

Amongst managerial employees, there appears to be a reduced emphasis on training within the United Kingdom and to a lesser extent some CMEs such as

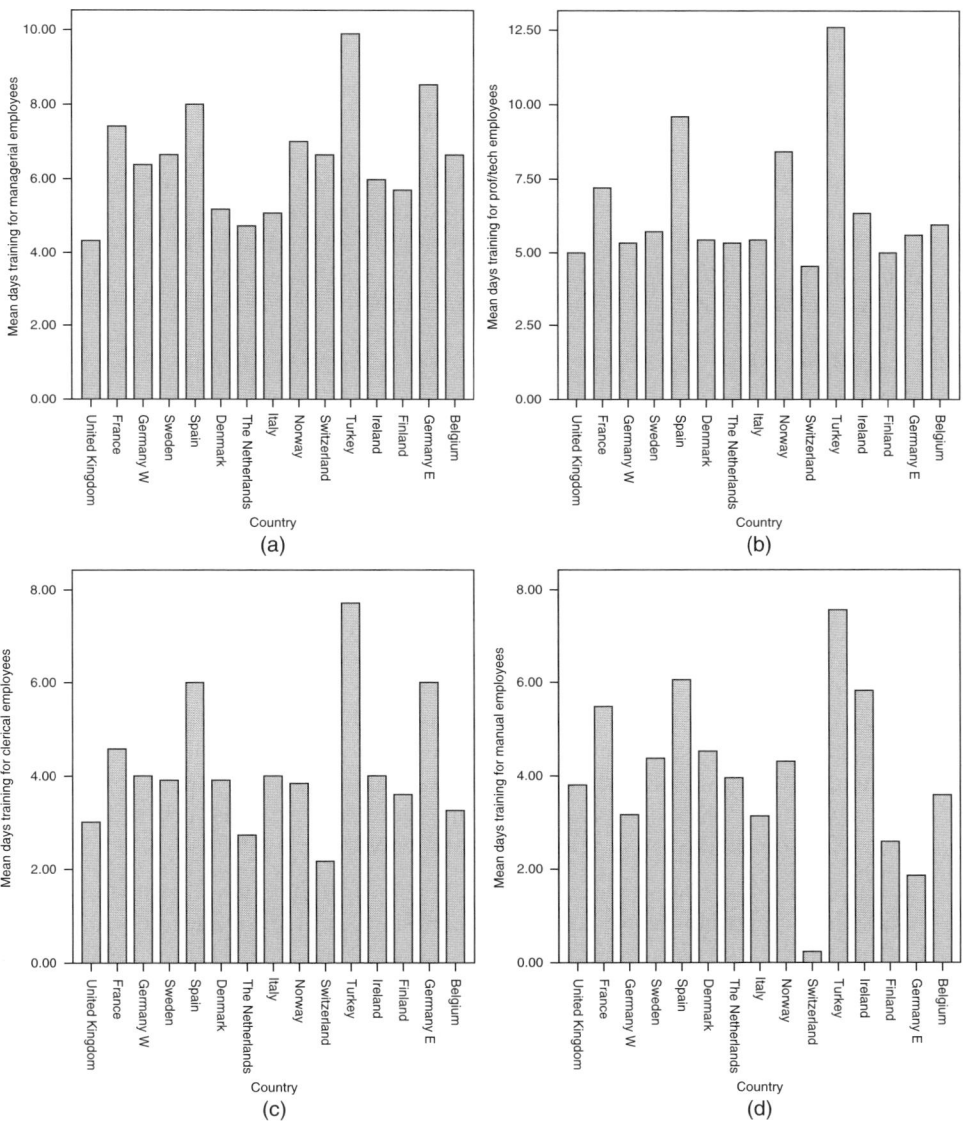

Figure 6.2 Average Days of Training in 1995
Source: Cranet, various dates

Denmark, the Netherlands as well as a more 'mixed' system, Italy (c.f. Whitley 1999). This shift could reflect a generally stronger shift towards the provision of management education by tertiary educational institutions by the mid-1990s, (Doyle 2001: 394–95). German spending also appeared relatively high: this may reflect growing needs for more generic managerial skills, given rising pressures to reorganise long-established conglomerates by the mid-1990s – in turn, driven by shifts in the German corporate governance system towards a greater responsiveness to the needs of owners and markets – which may have necessitated new managerial outlooks and skills sets (see Jurgens et al. 2000). It may also reflect the need for different managerial skills in the newly merged east German economy.

The days spent on the provision of training for professional and technical employees in the United Kingdom, a leading LME, dropped by more than one in 1995. This reflects the long term decline of British manufacturing, which, leads to a drop in the demand for technical skills. However, average training duration for manual employees was relatively high: as noted earlier, this probably reflects the need for basic induction training, given high staff turnover rates. Weak regulation of the employment contract via law – and few and weaker collective agreements with unions – results in firms being more able to readily adjust staff sizes: in turn, this is likely to be met by weaker organisational commitment by employees, (Harcourt and Wood 2007). Again, these trends reflect the predictions of Table 6.1.

The average duration of training was again high for transitional economies, and the Mediterranean economy of Spain (but not for Italy). This may reflect a possible mismatch between formal education and basic workplace training in a number of such countries, (Patiniotis and Stavroulakis, 1997; Holman 2001: 69). Ongoing modernisation places pressures on both small and medium family-owned businesses, and large formerly state-owned organisations, to modernise practices in order to compete. An exception to this general rule was Italy – this reflects the highly spatially segmented nature of the Italian economy, with the heavily industrialised northern regions differing strongly from the southern, more traditionally Mediterranean model of capitalism, even if the differences might not be so extreme as to mean that the country embodies two distinct and different business systems, (Whitley 1999: 45). Again, managerial education in a range of Mediterranean countries has, historically speaking, been rather patchy, necessitating further skills development, (c.f. Patiniotis and Stavroulakis 1997).

Compared to the two previous surveys, the 1999–2000 survey covers a significantly larger number of countries including four Mediterranean countries (Greece, Italy, Portugal and Spain), four Eastern European countries (Bulgaria, the Czech Republic, Estonia and Slovenia) as well as Turkey and Israel. The trends observed for 1995 generally continued into 1999–2000 (Figure 6.3). These include relatively long training periods for Mediterranean countries, again reflecting persistent training mismatches, and the pressures on organisations to update their practices in the light of intensifying overseas competition and reduced state interventionism, (see Holman 2001). Training levels in the UK remained relatively consistent, with a slight increase in the duration of training supplied to

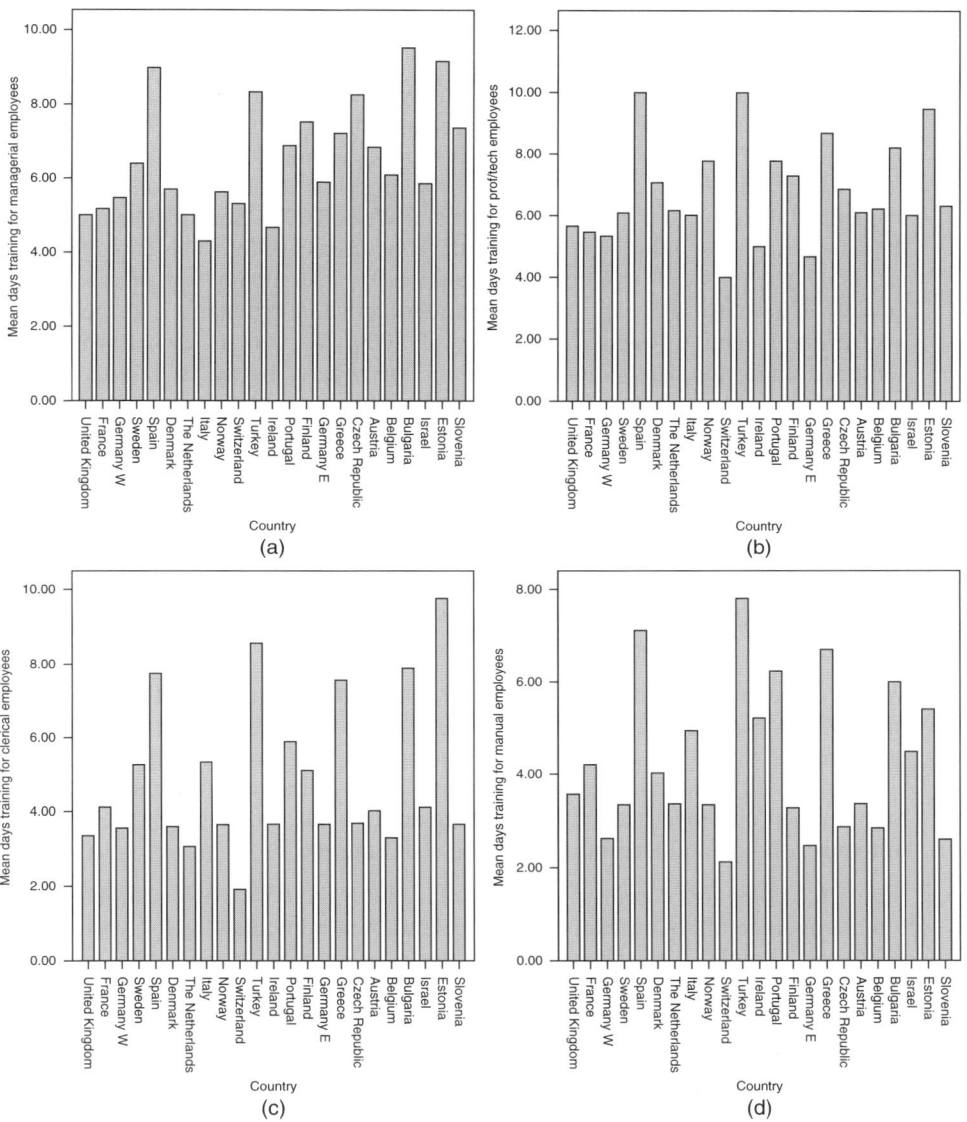

Figure 6.3 Average Days of Training in 1999–2000
Source: Cranet, various dates

clerical workers. The bigger panel of countries encompassed by this particular
round of the survey highlighted an important issue: that within a large number
of CME firms, training provided by the firms remains limited. Most probably, as
Supiot (2001: 29) argues, this reflects the continued presence of good vocational
training systems in many CMEs, including Austria and Germany. In other CMEs,
such as Denmark and the Netherlands, state provision aimed at upgrading workers'

skills throughout their working lives helps both individuals to compete in the wider labour market and firms to access needed skills as and when required (Euractiv, 2005). The remaining pressures on firms to provide training would be in four areas. First, the upgrading and topping up of industry specific skills to make them more focused on needs specific to individual organisations (c.f. Regini, 1997). Relatively long periods of tenure would mean that this process could take place over many years of an individual's career at the firm, making for a somewhat modest average annual duration of training, (Harcourt and Wood 2007). Second, changes in the structuring of conglomerates; whilst the economic base for a shareholder value economy in CMEs such as Germany is relatively low, company managers in a number of key firms have introduced "shareholder value orientated management control and incentive systems" (Jurgens et al. 2000: 75), which may necessitate some retraining amongst middle ranking and lower level managers. Third, relative weaknesses in competing in areas of high tech industry might place pressures on firms to develop skills in such areas, in a sector where CMEs have traditionally performed less well than LMEs, and where the national training system has been commensurately less developed, (Thelen 2001). Finally, the relationships between firms and unions in CMEs tends to be deeper and more wide ranging: higher levels of coordination between firms and unions are likely to help secure national level skills provisions well suited to the provision of vocational skills to workers on a pre-work basis, (Thelen 2001: 74–76, Harcourt and Wood 2007). Once more, these trends fit the predictions of Table 6.1.

Whilst more modest in other areas, resources devoted to training and development of clerical and manual workers were relatively high in the Republic of Ireland. In part, this might have reflected the nature of the restructuring of the Irish economy, with a move to neo-corporatism placing pressures on firms to invest more in their employees, even if they were not in a position to guarantee security of tenure, (Wood and Harcourt 2001; see also Figure 6.7).

Figure 6.4 compares countries for 2004–05. The 2004–05 wave has slightly different coverage of countries including Iceland, Northern and Greek Cyprus, Slovakia and Tunisia. Transitional and Mediterranean capitalist economies continued to place a relatively strong emphasis on training, in terms of average duration. This would indicate that such countries are not rapidly converging with other varieties of capitalism in this regard: either there is a serious backlog in this area, making for a relatively long transition, or such countries remain locked on a distinct (albeit internally changing) trajectory. The relative length of UK training for manual employees increased somewhat. However, there is considerable evidence to suggest that this remained focused on basic induction training, to compensate for high staff turnover rates (see also Figure 6.7), rather than the diffusion of enlightened HRM policies that have encompassed a stronger emphasis on human resource development, (Harcourt and Wood 2007). Within the CME category, there was some shift in the relative positions of different countries. However, most countries share some common features reflecting the need to develop generic (in terms of senior management) and top-up organisational specific (in the case of manual workers) skills, a long term process (particularly in the case of the latter) that would not necessitate unduly large resource outlays, given that such training would be spread over a typical individual's career life cycle

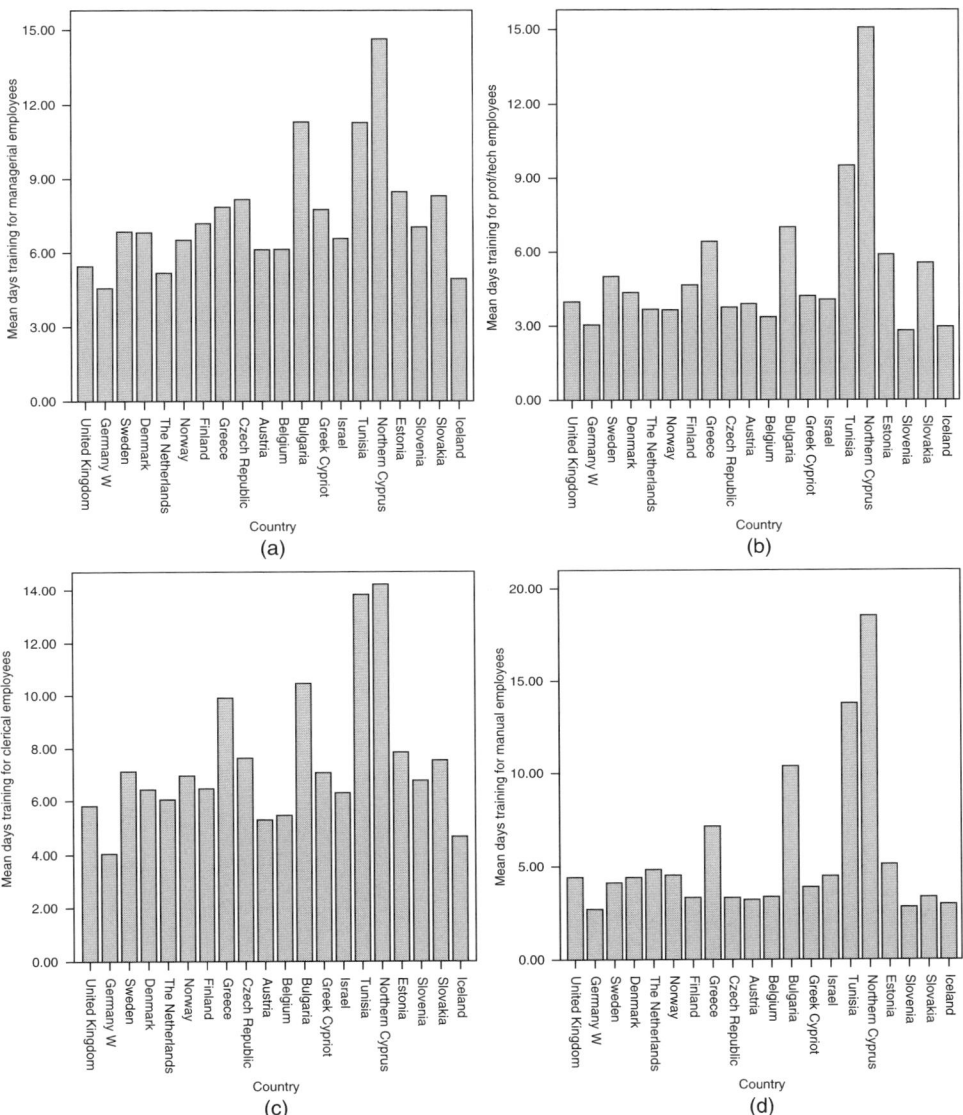

Figure 6.4 Average Days of Training in 2004–2005
Source: Cranet, various dates

(Harcourt and Wood 2007, c.f. Thelen 2001). However, there was no evidence of a smoothing of inter-country variations, reflecting both the uneven and episodic – and internally diverse – nature of systemic evolution, and strong pressures mitigating against a convergence with the LME model, (Boyer 2006).

Figure 6.5 compares changes in the amount spent on training as a percentage of overall salaries and wages in different national contexts. The United Kingdom has tended to hover around 3%, with the exception of the year 1999–2000, when

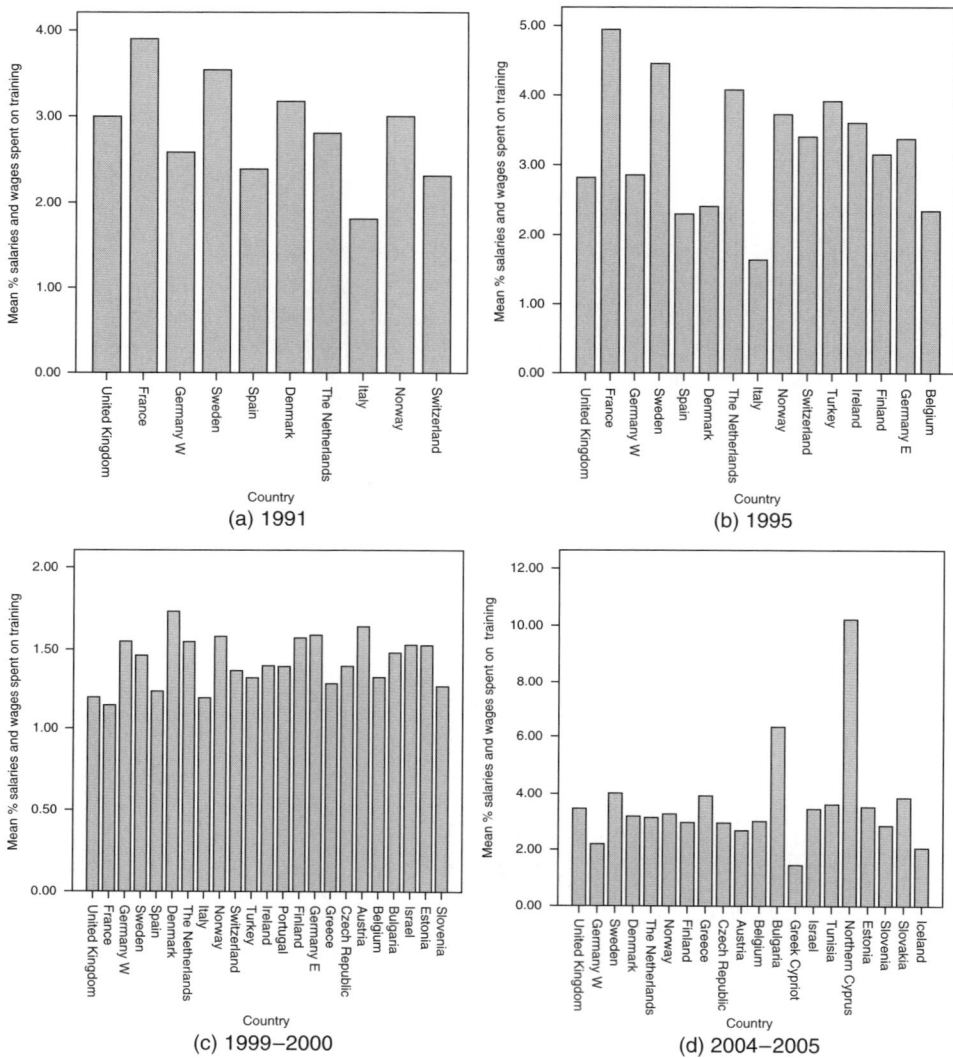

Figure 6.5 Percentage of Salaries and Wages Spent on Training
Source: Cranet, various dates

spending across the board was lower; in other words, the UK has had a middle to upper ranking spending profile when compared to other countries. The spending was somewhat higher for France in the early to mid-1990s, with a spend between 4% and 5% (no data were available for 2004–2005, although by 1999–2000 this figure had dropped substantially). Another relatively high spender was Sweden, with spending up to an equivalent of 4.5% of wages on training and development. In contrast, Germany was prominent among the relatively low spenders. What can explain this difference? Even when compared to other CMEs, Germany retains a strong vocational training system, providing good sets of industry specific skills (Thelen 2001; Harcourt and Wood 2007). This means that any in-firm training can be highly focused and cost effective. In contrast, among CMEs, Sweden has a relatively weak vocational training system (see Amable 2003: 161–2). This problem may be exacerbated by trends toward local bargaining: the latter would reduce the prospects for effective coordination of employer and employee interests, and hence for the development and enhancement of national and industrial vocational training systems (c.f. Thelen 2001: 79; Hall and Soskice 2001: 34). This would necessitate firms devoting more resources to internal skills development. Once more, these trends are per the predictions in Table 6.1.

Interestingly, by 1999–2000 the costs incurred by training were relatively high in two flexicurity economies, Denmark and the Netherlands. Flexicurity is a specific set of policies and practices encountered in a limited number of CMEs. Effectively, the system involves employees trading job security for employment security. Employees have access to continued training, through state provision, to upgrade their marketable skills – ensuring that they can be confident of employment if they should lose their jobs – in return for which statutory job protection is weaker. However, in practice, such systems operate not only via formal rules and structures, but also via informal conventions. Employers appear less likely to engage in opportunistic dismissals than in the case of LMEs (see Issacharoff 1996; Schwab 1993) and may be encouraged to help in the provision of lifelong learning. In turn, they can count on higher levels of employee commitment than might be expected in a system with relatively weak job protection, and are assured of state assistance in the provision of organisationally relevant skills (Harcourt and Wood 2007).

Finally, the percentage of salaries spent on training within Mediterranean and transitional economies was by no means always commensurate with the relative average duration: there were considerable variations within this category. This would suggest that much training is conducted on a relatively cost-effective basis, and may encompass informal on the job training as a means of bridging formal skills gaps.

Figure 6.6 compares trends in the use of external training providers. Private sector external training providers may be used to impart industry specific skills in the absence of an effective national vocational training system, whilst in some national contexts, the state plays an active role in plugging skills gaps, and ensuring individuals are in possession of worthwhile marketable skills. Hence, Denmark and the Netherlands had the highest percentage of firms relying on external providers for their training. Both countries also experienced a particularly pronounced increase in 2004–05, reflecting the increasing significance of state provided or sponsored labour market training programmes (see Harcourt and Wood 2007). In contrast, the number of firms increasing their use of external training providers was rather more modest in Germany, Finland and Sweden. In Germany, this reflects the primary focus of in-organisation training aimed at gradually developing organisation specific skills, building on the good base of industry specific skills provided by the vocational training system. Such training is difficult for external providers, whose focus would tend to be more generic. In the case of Finland and Sweden, the national vocational training system is rather

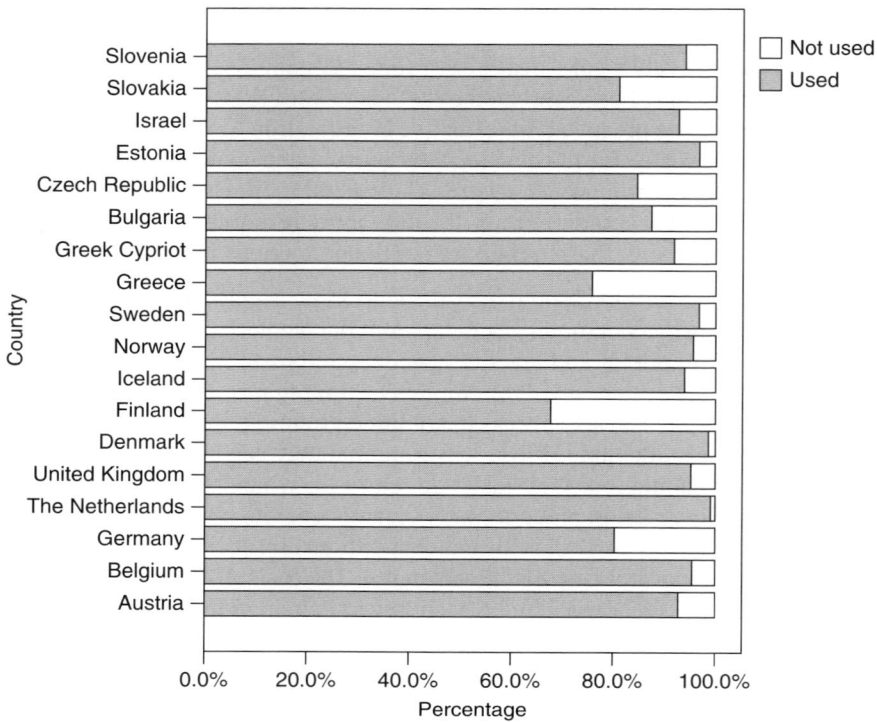

Figure 6.6 Use of External Providers for Training and Development, 2004–2005
Source: Cranet, various dates

less effective, (see Amable 2003). However, a similar emphasis on incrementally innovative manufacturing requires a combination of industry and organisation specific skills: again, the capacity of external providers to provide the latter would be limited.

The (LME) United Kingdom made fairly extensive use of external providers. This reflects the weaknesses in general vocational training (creating more demand for private sector external providers, given weakness in the state provision) being only partially mitigated by a general reluctance of firms to invest in developing their employees' skills, on account of the shorter time horizons of a shareholder value orientated model, and a reliance of firms on numerical flexibility as a basis of competitiveness, (Jessop 2001: 118–21). These trends reflect the predictions of Table 6.1.

No clear pattern emerged amongst transitional and Mediterranean capitalist based firms. This could reflect the fact that limitations in state provided pre-work vocational and labour market training programmes are not necessarily matched by the capacity of external non-governmental providers to keep pace with organisational needs.

A backlog in both private and official training provisions is not always easy to redress, given existing skill sets, with continuing national variations in regulation (some countries, such as Greece, have heavily restricted the role of private educational providers) making it harder or easier for the former to expand their role within this broad category, (c.f. Patiniotis and Stavroulakis 1997).

The 3 panels of Figure 6.7, a, b, and c, depicts staff turnover by country in 1995, 1999–2000 and 2004–5. As can be seen, although there is some volatility in the case of transitional and Mediterranean economies, there are certain strong continuities. First, staff turnover rates remain relatively low in most CMEs, despite periodic pressures towards labour market deregulation. This pattern may simply

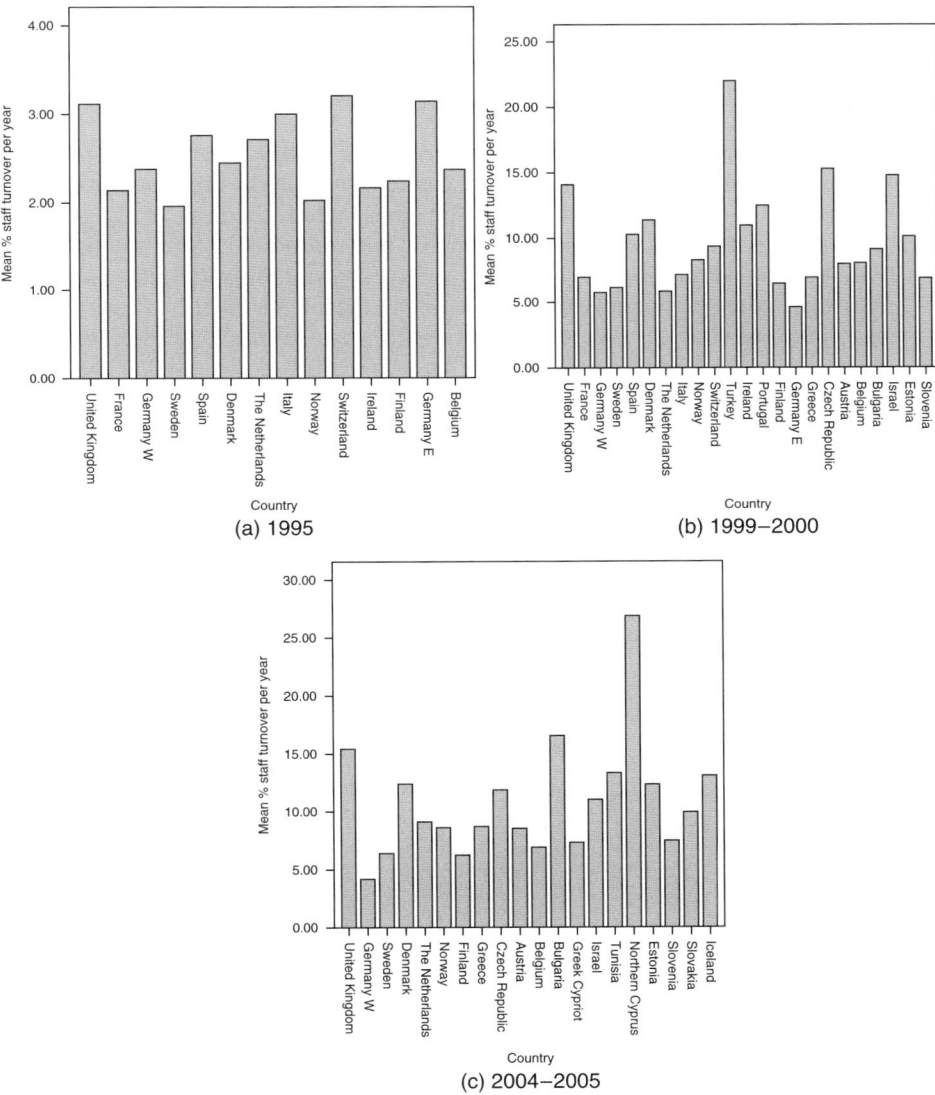

Figure 6.7 Staff Turnover
Source: Cranet, various dates

indicate a preference for continuity and familiarity in employment contracts, as a means of lowering transaction costs, (Marsden 1999), but may also reflect, as Harcourt and Wood (2007) note, underlying systemic complementarities. A stable workforce makes developing organisationally specific skills cost effective and worthwhile and allows for the gradual accumulation of organisational wisdom which, in turn, is highly conducive to incrementally innovative production, (Thelen 2001). It is also likely to be more conducive to collective employment relations and, hence, more effective coordination of employer and employee interests, again conducive to the efficient usages of skills. There are two notable exceptions to this general rule, the flexicurity economies of Denmark and the Netherlands. The former in all the years under review has generally been high in CME terms. In the case of the latter, there has been a tendency for staff turnover rates to rise, reflecting the gradual development and extension of flexicurity over the past few years in that country (see also Table 6.1).

Figure 6.8 depicts the main influences in defining training needs in 2004–05. Interestingly, the role of the individual seemed particularly strong in the UK, Ireland, and in certain types of CME. The latter include the flexicurity economies, such as the Netherlands and Denmark, and those CMEs with relatively weak vocational training systems, such as Sweden and Finland. In the case of the flexicurity economies, individuals have strong incentives to ensure that they are well equipped with up-to-date marketable skills, and access to relevant training

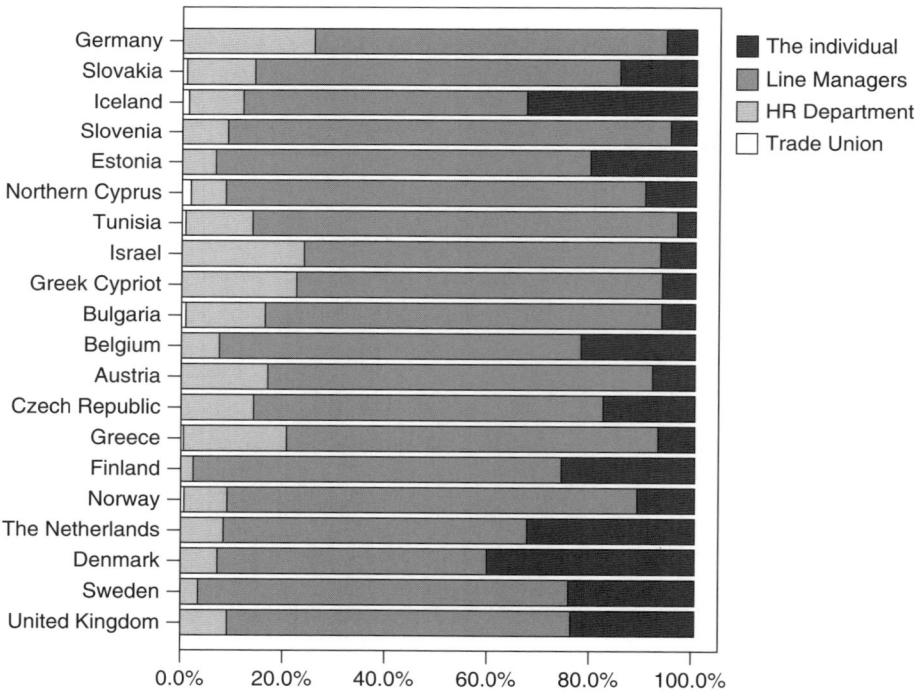

Figure 6.8 Main Influence on Defining Training Needs, 2004–2005
Source: Cranet, various dates

to do so. In contrast, the role of the individual was vary much less, and that of line managers more, in other CMEs such as Germany and Norway. On the one hand, it could be argued that some CMEs have become more LME-like, with a commensurate rise in an individualist culture. On the other hand, the CME model is underpinned by both formal rules and informal conventions and trade-offs (Bredgaardt et al. 2005). In other areas, such as in terms of the relative centralisation of collective bargaining, and implicit understandings between employees and firms, there is a stronger emphasis on collective rights and mutual obligations. Also, as is apparent from the above, in many other areas there is less evidence of convergence with the LME model, again as per the predictions of Table 6.1.

The most dominant characteristic of Mediterranean and transitional economies is that the role of HRM departments is relatively prominent. A case can be made for HRM departments to become more prominent in times of organisational crisis or transformation, given the linkage between high commitment and performance (Storey 2001: 364–67). Within Mediterranean economies, medium sized enterprises have had to contend with very much less state protectionism, and larger organisations with less active state involvement or backing. Whilst the outcome of such transformations is sufficiently varied to preclude a simple convergence with the LME model in this area, the role of HRM departments mirrors a wider environment of change. Within transitional economies, the process of organisational transformation has often been a highly complex process (Whitley 1999), again resulting in HRM departments becoming more prominent.

Apart from a small percentage of companies from Nordic countries and transitional economies, trade unions tend not to be the main influence on defining training needs. This would reflect the trend towards more decentralised collective bargaining in many such cases, especially when compared to 'Rhineland-type' CMEs: centralised bargaining (which in turn depends on good working relations between and within groupings of unions and employers) is more conducive to the type of national and industry-wide coordination that underpins strong vocational training systems, geared towards the provision of industry specific skills (see Hall and Soskice 2001: 34).

Figure 6.9 depicts the main influences in designing firm sponsored and implemented training activities. Here a very much more complex picture emerges. Across the board, the role of both individuals and unions is relatively weak, with decision making in this area being dominated by HRM departments or line managers. However, within CMEs, centralised neo-corporatist deals may place some broader pressures on firms to take stronger account of the interests and well-being of employees (as opposed to simply immediate organisational needs) than would otherwise be the case (Harcourt and Wood 2003).

There is considerable variation in the relative importance of the former versus the latter, given differences as to whether the HRM department plays a more strategic or hands-on operational role: in the case of the former, line managers are typically entrusted to a lot more day-to-day responsibility for handling the implementation of HRM systems, leaving the HRM department freer to engage at the policy level (Brewster et al. 2006). Similar to Figure 6.8, trade unions are relatively unimportant

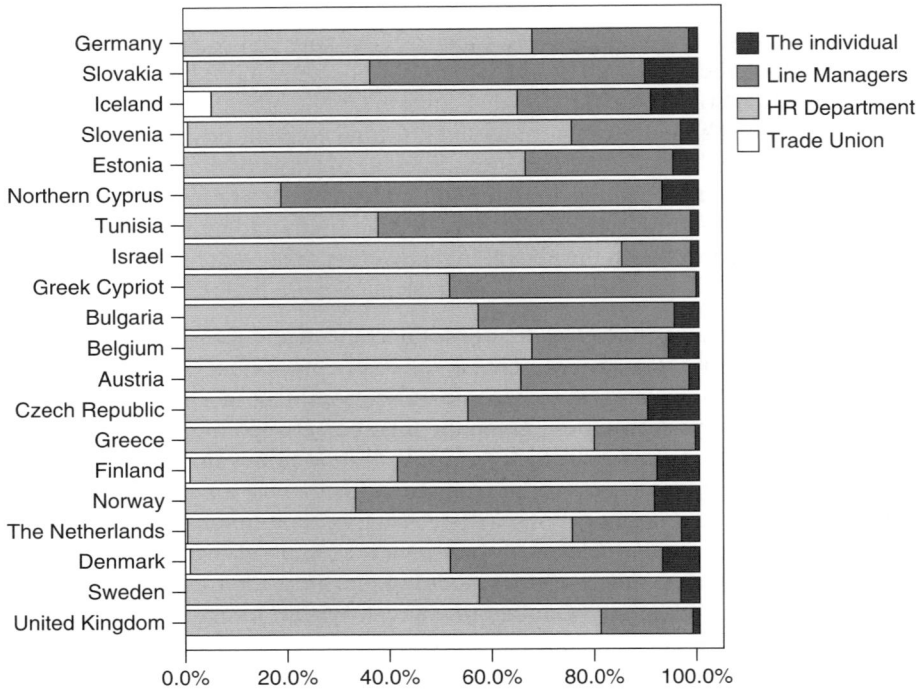

Figure 6.9 Main Influence on Designing Training Activities, 2004–2005
Source: Cranet, various dates

as they are the main influence in only a small percentage of companies from some Nordic countries, transitional economies, Germany and the Netherlands.

Figure 6.10 summarises the main influence on implementing training activities. A noticeable trend is the prominent role played by HRM departments in most transitional economies and in LMEs. Brewster et al. (2006) found that, when employment relations are standardised through collective trade union regulated contracts, HRM departments tend to be smaller. In contrast, they tend to be larger in situations – such as is the case of LMEs – where unions are weaker and individual contracts more common (Brewster et al. 2006: 3–21). The latter allows firms to adjust terms and conditions of services more readily; a larger and more proactive HRM department more frequently engaged in selection and recruitment (to deal with high staff turnover rates) and individual performance management systems is again more likely to have an active interest in training (even if it is only during the induction phase). In contrast, line managers seem to be more influential in a larger proportion of firms operating in CMEs. This would probably reflect the continued importance of manufacturing in such economies, which in turn is founded on the successful deployment of functionally flexible forms of manufacturing that require a close integration of design, implementation, on-going manufacturing and the maintenance and redesign of manufacturing systems, (see Hall and Soskice 2001: 44). Finally, individuals are more likely to have a stronger influence on designing training needs in flexicurity economies; this would reflect

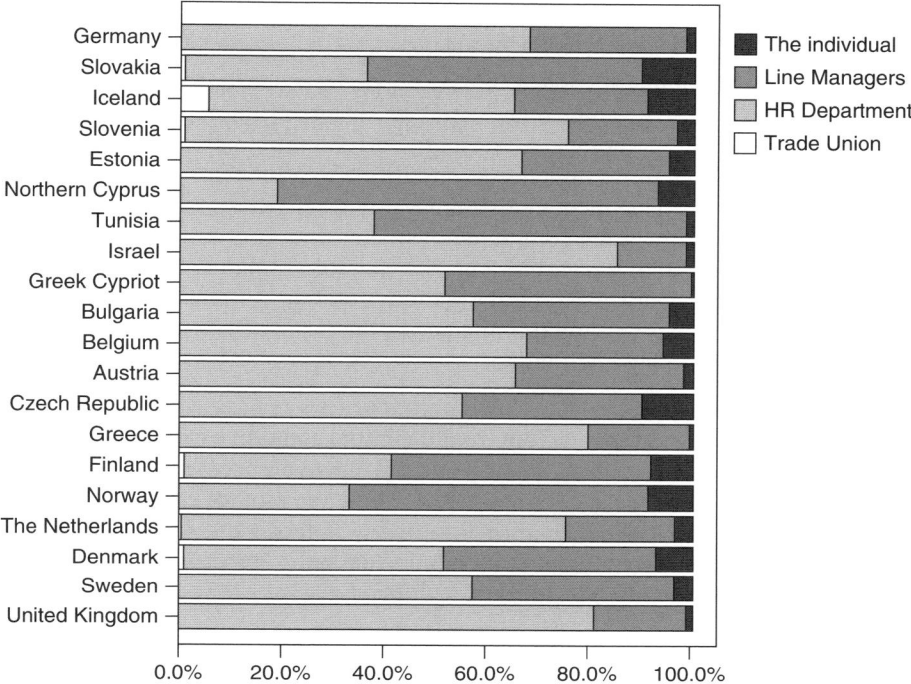

Figure 6.10 Main Influence on Implementing Training Activities, 2004–2005
Source: Cranet, various dates

the underlying philosophy of such systems, aimed at facilitating the ability of individuals to acquire skills to ensure their employability throughout their working lives (Bredgaardt et al. 2005).

Factor Analysis

The type of factor analysis we undertook is principal axis factoring, the purpose of which is structure detection, i.e. the detection of the underlying relationships between variables. In order to investigate which theory works best, the dichotomous version of the VOC approach or Whitley's multi-varieties approach, we not only include all the variables from the descriptive study in the factor analysis, but we also include three dummies which distinguish between LMEs, Mediterranean countries and transitional economies. If the dichotomous approach is valid, then we expect the two latter dummies to have no explanatory power. If Whitley's approach is correct, then the latter two dummies should explain a significant proportion of the variance in the training variables. The results from the factor analysis can be found in the appendix to this chapter.

The Kaiser–Meyer–Olkin measure of sampling adequacy has a value of 0.72 (see Table A1). This measure gives the proportion of the variance in the variables which may be explained by underlying factors. As the statistic has a measure fairly close to 1, a factor analysis should prove to be useful.[2] The Bartlett test of sphericity[3] is highly significant, providing further support for the usefulness of a structure detection factor analysis.

The initial communalities (see Table A2) give the proportion of variance in each variable explained by all the other variables. The four training durations for each of the four bands of employees have high initial communalities. The main influence on the design of training needs and the main influence on implementing the training activities have moderately high training activities. All the remaining variables have very low initial communalities. The extraction communalities, which give the proportion of the variance in each variable explained by the factors in the factor solution, are also high for the four duration variables as well as for the main influence on designing training needs, the main influence on implementing training needs and the LME dummy.

Table A3 in the appendix shows that only four factors have eigenvalues of more than 1 and that jointly the factors from the initial solution explain about 53% of the variance in the variables. Factor 4 has an eigenvalue just above 1 suggesting that this factor is of marginal importance. The scree plot reveals that the last major drop in terms of eigenvalues is between factors 3 and 4, confirming that it makes sense to focus on the first three factors only. Hence, we decided to constrain the factor analysis to three factors only.

The (unrotated) factor matrix (see Table A4) shows the variables underlying each of the three factors. Factor 1 is most highly correlated with the four training duration variables. The variable with the highest correlation (0.82) with factor 1 is the average number of training days for professional or technical employees. The average number of training days for manual employees has the lowest correlation of 0.65 of the four variables of training duration. No other variable has a correlation coefficient of 0.5 or greater. The second factor is mainly correlated with the main influence on designing training needs and the main influence on implementing training. The third factor is mainly composed of the LME dummy variable which has a correlation of just below 0.5. Interestingly, the dummy variables for the Mediterranean countries and the transitional economies are not highly correlated with any of the three factors. This suggests that the dichotomous approach works better with our data than Whitley's approach.

As a summary, factor 1 is composed of the four training duration variables, factor 2 is formed by the main influence on designing training needs as well as the main influence on implementing training, and factor 3 is composed of the LME dummy variable. However, the factor matrix shows that the factors are somewhat difficult to interpret. In particular, the main variable, the LME dummy, underlying factor 3 is negatively correlated with factor 1 but positively correlated with factor 2. Hence, it makes sense to study the rotated factor matrix (see Table A5).

Relationships are now easier to interpret. The rotated factor matrix reveals some interesting correlations as well as cross-correlations. As a rule of thumb, one normally considers correlations and cross-correlations of 0.2 or greater to be of interest. In what follows, we will refer to correlations in the region of 0.2 and 0.5 as moderate correlations. In detail, factor 3, is highly correlated with the

LME dummy, and it is also moderately and positively correlated with the annual percentage of staff turnover. This confirms one of the patterns uncovered by the univariate analysis: staff turnover tends to be higher in LMEs than in CMEs. Factor 3 is also positively correlated (albeit just below the typical threshold of 0.2) with the money spent on training. This suggests that the higher staff turnover makes the spend on training higher than it would otherwise be. Factor 1, the 'training duration' factor, is also moderately and positively correlated with the money spent on training. What accounts for the relatively high spend in the UK, which echoes one of the conclusions from the univariate analysis? It is likely that, given the higher turnover in this LME, much of this training is in fact induction training, rather than value-added skills development. There is also evidence that the design of training is more likely to be done centrally. Within LMEs, training is more likely to be done via the HRM department, which is both a reflection of the relatively greater size of HRM departments in such contexts (individual contracts mean that the process of people management is less regulated and more open ended), and the greater emphasis on induction training (which HRM departments are more likely to get directly involved in than specific skills-based, on-the-job training). The converse is true in CMEs, where line managers are more prominent, given the focus on enhancing organisation specific skills throughout an individual's working life. In flexicurity economies, training is likely to be even more decentralised, with individuals more likely to take an active role in their skills development. Conventional wisdom would suggest that within LMEs, firms rely on the external labour market to plug skills gaps, and there is a general lesser propensity to invest in people. However, Goergen et al. (2012) found that the converse was the case. This reflects not only persistent limitations in national vocational training frameworks, but also, as noted above, higher staff turnover rates, necessitating a greater spend on basic induction training, more than offsetting any savings in long term investment in people.

All in all, the factor analysis confirms the patterns uncovered by the univariate analysis. First, staff turnover tends to be higher in LMEs than in CMEs. Second, spend on training and training duration are higher in LMEs mostly because of the higher staff turnover. Third, while the LMEs and CMEs form fairly homogeneous groups, Mediterranean countries and transitional economies form much less consistent groups. This suggests that approaches such as Whitley's, which go behind the dichotomous approach, perform less well in explaining differences in training across countries than the latter.

Patterns

In view of the above, some important differences emerge in a range of different areas, closely in line with the propositions summarised in Table 6.1. A dominant theme from consecutive survey waves is that there is little evidence of homogenisation or convergence in most areas of training and development. This would reflect both the embedded nature of many norms and practices, and the complex nature of systemic evolution that may encompass rupture, continuity and recombination, rather than simply substitution of practices, (Boyer 2006). Any 'transition' within transitional – and indeed Mediterranean – economies seems to be rather protracted: there is little to suggest that practices are being simply supplanted with those found in another model of capitalism. Quite simply, the transition is a long one.

A second theme is that, whilst transitional economies share much in common with Mediterranean capitalism, important distinctions remain; within the former there is stronger evidence of flux and change. The independent family-owned SME that is central to Mediterranean capitalism is a well established and particularly resilient business model that is likely to survive all manner of external vicissitudes.

Third, there is much diversity within the CME model. CMEs with weak vocational training systems, and those that have followed the flexicurity model, differ in many areas from other CMEs. Whilst the former two categories are characterised by some LME-like behaviour in the area of training and development, they remain distinct, partially reflecting a deeply embedded model of co-determination and restraint in many other areas of work and employment relations, a model that is both resilient and flexible (Harcourt and Wood 2007).

Fourth, it is clear that whilst certain practices remain dominant in particular national settings, alternative clusters of practices exist. The fact that a sizable grouping of firms within a particular national setting follow a particular model does not mean that other sets of practices are not viable, or cannot operate in a complementary manner. Further analysis of the dataset revealed that sector and size both impact on firm level practices in a range of areas pertaining to employment and work (Brewster et al. 2007). The nature and extent of alternative training paradigms within different national settings could constitute a fruitful area for future research.

Finally, many of the differences between national training practices at firm level reflect the nature and depth of relations between a firm and its employees, and the relative strength and importance of unions. Centralised bargaining is conducive to greater coordination in national training provisions, reducing the need for firms to plug industry-wide gaps in training systems (Hall and Soskice 2001: 34). Moreover, greater regulation of the employment contract on a collective basis is likely to impart a greater stability to working life, and hence permit firm level training to be more incremental and cumulative (Harcourt and Wood, 2007).

Conclusion

This chapter confirms the continued diversity of national varieties of capitalism, and the persistence of distinct clusters of practices within the 'transitional' economies of Mediterranean and Eastern Europe. As predicted by the literature (see Table 6.1), firms are more likely to invest in training and development where security of tenure is stronger: not only will firms have to get more out of their existing human resources (as they cannot so easily resort to firing and hiring to plug skills and productivity shortfalls), but staff have stronger incentives to acquire organisation specific operational skills (and hence, are more likely to take company provided training more seriously). Again, specific production paradigms are dependent on particular skills sets: these can range from complex sets of skills conducive to high value added incrementally innovative production to the relatively limited aptitudes associated with low value added service sector activity (c.f. Thelen 2001). Individual nations have particular strengths in specific sectors and market segments: this will reflect both dominant regulatory and corporate governance paradigms, and firm level practices and the relationships between them. The survey findings highlight the national differences in these areas and shed further light on the nature of such relationships. For example, LME firms will tend to engage in larger amounts of shorter induction training given higher staff turnover rates, in turn a product of deregulated labour markets, and short-termism, imposed by a shareholder value dominated system of corporate governance. External private sector providers will play an important role in plugging skills gaps in the national vocational training system. In contrast, in CMEs, training is more likely to be geared to enhancing longer term organisation specific skills, reflecting a longer-term time horizon imposed by the corporate governance systems, and regulated labour markets; the role of the state is a more active one, geared to providing either pre-career vocational training and/or continuous labour market training.

Notes

1 France only has information on two of the categories (managerial and manual employees) for 1991. This was owing to the deletion of the third question from the French version of the questionnaire, in order to allow the insertion of a question of specific national interest, whilst keeping the questionnaire the same length.
2 Conversely, a value of less than 0.5 normally implies that a factor analysis will be of limited use.
3 This is a test of whether the null hypothesis that the correlation matrix is an identity matrix, that is the variables are unrelated to each other, is upheld. If the null cannot be rejected, then the variables will not be suitable for a structure detection.

References

Amable, B. (2003) *The Diversity of Modern Capitalism*. Oxford: Oxford University Press.

Boyer, R. (2006) 'How do institutions cohere and change?', in G. Wood and P. James (eds) *Institutions, Production and Working Life*. Oxford: Oxford University Press.

Bredgaardt, T., Larsen, F. and Madsen, D. (2005) *The Flexible Danish Labour Market: A Review*, CARMA Research Papers 1/2005, University of Aalborg, Denmark.

Brewster, C., Goergen, M., Wood, G. and Wilkinson, A. (2012) 'Varieties of capitalism and investments in human capital', *Industrial Relations* 51(s1): 501–27.

Brewster, C., Wood, G., Croucher, R. and Brookes, M. (2007) 'Collective and individual voice: Convergence in Europe?', *International Journal of Human Resource Management* 18(7): 1246–62.

Brewster, C., Wood, G., Van Ommeren, J. and Brookes, M. (2006) 'The determinants of HR size', *Human Resource Management* 45(1): 3–21.

Chandler, A.D. Jr (1977) *The Visible Hand: The Managerial Revolution in American Business*. Cambridge, MA: The Belknap Press of Harvard University Press.

Chandler, A.D. Jr (1984) 'The emergence of managerial capitalism', *Business History Review* 58: 473–503.

Daylan, F. (2004) 'The cooperation of small and middle-sized companies with universities in Turkey: Acquiring Enterprising Skills project', *European Journal of Industrial Training* 28(7): 587–97.

Dore, R. (2000) *Stock Market Capitalism: Welfare Capitalism.* Cambridge: Cambridge University Press.

Doyle, M. (2001) 'Management development', in I. Beardwell and L. Holden (eds) *Human Resource Management: A Contemporary Approach.* London: FT/Prentice Hall.

Euractiv (2005) 'Flexibility and social security key to employment, experts agree'. Accessed online at http:// www.Euractiv.com, 21 September 2005.

Goergen, M., Brewster, C. and Wood, G. (2009) 'Corporate governance and training', *Journal of Industrial Relations* 51(4): 459–87.

Goergen, M., Brewster, C., Wood, G. and Wilkinson, A. (2012) 'Varieties of capitalism and investments in human capital', *Industrial Relations* 51(1): 501–27.

Hall, P. and Soskice, D. (2001) 'An introduction to the varieties of capitalism', in P. Hall and D. Soskice (eds) *Varieties of Capitalism: The Institutional Basis of Competitive Advantage.* Oxford: Oxford University Press.

Hancke, B. (2001) 'Revisiting the French model', in P. Hall and D. Soskice (eds) *Varieties of Capitalism.* Oxford: Oxford University Press.

Harcourt, M. and Wood, G. (2003) 'Under what circumstances do social accords work?', *Journal of Economic Issues* 37(3): 747–67.

Harcourt, M. and Wood, G. (2007) 'The importance of employment protection for skill development in coordinated market economies', *European Journal of Industrial Relations* 13: 141–59.

Hicks, J. (1969) *A Theory of Economic History.* Oxford: Clarendon Press.

Holman, O. (2001) 'Semiperipheral Fordism in southern Europe', in B. Jessop (ed.) *Regulation Theory and the Crisis of Capitalism Volume 4 – Country Studies.* Cheltenham: Edward Elgar.

Issacharoff, S. (1996) 'Contracting for employment: The limited return of the common law', *Texas Law Review* 74: 1783–1812.

Jessop, B. (2001) 'Conservative regimes and the transition to post-Fordism', in B. Jessop (ed.) *Regulation Theory and the Crisis of Capitalism – Volume 4: Country Studies.* Cheltenham: Edward Elgar.

Jurgens, U., Naumann, K. and Rupp, J. (2000) 'Shareholder value in an adverse environment: The German case', *Economy and Society* 29(1): 54–79.

La Porta, R., Lopez-de-Silanes, F., Shleifer, A. and Vishny, R. (1997) 'Legal determinants of finance', *The Journal of Finance* 52: 1131–50.

La Porta, R., Lopez-de-Silanes, F., Shleifer, A. and Vishny, R. (1998) 'Law and finance', *Journal of Political Economy* 106: 1113–55.

Lincoln, J. and Kalleberg, A. (1990) *Culture, Control and Commitment: A Study of Work Organization in the United States and Japan.* Cambridge: Cambridge University Press.

Marsden, D. (1999) *A Theory of Employment Systems: Microfoundations of Societal Diversity.* Oxford: Oxford University Press.

Pagano, M. and Volpin, P. (2005) 'The political economy of corporate governance', *American Economic Review* 95: 1005–30.

Papelexandris, N. and Chalikias, J. (2002) 'Changes in training, performance management and communication among Greek firms in the 1990s', *European Journal of Industrial Training* 26(7): 342–52.

Patiniotis, N. and Stavroulakis, D. (1997) 'The development of vocational education policy in Greece: A critical approach', *Journal of European Industrial Training* 21(6–7): 192–202.

Regini, M. (1997) 'Different responses to different demands: Firms, institutions and training in Western Europe', *European Sociological Review* 13(3): 267–82.

Roe, M. (2003) *Political Determinants of Corporate Governance*. Oxford: Oxford University Press.

Schwab, S. (1993) 'Life Cycle Justice: Accommodating Just Cause and Employment at Will', *Michigan Law Review*, 92: 8–62.

Storey, J. (2001) 'Looking to the future', in J. Storey (ed.) *Human Resource Management: A Critical Text*. London: Thomson Learning.

Supiot, A. (2001) *Beyond Employment*. Oxford: Oxford University Press.

Thelen, K. (2001) 'Varieties of labor politics in the developed democracies', in P. Hall and D. Soskice (eds) *Varieties of Capitalism: The Institutional Basis of Competitive Advantage*. Oxford: Oxford University Press.

Whitley, R. (1999) *Divergent Capitalisms: The Social Structuring and Change of Business Systems*. Oxford: Oxford University Press.

Wood, G. and Harcourt, M. (2001) 'The consequences of neo-corporatism: A syncretic analysis', *International Journal of Sociology and Social Policy* 20(8): 1–22.

APPENDIX – Factor Analysis

Table A1 KMO and Bartlett's Test

Kaiser–Meyer–Olkin Measure of Sampling Adequacy.		.722
Bartlett's Test of Sphericity	Approx. Chi-Square	2613.684
	df	78
	Sig.	.000

Source: Brewster et al. (2012: 501–27).

Table A2 Communalities

	Initial	Extraction
DAYS TRAINING FOR MANAGERIAL EMPLOYEES	.487	.579
DAYS TRAINING FOR PROF/TECH EMPLOYEES	.546	.673
DAYS TRAINING FOR CLERICAL EMPLOYEES	.489	.585
DAYS TRAINING FOR MANUAL EMPLOYEES	.377	.446
% SALARIES AND WAGES SPENT ON TRAINING	.059	.086
CHANGEXT	.022	.016
% STAFF TURNOVER PER YEAR	.080	.084
NEEDS	.064	.083
DESIGN	.283	.528
Implementing the training activities	.262	.453
LME	.135	.347
Mediterranean	.042	.020
transitional	.116	.160

Extraction Method: Principal Axis Factoring.
Source: Brewster et al. (2012: 501–27).

Table A3 Total Variance Explained

Factor	Initial Eigenvalues			Extraction Sums of Squared Loadings			Rotation Sums of Squared Loadings		
	Total	% of Variance	Cumulative %	Total	% of Variance	Cumulative %	Total	% of Variance	Cumulative %
1	2.790	21.464	21.464	2.348	18.062	18.062	2.333	17.947	17.947
2	1.704	13.107	34.571	1.126	8.663	26.724	1.020	7.847	25.794
3	1.350	10.386	44.958	.585	4.502	31.227	.706	5.432	31.227
4	1.073	8.254	53.212						
5	.985	7.574	60.786						
6	.960	7.385	68.171						
7	.889	6.840	75.011						
8	.829	6.378	81.389						
9	.671	5.159	86.548						
10	.554	4.261	90.809						
11	.482	3.705	94.514						
12	.390	2.997	97.511						
13	.324	2.489	100.000						

Extraction Method: Principal Axis Factoring.
Source: Brewster et al. (2012: 501–27).

Table A4 Factor Matrix[a]

	Factor		
	1	**2**	**3**
DAYS TRAINING FOR MANAGERIAL EMPLOYEES	**.752**	.006	−.114
DAYS TRAINING FOR PROF/TECH EMPLOYEES	**.820**	.026	−.014
DAYS TRAINING FOR CLERICAL EMPLOYEES	**.759**	.019	.099
DAYS TRAINING FOR MANUAL EMPLOYEES	**.647**	.088	.140
% SALARIES AND WAGES SPENT ON TRAINING	.212	.045	.196
CHANGEXT	−.013	−.103	−.071
% STAFF TURNOVER PER YEAR	.066	.168	.226
NEEDS	.045	.225	−.173
DESIGN	−.113	**.716**	−.053
Implementing the training activities	−.034	**.647**	−.182
LME	−.137	.289	**.495**
Mediterranean	.083	.103	−.053
transitional	.157	.028	−.366

Source: Brewster et al. (2012: 501–27).

a. 3 factors extracted. 15 iterations required.

Table A5 Rotated Factor Matrix[a]

	Factor		
	1	**2**	**3**
DAYS TRAINING FOR MANAGERIAL EMPLOYEES	**.739**	.088	−.160
DAYS TRAINING FOR PROF/TECH EMPLOYEES	**.815**	.064	−.068
DAYS TRAINING FOR CLERICAL EMPLOYEES	**.764**	.005	.035
DAYS TRAINING FOR MANUAL EMPLOYEES	**.657**	.044	.111
% SALARIES AND WAGES SPENT ON TRAINING	.229	−.038	.178
CHANGEXT	−.019	−.061	−.108
% STAFF TURNOVER PER YEAR	.086	.052	.271
NEEDS	.028	.280	−.056
DESIGN	−.118	**.658**	.284
Implementing the training activities	−.051	**.658**	.131
LME	−.091	.031	**.582**
Mediterranean	.078	.119	−.008
transitional	.122	.195	−.326

Source: Brewster et al. (2012: 501–27).

a. Rotation converged in 5 iterations.

Table A6 Factor Transformation Matrix

Factor	**1**	**2**	**3**
1	.996	.042	−.082
2	−.001	.893	.449
3	.092	−.447	.890

Source: Brewster et al. (2012: 501–27).

7 Context and Working Time: Diversity in Practice

SUZANNE RICHBELL, CHRIS BREWSTER,
MICHAEL BROOKES AND GEOFFREY WOOD

This chapter compares the nature and extent of non-standard working time between liberal market (LMEs) and coordinated market economies (CMEs) in Europe. More specifically, we explore differences and commonalities in the usage of overtime, shiftworking and weekend working, controlling for sector, organizational size, and the presence of unions and collective bargaining.

Within the employment contract, a worker sells labour to be delivered over an agreed time period, in return for a wage. Not all jobs are associated with readily commodifiable labour time: this encompasses a range of occupations from traditionally organized postal delivery and refuse removal services to academic work. However, for many occupations, from face-to-face service sector occupations, through to administrative support functions, completion of the job is contingent on carrying out duties during specified and regular time periods. In others, such as manufacturing, the cost of machinery and technology may be amortized through continual use, necessitating after-hours working. What this would suggest is that non-standard working time is contingent not just on national context, but also on sector and organization type.

This chapter compares the implicit and explicit predictions of the literature on comparative capitalism as to the nature and extent of non-standard working time. After a brief review of the specific methods of data analysis deployed, we present our empirical findings, based, once more, on the Cranet surveys.

Working Flexibly and Working Time

Firms may utilize their workforces in a contingent manner in a range of ways. This can encompass any arrangement that departs from full time, permanent waged employment during the standard working day (Polivk and Nardone 1989: 10). This can include numerical flexibility, functional flexibility and flexibility in working time; the relative incidence and combination of these forms is likely to vary from context to context (Brewster 1998; Tregaskis and Brewster 2006).

When organizations can readily adjust workforce size because of ease in hiring and firing, they may be seen as being numerically flexible. This may, in part, be contingent on labour law, but also on the types of contract the firm chooses to adopt (e.g. temporary or permanent). Firms are functionally flexible when workers are able and permitted to carry out a range of tasks that cut across narrow skills sets (Wood et al. 2006). Meanwhile, temporal flexibility refers to the ability of the employer to readily adjust the hours worked and/or to extend or reconfigure working time to fall outside of the normal working day. This chapter focuses on temporal flexibility.

In the pre-industrial period, working time often corresponded with the length of daylight; in home-based production, craft work was carried out during specific seasons, or fitted around daily tasks centring on the production of foodstuffs. The early factories were characterized by the marshalling of labour into a confined physical space, and the monitoring and regulation of their working time. Increasing standardization in working time was not, however, possible in a range of basic service occupations, whilst factory owners soon sought to maximize the utilization of their machinery through standardized working.

Since the economic crisis of the early 1970s, there has been increasing pressure on firms to cut costs and enhance efficiency to cope with volatility in input costs, the emergence of new competitors and technological change. The rising importance of service sector work in LMEs has accelerated this trend. Within the public sector, the recasting of the public as consumers of services has again resulted in pressure to work on a more temporally flexible basis (Wilson et al. 2005). Whilst organizations may make savings and become more efficient through such adjustments, this imposes a cost on workers. The provision of educational services and, indeed, the ability to socialize beyond the family unit, is predicated on the bulk of society working during roughly similar hours. Whilst reducing working hours may free up more time for other activities, it may also result in an intensification of work, and the expectation that employees should be readily available, as and when the organization needs them, irrespective of personal obligations (Supiot 2001; Ackers and Al-Sawad 2006; Hollinshead et al. 1999).

There are two main underlying issues concerning working time: how long individuals work for, and during which periods of the day (Berg et al. 2005). Non-standard working time is work that takes place other than during or for the duration of the working day presumed to be experienced by the bulk of the labour force: in many developed national contexts, this involves eight hours of daily work over a five day week (McOrmond 2004). However, this assumption increasingly is at odds with reality: Boisard et al. (2002) found that a standard working day was only something experienced by a minority of the workforce in the EU.

In historical terms, overtime was the most common form of temporally flexible working (Supiot 2001: 62). Overtime simply refers to the hours worked beyond the standard day. Although it may attract a wage premium, this is not always the case, a good example being evening workers in the retail sector. Again, unpaid overtime may be driven by company norms (e.g. participation in 'cleaning parties' in the junk food sector) or personal ambition (common among certain categories of professional work). Not only does this save companies money, but it also frees them from having to renegotiate wage rates or depart from standardized contracts (Marsden 1999: 161). It also can result in savings in pensions and other benefits costs. In many countries, overtime is regulated through restrictions on the total number of hours that can be worked during a week and through requiring that specific procedures should be adhered to.

Shift working is widespread across the EU (Boisard 2003). This may involve working at periods during the day or night that fall outside the common working day. Individuals may, according to organizational need, or to spread the burden across the workforce, be rotated across different working time slots. Shift working, as noted, allows for the cost of plant or technology to be amortized, and/or to provide services at times customers demand. Modern IT has allowed firms to make use of quite complex systems for administrating and rewarding shift work (Brewster 1998). Again, this allows firms to make optimal usage of existing staff (Williams and Adams-Smith 2006: 229).

Weekend working is often instituted for a similar logic to that driving shift work. Some individuals may prefer weekend working, in order to fit other commitments (e.g. sharing childcare duties with a spouse), but, commonly, this is instituted to suit organizational, rather than individual, needs (Hollinshead et al. 1999: 483).

Given this, non-standard working time may suit or be detrimental to individual worker well-being (Martin 2006: 101). In practical terms, there is evidence to suggest that it often leads to higher levels of stress and general fatigue (Boisard 2003). Adjusting working time may erode worker solidarities and open the way for further adjustment in the nature and time of work (Marsden 1999). Non-standard working may also result in the introduction of more sophisticated systems for controlling working time; although it may allow workers some flexibility in line with personal domestic needs, genuinely 'negotiated flexibility' appears more common in some settings than others (Cousins and Tang 2004). Again, in some settings, firms devote more attention to ensuring work–life balance and support in coping with atypical work arrangements (Wilson et al. 2005).

Hence, the relative usage of non-standard working time is bound up with the relative usage of general flexibility in working arrangements and the relationship between the firm and other stakeholders. However, whilst there is little doubt that setting matters, the literature on comparative capitalism has tended to neglect the issue of variations in working time arrangements according to capitalist archetype, other than from an ideal type/broad brushstroke starting point.

Comparative Capitalism and Working Time

As outlined in the opening chapter, the literature on comparative capitalism centres on exploration of the nature and linkage of inter- and intra-firm relations according to national context and configurations (Lincoln and Kalleberg 1990;

Hall and Soskice 2001; Whitley 1999). This includes the relative countervailing power of employees and other stakeholders. Although there has been a proliferation of identified capitalist archetypes in recent years, the bulk of the literature has tended to cast LMEs and CMEs as common and unified categories, with the primary focus being on identifying specific forms of more peripheral capitalism (a notable distinction being Bruno Amable's [2003] work on the differences between Scandinavia and continental European 'Rhineland' economies). Berg et al. (2005) note that the relative usage of non-standard working time is affected by a combination of informal conventions, legislation, technology and production paradigms, firm size and employee voice. Hence, even within a specific capitalist archetype, there is likely to be some variation between firms. At the same time, national archetypes do have different strengths, and this is likely to be reflected in sectoral composition and specific production regimes.

As noted in preceding chapters, CMEs are characterized by more cooperative work and employment relations, generally better working conditions and more effective labour regulation than LMEs. This chapter only focuses on the more mature capitalist archetypes, and hence makes use of the LME/CME dichotomy. Although we recognize that there is room for more detailed analysis of the differences between continental 'Rhineland' and Scandinavian capitalism, these economies share a tendency to more centralized bargaining, and industry-wide cooperation rather than adverserial competition, both of which would help maintain working standards (Amable 2003). Again, the relatively greater importance attached to incrementally innovative manufacturing in CMEs – where employees tend to enjoy relatively good terms and conditions of work and working life – would suggest that the use of non-standard work in such a context would be instituted with a greater regard to employee well-being (Sayer 2006; Thelen 2001).

In CMEs, adjustments in the length of time worked may allow firms to reduce their workforce without having to resort to redundancies and to upsize without hiring those with unproven abilities (Tregaskis et al. 1998). This allows firms to be numerically flexible, whilst at the same time adhering to stricter employment protection legislation (Wood et al. 2006). Whilst there are often restrictions governing the use of overtime, firms can and regularly do adjust the length of the working week to retain jobs when demand is reduced; by 'parking' labour in this manner, the expertise of skilled workers is retained, and there is less chance of premature upsizing (Harcourt and Wood 2007). When workers are better informed about, and have clearer protection by, the law, workers can cope better with unexpected changes in circumstances (Marsden 1999: 77). Furthermore, within these CMEs, non-standard working arrangements are more likely to represent the outcome of negotiations and, hence, in part reflect union power and the collective bargaining process. Normally, within such contexts, there is some pre-agreed specification as to the maximum allowed adjustable working time (Berg et al. 2005). Hence, any major adjustment in working time is likely to require a negotiated agreement. In practice, unions are likely to accede to reduced working hours in order to avoid redundancies, but may be less inclined to agree to the extensive use of overtime (Harcourt and Wood 2007). Indeed, ad hoc extensions in working time beyond pre-agreed norms may be difficult to introduce without extensive bargaining. The latter would suggest that pay is more important than quality of working life; should workforces hold such instrumental views, union organizing becomes very much more difficult (see Waddington and Whitston 1997). In addition, firms may lose out, as employees are less likely to invest in their organization-specific human capital when working life has less meaning (Sayer 2006: 209–12).

In contrast, in LMEs, firms are more likely to use redundancies extensively (Hall and Soskice 2001). Weaker job protection allows firms to readily dispose of workers, whilst there are similarly likely to be weaker restrictions on the use of overtime. As unions are weaker in LMEs, managers have more room to adjust working arrangements unilaterally. Even if employees may at times welcome the opportunities for additional income earning provided by overtime, any increase in instrumentalism will further erode the meaning attached to working life. This may weaken the willingness of employees to engage, which, in turn, may make the implementation and sustaining of higher value added production paradigms more difficult.

In any event, as the balance of power is more firmly weighted towards management in LMEs, employers have considerably more room to amend working arrangements. Not only do employees have fewer rights under the law, but also the countervailing power of unions is less. Existing empirical evidence would support the view that the use of overtime is greater in LMEs (Ackers and Al-Sawad 2006). The aggressive lobbying by successive UK governments against further EU-wide restrictions on the use of overtime would again suggest that the UK relies a lot more on it than CMEs (Ewing 2003: 151). Indeed, working time in Britain is among the longest in the EU (Ewing 2003: 151).

Core Propositions

Given the above, it is likely that not only context, but also sector and firm size will impact on the use of non-standard working time. Our first proposition is that overtime and shift working are more common in LMEs.

> 1. *Overtime and shift working are more common in LMEs.*

It will also reflect variations in the state of external labour markets, an issue that falls beyond the scope of this study. On sectoral lines, certain types of personal services are particularly associated with non-standard working arrangements. There is a wide body of literature that suggests that low value added services of this nature are particularly common in LMEs (Hyman 2006). Within other sectors, specific production processes are likely to impact on time worked. This suggests two sub-propositions:

> 2a. *The extent of non-standard working time will be contingent on sector.*
> 2b. *Non-standard working time is more common in the service sector.*

Non-standard working arrangements are more likely to be encountered when unions and collective representation and voice arrangements are weaker. Although no single capitalist archetype is monolithic or uniform, embedded systemic differences in the regulation of labour, and the nature and extent of employee voice are likely to impact on practice.

This leads to our third proposition:

> 3. **_The extent of non-standard working time will be contingent on the relative extent of collective bargaining, and whether or not works councils are present._**

This study controls for the size of the organization. This is on account of the fact that in smaller firms, working hours are very much less likely to be standardized. Examples would include family run 'corner shop' businesses, specialized subcontractors, craft industries and other such concerns (Supiot 2001: 63). Smaller firms often rely on meeting short term needs of customers, are on short term or subordinate contracts with larger firms, and/or may compete by offering services when others are closed. Any pressures posed by legal requirements will be matched through the greater use of informal ad hoc solutions (Webster and Wood 2005). Unions are likely to be relatively weak in the small business sector, even when their rights are secured by law.

Method

Once more based on the Cranet survey, this chapter focuses on the case of five European countries, namely the United Kingdom (LME) and Germany, Austria, Sweden and Denmark (CMEs). The analysis excludes SMEs. We looked at the relative incidence of three kinds of non-standard work: weekend work, shift work and overtime. In each case, the questionnaire calls for firms to list the proportion of employees undertaking each of these three working arrangements. Each of these continuous variables was then used as the dependent variable in an OLS regression model. The following were the principle independent variables:

- A dummy separating CMEs from the reference LME country.
- A set of dummy variables separating the data into 16 different industries, the traditionally heavily unionized metal industry being the base category.
- A continuous variable based on the size of the organization defined as the total number of employees.
- Management communicating with the workforce through works councils and trade unions.

The study encompassed 1,642 different organizations, with the median organization having 450 employees, of which 90% are full time workers.

Findings

Table 7.1 summarizes the extent of the usage of non-standard working arrangements. Many companies made use of more than one arrangement.

Table 7.1 NSWT in Five Selected EU Countries.

	Proportion of employees working under specified work pattern						
	Not used	<1–5%	6–10%	11–20%	21–50%	>50%	Total
Overtime Working (extra time beyond an employee's normal time, added to a day or shift)							
n	184	323	243	256	319	317	1642
%	11.2	19.7	14.8	15.6	19.4	19.3	100
Shift Working (working one of a set of consecutive periods into which a 24 hour working day is divided)							
n	481	255	154	163	242	347	1642
%	29.3	15.5	9.4	9.9	14.7	21.1	100
Weekend Working (working Saturday or Sunday)							
n	649	452	165	94	141	141	1642
%	39.5	27.5	10.0	5.7	8.6	8.6	100

Source: Cranet

Non-standard working arrangements proved to be widespread. Almost all the organizations studied made use of overtime (89%). Some 71% made usage of shift working and 60% of weekend working.

In Table 7.2, the usage of overtime is the dependent variable, in Table 7.3 shift work, and in Table 7.4 weekend working. We report on the results for the whole sample, and then according to capitalist archetype.

Our first proposition was that non-standard working was more common in liberal markets, given structural weaknesses in unions and lighter employment regulation. We tested this by using overtime as a function of the explanatory variables (including the CME dummy variable), then estimating it separately for the two sub-samples (LME and CME) – see Table 7.2. It would seem that the first proposition has been confirmed, given that the CME dummy variable is negative (–4.16) and significant ($p < 0.01$) in the combined data, once controls have been introduced for industry, collective representation and size. However, little of the variation in the dependent variable can be explained through the independent variables, and there is a very low r-squared result (0.03).

This could reflect the fact that overtime may mean very different things in different settings. This could range from collectively and legislatively regulated overtime, for which there are clear maximum limits, to arbitrarily forced increases in working time. Again, some organizations may require employees to participate in 'voluntary' quasi leisure activities that are clearly directed to serve a particular organizational aim. Here it is worth noting that total annual working hours is higher in LMEs than CMEs (Ewing 2003: 151; Williams and Adams-Smith 2006: 231–3). The relative incidence of weekend working between the two types of economies was not significant.

We found very much stronger results when we turned to shift working, with an r-squared of 0.20 in the combined model that encompasses both LMEs and CMEs

Table 7.2 OLS Models of Overtime

	Combined			LME			CME		
	Coeff.	t-ratio	Mean	Coeff.	t-ratio	Mean	Coeff.	t-ratio	Mean
Constant	20.60***	9.87		27.43***	9.95		17.02***	5.13	
Total employees (000s)	0.03	0.44	1.91	0.13	1.52	2.32	−0.08	−0.70	1.59
Energy and water	−1.68	−0.37	0.03	−0.17	−0.02	0.02	−0.35	−0.06	0.03
Chemical products	−0.84	−0.22	0.04	3.89	0.45	0.01	0.76	0.17	0.05
Other manufacturing	3.56*	1.71	0.21	0.59	0.20	0.24	4.03	1.42	0.19
Building	6.26*	1.66	0.04	−8.40	−1.58	0.01	15.89***	3.08	0.04
Retail and distribution	−0.10	−0.04	0.11	−8.91***	−2.46	0.13	4.46	1.28	0.10
Transport	1.80	0.55	0.05	−6.93	−1.35	0.04	7.14*	1.68	0.06
Banking and finance	−0.16	−0.06	0.13	−14.10***	−3.95	0.14	10.08***	2.99	0.11
Personal services	−10.33	−1.41	0.01	−19.44	−0.78	0.002	−6.47	−0.82	0.01
Health services	−7.08	−1.35	0.02	−8.98	−0.99	0.01	−5.52	−0.86	0.02
Other services	−3.79	−0.81	0.02	−22.38***	−2.60	0.01	3.36	0.60	0.03
Education	−14.24	−1.57	0.01	−25.42**	−2.24	0.01	−5.70	−0.41	0.005
Social services	−2.66	−0.20	0.003	−20.03	−0.80	0.002	5.01	0.31	0.003
Public administration	2.38	0.45	0.02	−5.75	−1.09	0.04	18.51	0.94	0.002
Other	3.15	1.15	0.09	−9.36***	−2.44	0.10	11.63***	3.07	0.08
Collective voice	8.55***	4.82	0.75	8.06***	3.70	0.57	3.99	1.36	0.88
CME	−4.16***	−2.75	0.57						
Dependent Variable	Overtime			Overtime			Overtime		
Mean	25.59			26.84			24.66		
Number of observations	1530			656			874		
R-squared	0.03			0.11			0.04		

Source: Richbell et al. (2011: 945–62).

*, ** and *** denotes significance at the 10, 5 and 1% levels respectively.

Table 7.3 OLS Models of Shift Work

	Combined			LME			CME		
	Coeff.	t-ratio	Mean	Coeff.	t-ratio	Mean	Coeff.	t-ratio	Mean
Constant	21.86***	10.71		19.45***	6.68		21.33***	6.81	
Total employees (000s)	0.06	0.86	1.91	0.07	0.84	2.32	-0.02	-0.15	1.59
Energy and water	-15.24***	-3.44	0.03	-15.99*	-1.85	0.02	-14.85***	-2.89	0.03
Chemical products	9.14***	2.43	0.04	9.86	1.08	0.01	8.97**	2.16	0.05
Other manufacturing	11.83***	5.82	0.21	8.82***	2.81	0.24	14.62***	5.45	0.19
Building	-16.92***	-4.60	0.04	-18.94***	-3.37	0.04	-15.08***	-3.09	0.04
Retail and distribution	-7.61***	-3.07	0.11	-1.65	-0.43	0.13	-12.78***	-3.89	0.10
Transport	3.26	1.01	0.05	3.29	0.61	0.04	3.72	0.93	0.06
Banking and finance	-22.60***	-9.33	0.13	-19.93***	-5.29	0.14	-23.87***	-7.49	0.11
Personal services	-10.82	-1.51	0.01	-19.46	-0.74	0.002	-9.85	-1.33	0.01
Health services	2.74	0.53	0.02	-6.22	-0.65	0.01	6.60	1.09	0.02
Other services	-15.32***	-3.33	0.02	-20.53**	-2.26	0.01	-13.65***	-2.57	0.03
Education	-19.74**	-2.23	0.01	-14.83	-1.23	0.01	-25.25*	-1.92	0.005
Social services	-8.25	-0.63	0.003	-33.32	-1.26	0.002	0.10	0.01	0.003
Public administration	-10.85**	-2.11	0.02	-12.82**	-2.29	0.04	13.05	0.71	0.002
Other	-8.82***	-3.30	0.09	-6.54*	-1.61	0.10	-10.53***	-2.95	0.08
Collective voice	10.24***	5.89	0.75	13.85***	6.01	0.57	6.24**	2.24	0.88
CME	-4.15***	-2.80	0.57						
Dependent Variable	Shift work			Shift work			Shift work		
Mean	23.97			24.07			23.89		
Number of observations	1530			656			874		
R-squared	0.20			0.23			0.20		

Source: Richbell et al. (2011: 945–62).

*, ** and *** denotes significance at the 10, 5 and 1% levels respectively.

Table 7.4 OLS Models of Weekend Working Time

	Combined			LME			CME		
	Coeff.	t-ratio	Mean	Coeff.	t-ratio	Mean	Coeff.	t-ratio	Mean
Constant	3.96***	2.49		4.67**	2.09		2.13	0.87	
Total employees (000s)	0.21***	4.01	1.91	0.18***	2.60	2.32	0.26***	2.98	1.59
Energy and water	3.34	0.97	0.03	-6.54	-0.99	0.02	6.93*	1.72	0.03
Chemical products	10.09***	3.45	0.04	2.46	0.35	0.01	11.93***	3.68	0.05
Other manufacturing	4.51***	2.85	0.21	3.24	1.34	0.24	5.37***	2.56	0.19
Building	2.51	0.88	0.04	3.18	0.74	0.04	1.85	0.49	0.04
Retail and distribution	20.79***	10.76	0.11	23.55***	8.01	0.13	18.18***	7.08	0.10
Transport	14.74***	5.87	0.05	11.61***	2.79	0.04	16.34***	5.20	0.06
Banking and finance	-2.67	-1.42	0.13	-3.54	-1.22	0.14	-1.96	-0.79	0.11
Personal services	21.62***	3.88	0.01	-4.69	-0.23	0.002	24.22***	4.17	0.01
Health services	21.90***	5.46	0.02	-1.70	-0.23	0.01	31.65***	6.66	0.02
Other services	4.28	1.20	0.02	-3.81	-0.55	0.01	7.32*	1.76	0.03
Education	-3.20	-0.46	0.01	-2.10	-0.23	0.01	-5.04	-0.49	0.005
Social services	15.48	1.51	0.003	-0.82	-0.04	0.002	21.18*	1.79	0.003
Public administration	6.89*	1.72	0.02	4.18	0.97	0.04	33.49**	2.31	0.002
Other	5.45***	2.62	0.09	6.74**	2.16	0.10	4.08	1.46	0.08
Collective voice	3.65***	2.70	0.75	4.09**	2.31	0.57	3.65*	1.68	0.88
CME	-1.18	-1.03	0.57						
Dependent Variable	Weekend working			Weekend working			Weekend working		
Mean	12.10			12.06			12.13		
Number of observations	1530			656			874		
R-squared	0.14			0.17			0.15		

Source: Richbell et al. (2011: 945–62).

*, ** and *** denotes significance at the 10, 5 and 1% levels respectively.

(Table 7.3). A highly significant (p < 0.01) negative coefficient (−4.15) demonstrates that atypical shift working is less common in CMEs, even when we control for size, collective representation and industry.

We then turned to exploring our second (two) sub-propositions, with the incidence of overtime estimated as a function of the explanatory variables including industry. We found that there was much sectoral variation, with greater overtime working in building (p < 0.01) and banking and finance (p < 0.01) in the CME sub-sample than the base category (metal manufacturing). This would reflect the greater use of call centres in banking, and a culture of long working hours in financial services (Hollinshead et al. 1999). The services sector is a very diverse broad category, encompassing outsourced public functions, high technology support, financial services, through to low value added personal services (e.g. 'junk food'). In the case of LMEs, it appears that much of the flexibility is attained through contingent and part time working, rather than through conventional employees extending their working time. We then tried a simplified model, comparing services combined, against all other sectors. Here, again, we found that sector was not significant in the case of the combined data. However, in LMEs, the service sector was less likely to use overtime.

We found that shift working was more likely in the manufacturing sector in both LMEs and CMEs. This would confirm the extent to which the need to amortize the cost of plant and technology is likely to result in firms maximizing working time whilst, at the same time, seeking to reduce the fatigue and possibility for error that may be associated with overtime work. We found that weekend working was more common in both transport and retailing, given customer demand in both these periods.

We then looked at non-standard working in smaller firms. Firm size appears to only have limited impact on the relative incidence of non-standard working, with size failing to show a significant coefficient in either the shift working or overtime models (see Tables 7.2 and 7.3). However, weekend working becomes more common as firms get larger rather than less, contrary to Proposition 3. This would highlight the extent to which weekend working may be becoming common, given the rise of a '24/7' society; many large supermarkets are now open on a 24 hour basis for example (Richbell and Kite 2007). It is also worth noting that the study did not encompass the smallest firms, where weekend working may be even more common.

Finally, in testing our third proposition, we looked at the relationship between the different measures of non-standard working time and the nature and extent of employee voice. We confirmed our proposition here: there was a difference according to the extent of collective voice, which was more significant in the case of shift working.

Conclusions

This paper only looks at formalized non-standard working time arrangements. Particularly within certain sectors, occupations and locales, unpaid non-standard working may be expected of employees, without this being paid for or formally recorded. Such working may be particularly widespread when law enforcement is weak, according to the sub-culture of the sector, and where labour law does not cover particular situations.

Non-standard working may diminish the quality of working life. However, it also allows firms to adjust payrolls without having to make use of redundancies, with benefits in terms of improved employee security. It also allows for plant and machinery to be used more effectively, which is particularly useful in the case of specific areas of manufacturing. The scope of such arrangements is often negotiated with employees, and indeed, shift working was found to be more common in manufacturing, and in contexts where employee voice was stronger.

We did not find a relationship between capitalist archetype and the extent of overtime working. This may reflect the extent to which overtime may encompass many different types of practice, ranging from non-voluntary increases in working hours through to modest increases that allow firms to adjust the amount of labour without recourse to premature hirings and firings. Indeed, whilst there was no relationship between the use of overtime and context, the amount of hours worked remains very much higher in LMEs (c.f. Williams and Adams-Smith 2006: 231–3). Again, weaker regulation and employee voice means that the incidence of unrecorded overtime may be higher in LMEs (c.f. Ackers and Al-Sawad 2006).

A counter-intuitive finding was that larger, rather than smaller, firms were more likely to use non-standard working time arrangements. More specifically, they were more likely to make use of weekend working, probably reflecting the need for manufacturing firms to amortize for the cost of plant and machinery, and the growing demand for retail and services such as call centres at all hours (Kreitzman 1999).

Other than in the case of overtime, collective voice was found to be associated with non-standard working, reflecting the above-mentioned tendency for greater use of shift working in manufacturing, a sector traditionally more unionized than many areas of the service sector.

A broader finding is of much diversity in working arrangements according to firm characteristics. Reflecting this, working outside of the 'normal' working day may be a reflection of a desire by firms to use plant and machinery more effectively, to avoid unnecessary hiring and terminations (and hence signal commitment to existing workers), or as arbitrarily imposed extra working arrangements.

References

Ackers, P. and Al-Sawad, A. (2006) 'Family-friendly policies and work–life balance', in A. Redman and A. Wilkinson, *Contemporary Human Resource Management*. London: FT/ Prentice Hall.

Amable, B. (2003) *The Diversity of Modern Capitalism*. Oxford: Oxford University Press.

Berg, P., Appelbaum, E., Bailey, T. and Kalleberg, A. (2005) 'Contesting time: International comparisons of employee control of working time', *Industrial and Labor Relations Review* 57(3): 331–349.

Boisard, P. (2003) *Time Constraints and Health Risks in Europe*. Dublin: European Foundation for the Improvement of Living and Working Conditions.

Boisard,P., Cartron, D., Gollac, M. and Valeyre, A. (2002) *Temps et Travail: La Durée du Travail*. Dublin: European Foundation for the Improvement of Living and Working Conditions.

Bratton, J. (2003) 'The context of human resource management', in J. Bratton and J. Gold (eds) *Human Resource Management: Theory and Practice*. London: Palgrave.

Brewster, C. (1998) 'Flexible working in Europe: extent, growth and challenge for HRM', in P. Sparrow and M. Marchington (eds) *HRM, the new agenda*. London: Pitmans.

Cousins, C.R. and Tang, N. (2004) 'Working time and work and family conflict in the Netherlands, Sweden and the UK', *Work, Employment and Society* 18(3): 531–49.

Ewing, K. (2003) 'Labour law and industrial relations', in P. Ackers and A. Wilkinson *Understanding Work and Employment*. Oxford: Oxford University Press.

Hall, P. and Soskice, D. (2001) 'An introduction to varieties of capitalism', in P. Hall and D. Soskice (eds) *Varieties of Capitalism: The Institutional Basis of Competitive Advantage*. Oxford: Oxford University Press.

Harcourt, M. and Wood, G. (2007) 'The importance of employment protection for skill development in coordinated market economies', *European Journal of Industrial Relations* 13(2): 141–59.

Harcourt, M., Harcourt, S. and Wood, G. (2004) 'Do unions affect employer compliance with the law?', *British Journal of Industrial Relations* 42(3): 527–41.

Hollinshead, G., Nicholls, P. and Tailby, S. (1999) *Employee Relations*. London: FT/Pitman.

Hyman, J. (2006) 'Remaking of work: Empowerment or degradation?', in G. Wood and P. James (eds) *Institutions, Production and Working Life*. Oxford: Oxford University Press.

Kreitzman, L. (1999) *The Twenty Four Hour Society*. London:Profile Books.

Lincoln, J. and Kalleberg, A. (1990) *Culture, Control and Commitment: A Study of Work Organization in the United States and Japan*. Cambridge: Cambridge University Press.

McOrmond, T. (2004) 'Changing working trends over the past decade', *Labour Market Trends* January: 25–35. Newport: Office for National Statistics.

Marsden, D. (1999) *A Theory of Employment Systems*. Oxford: Oxford University Press.

Martin, G. (2006) *Managing People and Organizations in Changing Contexts*. London: Butterworth Heinemann.

Polivk, A.E. and Nardone, T. (1989) 'The definition of contingent work', *Monthly Labour Review*, 112: 9–16.

Richbell, S. and Kite, V. (2007) 'Night shoppers in an "Open 24 Hours" supermarket: A profile', *International Journal of Retail and Distribution Management* 35(1): 54–68.

Richbell, S., Brewster, C., Brookes, M. and Wood, G. (2011) 'Non-standard working time: an international and comparative analysis', *International Journal of Human Resource Management* 22(4): 945–62.

Sayer, A. (2006) 'Organizational life: The good, the bad, and the instrumental', in G. Wood and P. James (eds) *Institutions, Production and Working Life*. Oxford: Oxford University Press.

Supiot, A. (2001) *Beyond Employment: Changes in Work and the Future of Labour in Europe*. Oxford: Oxford University Press.

Thelen, K. (2001) 'Varieties of labor politics in the developed democracies', in P. Hall and D. Soskice (eds) *Varieties of Capitalism: The Institutional Basis of Competitive Advantage*. Oxford: Oxford University Press.

Tregaskis, O. and Brewster, C. (2006) 'Convergence and divergence: The example of contingent employment practices over a decade', *Journal of International Business Studies* 37: 111–26.

Tregaskis, O., Brewster, C., Mayne, L. and Hegewisch, A. (1998) 'Flexible working in Europe: the evidence and the implications', *European Journal of Work, Organisation and Psychology* 7(1): 61–78.

Waddington, J. and Whitston, C. (1997) 'Why do people join trade unions in a period of membership decline?', *British Journal of Industrial Relations* 35(4): 515–46.

Webster, E. and Wood, G. (2005) 'Human resource management practice and institutional constraints', *Employee Relations* 27(4): 369–85.

Whitley, R. (1999) *Divergent Capitalisms*. Oxford: Oxford University Press.

Williams, S. and Adams-Smith, D. (2006) *Contemporary Employment Relations*. Oxford: Oxford University Press.

Wilson, M.G., Polzer-Debruyne, A., Chen, S. and Fernandes, S. (2005) 'Shift work interventions for reduced work–family conflict', *Employee Relations* 29(2): 162–77.

Wood, G., Harcourt, M. and Roper, I. (2006) 'The limits of numerical flexibility: Continuity and change', in G. Wood and P. James (eds) *Institutions, Production and Working Life*. Oxford: Oxford University Press.

8 Diversity Between and Within Varieties of Capitalism

CHRIS BREWSTER, JAMES WALKER,
GEOFFREY WOOD AND MICHAEL BROOKES

Introduction

This chapter explores the nature and extent of diversity within capitalism. This has long been, and remains, a keenly contested topic in contemporary socio-economics (see e.g. Albert 1991; Deeg and Jackson 2007; Hall and Soskice 2001; Lincoln and Kalleberg 1990). As we noted in Chapter 1, the debates following the collapse of communism in eastern Europe about the relationship between specific national institutional configurations and firm practices led to the development of an extensive literature on comparative capitalisms (Aoki 2010; Boyer 2006; Deeg and Jackson 2007). These included several meta-frameworks for analyzing the forces underlying diverse global systems (Amable 2003; Hall and Soskice 2001; Morgan et al. 2010; Whitley 1999). Central to this literature is the notion that specific market economies (clusters of countries) are likely to be associated with specific sets of firm level practices, creating – and continuing – distinctly different varieties of capitalism. Thus, a fundamental assumption is that the differences between the types of capitalism are more important than the differences within them.

These differences may of course be between the countries within the cluster; or they may be between different sectors or industries; or between different sizes of firms; or they may indeed be between different organizations with different circumstances and different strategies.

Critics have, inter alia, challenged these assumptions and asked whether variations in institutional configurations are most likely to be encountered between, rather than within, the varieties of capitalism (Boyer and Hollingsworth 1997; Hollingsworth 2006; Streeck 2005). Firms are for the most part, it is argued, embedded in a national institutional context that makes them likely to resist global pressures to homogenization and to persist with nationally distinct practices (Ahmadjian and Robbins 2005: 451–2), although the relative openness of societies to foreign capital inflows may shape the degree of adaptation of systems to external forces (Bandelj 2009: 128–29).

As elsewhere with much of the debate about comparative capitalisms, the literature has tended to draw evidence either from material eclectically selected from a variety of non-comparable sources or case studies and/or from broad OECD data. Whether using the dichotomous approach (Dore 2000; Hall and Soskice 2001) or the more elaborate approaches with more clusters, the process of generalizing and 'averaging' involved in such evidence inevitably tends to downplay variations within each particular strand of capitalism. This outlines a first step towards overcoming these shortcomings.

Diversity Within the Varieties

We lack a proverbial 'Mendelief table' of all possible mixes of institutional arrangements, practices and outcomes (Boyer 2005b), even though we know that more than one possible set of complementarities may coexist in a particular context, and that the number of combinations is bounded. Do the internal differences within the national business system archetypes exceed the differences between them (as Jacoby [2004: 12] suggests)? Diversity within clusters may arise from a number of sources. First, and most obviously, the process of grouping or clustering of countries, for example, contains within it the notion of internal diversity, since axiomatically countries are never identical (Amable 2003; Edwards and Kuruvilla 2005). Hence, within any identified variety of capitalism, there will be at least some variations between countries in their institutional contexts. But do the variations between countries in a cluster outweigh the variations between the clusters?

Second, it is well-known, because much within-country research has focused on this topic, that centrifugal and centripetal pressures make for internal sectoral clusters of firms even within particular national contexts (Katz 2005) or, to put it another way, it is more than possible that a specific national institutional context may provide opportunities for more than one set of workplace practices that may be optimal for different sectors of the economy. Firms may form relationships within sectors that are distinct from the relationships formed in other sectors, so that sectors differ (Crouch and Voelzkow 2004; Hudson 2006). Katz and Darbishire (2000), examining the automobile industry in Australia, Germany, Italy, Japan, Sweden, the UK and the USA, found some commonalities, including particularly the deteriorating bargaining position of trade unions, but also found increasing diversity in many areas, producing variation within employment relations between these countries. Third, organizational size is likely to make a significant difference to management practices within a national context; larger firms are more likely to have greater resources to devote to people management.

Beyond these broad-ranging distinctions of country, sector and size, other literature has highlighted the likelihood of differences between firms (Streeck and Thelen 2005; Crouch 2005; Boyer 2006; Brewster et al. 2006a; Lane and Wood 2009). Thus, within any particular variety of capitalism, there will be differences between the management practices of different firms based on criteria such as differences in governance mechanisms, the uneven nature of systemic change, and the operation of complementarities that both build on existing systemic strengths and compensate for failures.

Intensifying competition and macro-economic crises may force firms to experiment with alternatives: innovations or hybridization with aspects of other models and institutional restraints may be weakened as a result of liberal market reforms (Katz 2005). Overall, a diverse range of complementarities may be possible within contexts, allowing for the possibility of building on system strengths and of compensating for systemic weaknesses (Crouch 2005).

Because the VoC theories understand national economies in mechanistic and functionalist terms – sub-systems are seen as working together and reinforcing each other (Hollingsworth 2006) – they fail to take account of both continuities and continuous change (Streeck 2005: 580). This means that even if economies continue to evolve on distinct lines, any pattern of relationships and associated practices that can be discerned at one point in time is liable to change and prone to ongoing revaluation and reformulation. Thus we find, for example, that leading CMEs, such as Germany and Japan, are characterized by complex and often provisional institutional solutions, rather than being the coherent whole so often depicted by the VoC literature. A key critique of that literature is that it is unable to account for action, opportunism and change (Hollingsworth 2006). Hall and Thelen (2009: 14) have mounted a defence, arguing that the VoC literature does not assume that institutional arrangements only persist to promote aggregate economic welfare, but are also due to the consequences of competition between key actors and that institutions do not always end up serving the interests of those they were designed to serve. Such a defence focuses attention on the possibility of diversity within each VoC, the question we address in this chapter. Other approaches, by Amable (2003: 253) for example, include a broader focus on societal features and relative societal compromises than the dichotomous approach and, by offering varieties of capitalism that are not on the LME–CME axis, implicitly include greater room for firm level heterogeneity and suggest that organizations or even countries can change without necessarily moving toward either the LME or CME model. Amable (2003) indicates that although the diffusion of voluntaristic models in employment relations may lead to the spread of a 'contract culture' beyond the LMEs, which would suggest that increasing numbers of firms depart from established norms, any liberalization process is likely to be uneven and contested, suggesting that such a process may be characterized by variety and diversity rather than coherence and uniformity (see 2003: 260–65).

Hypotheses

On the basis of the discussion above, we develop two general hypotheses, one with a sub-hypothesis, which we can test across these elements of interdependence and delegation. Tables 8.1 and 8.2 record the individual components used to measure interdependence and delegation respectively.

Table 8.1 Measures of Interdependence.

Area	Training	Staffing
Measures	External training usage	Redundancies made
	Training days spent	Compulsory redundancies made
	Training financial spend	Contracts of a temporary nature

Table 8.2 Measures of Delegation.

Area	Pay/ compensation	Financial Partic.	Direct Involvement	Representative Participation
Measures	Senior staff: Usage of performance based pay	Senior staff: Usage of share ownership schemes	Team briefings, general workplace meetings, quality circles	Works councils/ JCCs, collective bargaining

We test the argument that all VoCs are equal or, in other words, that employment practices are globally identical and that the VoC has no influence on employment practices. Hence,

Hypothesis 1. The employment practices of organizations differ between 'varieties' of capitalism (as represented by country clusters).

Against the benchmark of this strong hypothesis we then ask whether specific employment practice between any pair of VoCs is equivalent thus, simultaneously, also testing whether diversities within capitalisms play a, or the, critical role. Hence, we test whether,

Hypothesis 1.1. The combination of employment relations practices of organizations in any one 'variety' of capitalism is distinctly different from those operating in any other specific 'variety' (or cluster).

Given that, as we have argued above, there are compelling reasons to consider that centrifugal and centripetal pressures make for internal sectoral clusters of firms even within particular national contexts, we examine the extent to which there is diversity *within* clusters. To do this we test our second hypothesis:

Hypothesis 2. The employment relations practices encountered in organizations *within* any specific variety of capitalism will be similar.

As we will detail below, we jointly examine each hypothesis across a variety of elements of interdependence and delegation. Our purposes here are, first, to examine whether each hypothesis is supported across each element and then, second, to explore the relative *extent* to which differences *between* varieties of capitalism are more or less empirically important drivers of differences in employment practices than the differences *within* varieties.

Data and methods

We test these hypotheses using data from the 2004/5 Cranet survey. This allows us to use a representative sample of organizations in 27 countries containing 6,503 firms.

Variables and Descriptive Information

By using the Cranet data on firm employment practices, we are able to build up a broad picture of the relative behaviours of organizations *between* and *within* a set of capitalistic varieties. Therefore, unlike nearly all previous work, our findings are generalizable. The employment practices we analyze are grouped around four key themes: compensation, delimitating between two different occupational groups (MANAGEMENT STOCK OPTIONS, and PROFESSIONAL/TECHNICAL STOCK OPTIONS; PERFORMANCE PAY TO MANAGERS and PERFORMANCE PAY TO PROF/TECH); communication within the organization (WORKFORCE MEETINGS, TEAM BRIEFINGS, WORK COUNCILS); employee development [log(TRAINING EXPENDITURE); log(% EXTERNAL TRAINING); DAYS OF TRAINING BY MANUAL WORKERS; DAYS OF TRAINING BY PROF/TECH WORKERS]; and three elements of staffing practices employed by these organizations (PROPORTION ON FLEXIBLE CONTRACTS, log(PROPORTION OF REDUNDANCY), and COMPULSORY REDUNDANCY).

Our typology of comparative capitalisms is largely based on Amable (2003), but with the addition of an additional analytical category to cover the transitional economies of central and eastern Europe. There is a growing body of literature that points to the limitations of dichotomous approaches, which fail to take account of variations in, and changes to, inter alia, the role of organized labour and employer associations, corporate governance and state policy (Crouch 2005; Goergen et al. 2009; Goergen et al. 2012; Morgan et al. 2010; Streeck 2008). Hence, we preferred the Amable categorization. We have, however, departed from his categorization in two respects: first, by elaborating the Mediterranean category and then, in the case of the post-socialist economies of eastern and central Europe. In the first case, some of the Mediterranean states were members of the European Union (EU) at the date of the survey, whereas others were not. Because membership of the EU meant accepting the EU's social policy and relevant legislation on employment matters, we decided to sub-divide these states into those in the EU prior to the survey (Italy, Spain and Greece) and those that at the time of the survey were outside (Cyprus, northern Cyprus, Turkey and Israel). In the second case, that of the ex-communist countries of central and eastern Europe, there is a growing literature arguing that economies in the region retain distinct features that continue to set them apart from the more mature models encountered elsewhere in the developed world (Hall and Soskice 2001; Whitley 1999; Morgan et al. 2010). This may reflect either a very protracted transition towards one or other of the existing archetypes, this often, with the exceptions of Slovenia and possibly, Slovakia, being taken to be the liberal market model. Alternatively, it may represent a sustained interregnum, with a new hybrid model ultimately emerging. Whilst this chapter does not seek to reach any final conclusions in this regard, we retain this cluster of countries as a distinct category. Whilst excluding this grouping of countries would more neatly confine the analysis to those countries encompassed in Amable's (2003) categorization, their incorporation allows for a broader base of comparisons.

Therefore, using Amable (2003) and Lane (2007) we adopt six specific 'capitalist varieties' – Nordic SOCIAL DEMOCRATIC (Sweden, Denmark, Norway and Finland), CONTINENTAL EUROPE (Germany, France, the Netherlands, Belgium, Austria and Switzerland), TRANSITION ex-communist central and eastern European countries (the Czech Republic, Bulgaria, Hungary, Estonia and Slovenia), the LIBERAL market economies (USA, UK, Canada, Australia and New Zealand), and the Mediterranean states, divided into those in the EU prior to 2004 (Italy, Spain and Greece) and those that, at the time of the survey, were outside (Cyprus, northern Cyprus, Turkey and Israel).

The literature on comparative capitalism transcends geographic classifications (liberal markets are encountered in North America, the UK and Australia and New Zealand). Alternative approaches to institutions noted in Chapter 1, such as the legal 'families' of La Porta et al.'s (1999) clustering of countries or the political approaches (Pagano and Volpin 2005; Roe 2003) giving primacy to political systems or governmental leaning, would represent a fertile ground for future enquiry, but this chapter concentrates on those approaches grounded within the socio-economic tradition.

We use a further country-specific variable, GDP per capita, to control for differences in levels of economic development. And we use a full set of industry dummies based on the European Union NACE categories at the two-digit level to capture differing compositions of economic activity across countries. (The sectors in NACE are: Agriculture, hunting, forestry, fishing; Energy and water; Chemical products; Other manufacturing; Building and civil engineering; Retail and distribution; Transport and communication; Banking, finance, insurance; Personal, domestic, recreational services; Health services; Other services; Education; Local Government; Central Government; and Other). We also test for the effects of size of the organization (proxied by number of employees: log[Employee]); and whether the organization operates in the public or private sector (Public), since it is plausible that firms operating in different industries and sectors, and of different sizes (above our minimum of 100 employees) exhibit differing human resource management strategies. Descriptive statistics are found in Appendix B.

The degree to which different patterns of employment practice can be discerned in the data is given in Table 8.3, which illustrates the relative extent to which each practice was invoked (as a percentage) and also ranks each of the ten practices across the 27 countries included in the sample. This clearly suggests that there are clustering tendencies. The latter are more likely to use management orientated financial incentives, reflecting the concern of shareholders to ensure that managers' objectives are more closely aligned with their own, even if at the expense of the rights and well-being of other stakeholders (c.f. Dore 2000). For example, organizations in Social Democratic nations are more likely to use WORKFORCE MEETINGS and TEAM BRIEFINGS and WORK COUNCILS to communicate with management than those in Liberal Market Economies. Interestingly, such

Table 8.3 Rankings

		Financial Incentives								Communication with Management					
		Management Stock Options		Prof/Technical Stock Options		Management Performance Pay		Prof/Technical Performance Pay		Via Workforce Meetings		Via Team Briefings		Via Work Councils	
		%	Rank	%	Rank	%	Rank	%	Rank	%	Rank	%	Rank	%	Rank
Liberal	USA	31.1	2	15.2	2	26.7	23	31.5	20	84.1	13	84.1	12	27.4	18
	UK	21.1	7	8.4	4	38.4	20	34.8	18	77.7	17	89.4	9	31.9	17
	Canada	16.1	11	6.4	7	32.8	21	25.9	23	86.7	11	88.1	11	55.0	11
	Australia	14.0	13	3.5	20	39.2	17	26.9	21	92.3	4	94.4	3	42.7	15
	New Zealand	62.9	14	1.8	24	39.2	18	33.6	19	77.4	18	90.5	6	23.0	20
Social	Sweden	11.1	20	4.5	15	22.2	25	14.8	26	97.1	1	96.0	2	90.5	2
Democratic	Denmark	13.3	16	5.3	10	47.1	14	35.3	17	95.3	2	73.5	21	82.9	7
	Norway	5.7	26	1.1	26	49.1	13	41.7	13	89.7	6	94.3	4	79.4	8
	Finland	13.8	14	6.6	6	26.3	24	26.6	22	94.5	3	89.6	8	40.1	16
Continental	Germany	12.1	19	2.2	22	56.5	8	49.8	9	91.4	5	71.2	22	89.8	3
European	France	27.7	3	4.4	16	76.6	2	45.3	11	89.1	7	89.8	7	94.2	1
	Holland	12.9	17	4.2	18	41.6	16	35.5	16	84.2	12	92.9	5	88.9	4
	Belgium	22.7	5	5.8	9	54.2	9	44.0	12	87.1	10	81.8	13	75.1	9
	Austria	13.9	14	4.9	12	46.2	15	38.7	14	75.6	19	75.9	19	86.1	5
	Switzerlandv	13.4	15	4.6	14	62.2	6	46.6	10	63.2	22	79.5	14	43.6	14
Transition	Czech Republic	7.0	22	2.8	21	50.7	10	63.4	2	88.7	8	78.9	16	8.5	25
	Bulgaria	21.6	9	15.0	3	49.7	12	52.3	7	52.3	24	40.5	27	22.9	21
	Hungary	20.3	8	0.0	27	39.0	19	37.3	15	39.0	27	78.0	17	52.5	12
	Estonia	6.8	23	1.7	25	32.5	22	51.3	8	80.3	16	96.6	1	3.4	27
	Slovenia	7.5	24	4.3	17	72.0	3	78.9	1	80.7	15	88.2	10	60.9	10
Mediterranean	Spain	17.2	10	5.1	11	58.0	7	56.7	3	87.3	9	79.0	15	86.0	6
(European	Italy	25.0	4	4.6	13	77.8	1	52.8	6	65.7	20	77.8	18	50.9	13
Union)	Greece	32.1	1	17.3	1	66.0	5	53.8	5	46.8	26	62.8	24	26.3	19

Mediterranean (Non-European Union)	%	Rank	%	Rank	%	Rank	%	Rank	%	Rank	%	Rank	%	Rank
Turkey	24.7	5	9.0	8	67.3	4	54.4	4	66.6	48	73.2	19	21.3	22
Cyprus	6.0	25	3.6	19	17.9	26	21.4	24	63.1	23	69.0	23	20.2	23
Israel	15.2	12	7.6	5	50.7	11	63.4	2	82.5	14	75.4	20	5.8	26
Turkish Cyprus	22.5	6	6.3	8	17.0	27	16.4	25	47.5	25	50.0	26	12.5	24

Ranking (rank averages by capitalism)

	Rank	Rank	Rank	Rank	Rank	Rank	Rank
Liberal	2	2	5	5	2	1	4
Social Democratic	6	6	4	4	1	1	2
Continental European	3	4	3	3	3	3	1
Transition	5	5	2	2	6	4	5
Med (EU)	1	1	1	1	4	5	3
Med (Non-EU)	4	3	6	6	5	6	6
N	6,503	6,503	6,503	6,503	6,503	6,503	6,498

	Training						Contractual & Redundancy Arrangements					
	Training Expenditure		Proportion External Training		Training Days (Manual Workers)		Proportion Temporary Contracts		Proportion Redundancy		Compulsory Redundancy	
	%	Rank	%	Rank	%	Rank	%	Rank	%	Rank	%	Rank
Liberal												
USA	1.45	20	10.6	24	5.1	7	10.1	20	16.0	10	60.9	18
UK	1.76	16	13.3	16	4.1	12	9.6	16	15.9	11	88.6	5
Canada	2.27	7	12.4	19	4.2	10	9.2	20	31.1	1	75.0	11
Australia	2.29	6	17.6	8	5.7	6	8.9	21	13.7	18	57.1	21
New Zealand	1.85	12	11.8	11	4.0	13	10.1	14	17.5	9	86.8	7
Social Democratic												
Sweden	1.33	23	9.4	25	3.9	16	15.4	3	19.7	4	88.4	6
Denmark	1.65	18	18.0	7	4.1	11	6.2	26	14.5	16	86.5	8
Norway	2.71	2	15.3	12	3.9	15	12.0	8	13.6	19	59.3	19
Finland	1.90	11	21.0	2	3.2	21	17.3	2	19.0	7	71.3	12

Continental European	Germany	1.23	25	10.7	23	2.4	27	11.7	11	11.0	26	56.9	22
	France	3.01	1	19.9	5	3.5	18	9.9	15	10.6	27	63.6	16
	Holland	2.21	8	15.7	11	4.6	8	7.6	24	13.7	17	70.4	14
	Belgium	1.84	13	17.1	9	3.0	24	10.6	13	14.8	13	69.5	15
	Austria	1.30	24	10.9	22	2.9	25	9.5	18	12.6	22	44.4	25
	Switzerland	1.96	10	11.7	20	3.3	20	7.9	23	15.8	12	80.0	9
Transition	Czech Republic	1.78	15	18.1	6	3.2	22	13.2	5	17.8	8	97.7	1
	Bulgaria	2.46	4	7.1	26	9.5	1	8.8	22	19.7	3	71.1	13
	Hungary	2.72	2	21.0	3	3.6	17	14.0	4	12.2	23	78.3	10
	Estonia	2.35	5	27.2	1	4.4	9	11.4	12	12.8	21	96.2	2
	Slovenia	1.82	14	20.1	4	2.8	26	17.5	1	19.4	5	31.4	27
Mediterranean (European Union)	Spain	1.67	17	13.8	15	5.8	5	12.2	7	14.5	15	63.2	17
	Italy	2.64	3	12.8	17	3.5	19	13.0	6	19.1	6	50.0	23
	Greece	2.12	9	12.6	18	6.0	4	11.8	9	11.2	25	59.1	20
Mediterranean (Non–European Union)	Turkey	1.41	21	13.1	17	6.9	3	12.4	7	19.7	5	57.4	20
	Cyprus	0.80	26	14.7	13	3.1	23	11.8	10	13.6	20	35.7	26
	Israel	1.64	19	13.8	14	4.0	14	13.2	25	14.7	14	90.7	3
	Turkish Cyprus	1.41	22	3.5	27	8.2	2	9.6	17	19.9	2	46.2	24

Ranking (rank averages by capitalism)

Liberal	1	5	5	6	1	2
Social Democratic	3	3	2	3	2	1
Continental European	3	4	6	5	6	5
Transition	5	2	1	2	3	3
Med (EU)	1	1	3	1	5	6
Med (Non–EU)	6	6	4	4	4	4
N	6,503	6,503	6,150	6,615	1,284	1,990

practices have made only limited inroads into the ex-communist, or Transitional, economies of central and eastern Europe (c.f. Lane 2007).

Organizations in these transitional economies were much less likely to have WORKS COUNCILS, with the exception of Slovenia. In contrast, Estonia seemed to be an extreme example of a lack of collective representation. This would support the existing literature (Buchen 2007) that suggests that Slovenia has moved close to continental European capitalism, whilst Estonia has moved towards the liberal market model. Indirect worker representation seems somewhat more common in Mediterranean capitalist countries that were EU members than those that were not: this is likely to be, at least partially, evidence of the consequences of the implementation of European Union directives requiring consultation in certain circumstances. The figures for TRAINING EXPENDITURE reveal some interesting trends. First, spending in the Liberal Market Economies is relatively high, whereas the number of TRAINING DAYS is relatively low. This reflects the need for more basic training, given high staff turnover rates in such contexts (Goergen et al. 2009). Training spend is limited in both Continental European and Social Democratic capitalism, given the good vocational training systems in many categories in the former, and the role of the state in underwriting training in the latter. In contrast, limits in state provision and vocational training emphasize company training. In the more developed EU Mediterranean capitalist countries the pressure for skilled labour combined with the limits of state provision provides an incentive for company training. In the non-EU states and in the transitional economies, the constrained training spend probably reflects limited organizational resources. REDUNDANCY is, as might be expected, considerably more common in the Liberal Market Economies. It is also high in the Social Democratic systems, although here the flexicurity system operative in several countries, through which ease of dismissal operates alongside extensive state support for the unemployed (see Chapter 1), ameliorates the effects for individuals. Again, Slovenia seemed to be close to this model, whether because of liberalization or the infusion of aspects of flexicurity; the country has made slow progress towards the latter model (Kajzer and Brezigar-Masten 2008).

Descriptive statistics, however, conceal a great deal of information about the distribution of observations and are unable to control other variables, such as differences in economic structure, that are known to influence employment practices, so a more complete analysis of the data is required.

Analytical Approach

We attempt to explore simultaneously 'varieties of capitalism' and country-specific effects for each of the thirteen employment practices econometrically, allowing us to address empirically the three questions in our hypotheses:

1 'are there differences *between* varieties of capitalism?';
2 'are there differences *between specific* varieties of capitalism?; and,
3 'are there differences *within* varieties of capitalism?'

Since the survey questions classify the data in differing data structures we cannot employ the same estimation strategy uniformly. As Table 8.4 shows, seven of the fourteen variables are binary, five are continuous and one is ordinally discrete. We therefore utilize three estimators – binary probit, a Generalized Least Squares (GLS) estimator for the continuous variables, and an ordinal logit estimator for the ordinally discrete estimator.

We experimented with a set of alternative estimators. We also examined binary logit estimators but found the log likelihood statistics to be near identical to the binary probit results presented. We experimented with alternative assumption concerning the distribution of the generalized linear model (namely an inverse Gaussian error term distribution), but the results were not affected. Our preference for the GLS estimator over simple OLS is based on the enhanced efficiency of the GLS estimator and because it is estimated by maximum likelihood we are able to compare its log likelihood functions across alternative estimations.

Each estimator utilizes maximum likelihood and to facilitate comparability we report marginal effects, i.e. the change in probability of a change to a labour market practice to an infinitesimal change in the independent variables. The exception is the results from the ordered logit, which are provided in odds ratios, as marginal effects are indeterminable. Since ordered models examine the effects of each independent variable on multiple responses, in this case there are six possible outcomes, and there are differing marginal effects of each independent variable for each of the six outcomes, which is cumbersome and would make direct comparison between models less feasible.

The analysis directly addresses the hypotheses head on, after capturing a set of controls reflecting heterogeneity within countries. The results are reported in Table 8.4. We use the LIBERAL, Market-Based Economies (Canada, Australia, New Zealand, the USA and the UK) as the reference group to analyze the differences *between* the Varieties of Capitalism. To compare *within* each group we take the largest economy, in economic size, as the reference country (Sweden for the SOCIAL DEMOCRATIC, Germany in CONTINENTAL EUROPE, the Czech Republic in the TRANSITION category, Italy in the MEDITERRANEAN (EU) and Turkey for MEDITERRANEAN EUROPE (non-EU). We experimented extensively with the clusters and find that the removal of individual nations from VoC clusters does not qualitatively alter our findings. For the LIBERAL VoCs we take the UK economy as reference group partly because the sample size in the UK was greater than elsewhere, making up 16.7% of the sample, and partly because, along with the USA, the UK is seen to typify liberal market practices. We also include a further country-specific variable, GDP per capita, to control for differences in levels of economic development. Again, conducting extensive further robustness analysis on the results by excluding controls where these were insignificant shows the results to be qualitatively unaltered.

Before turning to discussion of the key varietal and country dummies we comment broadly on control variables. First, the size of the organization (log[employee]) has a robust impact in eight of the fourteen cases. Size has a positive impact on communication within organizations (WORKFORCE MEETINGS, TEAM BRIEFINGS, and WORK COUNCILS). There is much research (Brewster et al. 2006b) on the

Table 8.4 Analyzing Variety of Capitalism.

		Financial Incentives			Communication with Management			
		Management Stock Options	Prof/Technical Stock Options	Management Performance Pay	Prof/Technical Performance Pay	Via Workforce Meetings	Via Attitude Surveys	Via Work Council
Capitalisms Ref Liberal economies	Social Democratic	-0.090*** (5.38)	-0.151*** (4.53)	-0.176*** (5.43)	0.189*** (7.49)	0.124*** (4.81)	0.522*** (16.14)	-0.032*** (3.80)
	Continental European	-0.051* (2.23)	0.234*** (5.60)	0.268*** (6.36)	0.131*** (5.00)	-0.253** (7.06)	0.555*** (16.82)	-0.028* (2.22)
	Transitional	0.27 (1.60)	0.439** (2.59)	0.653*** (4.21)	0.168* (2.11)	-0.494** (2.82)	0.434*** (11.75)	0.19 (1.55)
	Mediterranean (EU)	0.165** (2.76)	0.483*** (6.64)	0.364*** (4.70)	-0.04 (0.80)	-0.261*** (3.74)	0.285*** (5.90)	0.02 (0.63)
	Mediterranean (Non-EU)	0.37 (1.75)	0.20 (0.91)	0.35 (1.65)	0.09 (0.77)	-0.729** (3.61)	0.397** (6.26)	0.370* (2.12)
Social Democratic Ref Sweden	Denmark	-0.02 (0.72)	0.270*** (5.30)	0.233*** (4.42)	-0.087 (1.64)	-0.286*** (5.40)	-0.06 (1.02)	-0.01 (0.74)
	Norway	-0.109** (3.52)	0.12 (0.99)	0.08 (0.72)	-0.271* (2.29)	0.11 (1.78)	0.05 (0.43)	-0.040*** (3.44)
	Finland	0.172*** (4.23)	0.156*** (3.22)	0.264*** (5.34)	-0.04 (0.85)	-0.164** (3.25)	-0.529*** (12.89)	0.095*** (3.63)
Continental European Ref Germany	France	0.03 (0.95)	0.419*** (7.80)	0.207*** (3.73)	0.092** (2.92)	-0.03 (0.75)	0.437*** (9.48)	-0.02 (1.26)
	Holland	-0.097 (1.66)	-0.23 (1.58)	-0.334*** (3.55)	-0.099** (2.53)	0.134* (2.07)	-0.01 (0.24)	-0.039* (1.87)
	Belgium	0.05 (1.67)	-0.080** (1.96)	-0.085** (2.25)	-0.22 (1.44)	0.144*** (7.88)	0.464*** (4.49)	0.04 (1.52)
	Austria	0.02 (0.67)	-0.094** (2.16)	-0.114** (2.87)	-0.217*** (4.96)	0.04 (1.44)	-0.06 (0.96)	0.03 (1.20)

	(1)	(2)	(3)	(4)	(5)	(6)	(7)
Switzerland	-0.116** (3.21)	-0.15 (1.16)	-0.245* (2.40)	-0.502*** (3.73)	0.146* (2.98)	-0.322*** (2.37)	-0.039* (2.44)
Transition Ref Czech Republic							
Bulgaria	0.541*** (4.86)	0.13 (1.51)	0.04 (0.44)	-0.328*** (3.75)	-0.462*** (5.50)	0.2111*** (2.08)	0.466*** (3.72)
Hungary	0.367** (3.42)	-0.03 (0.35)	-0.165** (2.21)	-0.521*** (5.59)	-0.01 (0.09)	0.404*** (4.48)	
Estonia	0.184* (1.98)	-0.04 (0.44)	-0.01 (0.18)	-0.06 (0.88)	0.131** (3.40)	-0.087*** (2.93)	0.06 (0.89)
Slovenia	0.08 (1.12)	0.296** (4.07)	0.241** (3.11)	-0.117* (1.75)	0.07 (1.74)	0.427*** (5.68)	0.07 (1.11)
Mediterranean (EU) Spain	-0.04 (0.98)	-0.190** (2.59)	0.11 (1.43)	0.135** (4.31)	-0.05 (0.92)	0.326*** (4.97)	0.00 (0.14)
Ref Italy							
Greece	0.196*** (3.08)	-0.05 (0.62)	0.13 (1.66)	-0.09 (1.58)	-0.221*** (3.27)	-0.308*** (3.90)	0.281*** (4.25)
Mediterranean (Non-EU) Cyprus	-0.105* (2.13)	-0.24 (1.48)	-0.21 (1.47)	-0.22 (1.37)	0.143** (2.50)	0.25 (1.45)	-0.037* (2.09)
Ref Turkey Israel	0.00 (0.04)	-0.14 (1.30)	-0.16 (1.71)	0.04 (0.61)	0.131** (3.20)	-0.18 (1.46)	-0.02 (0.57)
Turkish Cyprus	0.466*** (4.96)	0.187* (2.12)	0.225** (2.64)	-0.109 (1.88)	-0.01 (0.16)	0.09 (0.92)	0.09 (1.60)
Liberal Ref UK US	0.097* (2.13)	0.09 (1.48)	0.08 (1.47)	-0.02 (0.50)	-0.112* (2.50)	-0.252*** (4.49)	0.053* (2.09)
Canada	0.100* (2.49)	0.208*** (3.75)	0.144** (2.60)	0.100** (3.47)	0.03 (0.56)	0.173*** (3.32)	0.05 (1.95)
Australia	0.08 (1.53)	0.232** (3.29)	0.247** (3.45)	0.127*** (3.74)	0.03 (0.56)	0.00 (0.03)	0.04 (1.17)
New Zealand	0.258** (2.63)	0.361** (3.50)	0.388*** (3.66)	0.08 (1.45)	-0.14 (1.50)	-0.213* (1.93)	0.08 (1.55)
Employees (000s)	0.035***	0.05***	0.0371***	0.009*	0.008*	0.062***	0.011***

(10.63)	(9.46)	(7.34)	(2.44)	(2.24)	(10.24)	(5.65)
Public sector −0.138*** (11.25)	−0.106*** (5.36)	−0.1179*** (6.30)	0.01 (0.57)	0.01 (0.48)	0.145*** (6.67)	−0.046*** (6.53)
GDP per capital (bn) 0.015*** (3.72)	0.0146* (2.15)	0.017* (2.59)	0.00 (1.39)	0.00 (1.89)	−0.011*** (9.70)	0.0066** (3.41)
Industry Dummies YES	YES	YES	YES	YES	YES	YES
Estimator Binary Probit	Binary Probit	GLS (Gaussian)	Binary Probit	Binary Probit	Binary Probit	Binary Probit
N 5,480	5,736	5,736	5,736	5,736	5,736	5,423
Log pseudo likelihood −2029	−3472	−3382	−2428	−2360	−2735	−1065
Pseudo R² 0.162	0.112	0.097	0.1228	0.110	0.309	0.1229

Table 8.4 Analyzing Variety of Capitalism. (Continued)

		Training			Contractual & Redundancy Arrangements		
		log (Training Expenditure)	log (% External)	Training Days (Manual)	Proportion on Temporary contract	Proportion on Fixed Term Contract	Compulsory Redundancy
Capitalisms	Social Democratic	0.223*	−0.03	−0.08	0.209**	−0.162	0.07
		(2.16)	(0.37)	(0.98)	(3.09)	(1.77)	(1.44)
Ref Liberal economies	Continental European	−0.218	−0.348**	−0.539***	−0.482***	−0.440***	−0.394***
		(1.76)	(3.39)	(5.36)	(5.43)	(4.01)	(5.92)
	Transitional	1.99**	−1.58**	−0.638**	−0.618	−0.24	−0.828**
		(2.63)	(2.84)	(3.03)	(1.97)	(0.38)	(2.54)
	Mediterranean (EU)	0.20	−0.513*	0.02	−1.045***	−0.588**	−0.611***
		(0.05)	(2.56)	(0.10)	(6.54)	(2.58)	(4.45)

	(1)	(2)	(3)	(4)	(5)	(6)
Mediterranean (Non-EU)	1.66 (1.22)	−1.160* (2.17)	1.199* (2.29)	−1.705*** (3.98)	−0.36 (0.58)	−0.68 (1.80)
Social Democratic Ref Sweden Denmark	−0.458** (3.02)	0.256** (2.04)	−0.08 (0.73)	−0.425*** (4.22)	−0.02 (0.12)	0.140** (2.33)
Norway	−0.988** (2.51)	−0.11 (0.39)	−0.54 (1.88)	−0.12 (0.52)	0.05 (0.15)	0.12 (0.91)
Finland	−0.214** (2.65)	0.246* (2.09)	−0.08 (0.83)	−0.531*** (5.62)	−0.24 (1.82)	−0.296** (3.48)
Continental European Ref Germany France	0.437* (2.11)	0.936*** (5.11)	−0.21 (1.77)	0.07 (0.59)	0.24 (1.11)	0.12 (1.40)
Holland	−2.085** (2.99)	1.653** (3.22)	−1.955*** (3.92)	0.27 (0.79)	−0.14 (0.24)	0.231* (1.84)
Belgium	0.450*** (4.59)	0.244* (2.53)	0.629** (6.57)	0.782*** (8.73)	0.20 (1.75)	0.108** (2.32)
Austria	0.13 (1.20)	0.10 (0.99)	0.16 (1.79)	−0.351*** (3.74)	−0.13 (1.00)	−0.09 (1.44)
Switzerland	−0.51 (1.11)	0.40 (1.20)	−0.11 (0.34)	−0.14 (3.74)	0.33 (0.86)	0.252*** (3.16)
Transition Ref Czech Republic Bulgaria	−1.196*** (4.64)	1.240*** (6.15)	−1.261*** (6.73)	−0.66 (3.63)	0.15 (0.69)	0.217*** (3.06)
Hungary	−1.108*** (3.94)	1.036*** (5.07)	−1.016*** (4.77)	−0.54 (2.81)	0.29 (1.47)	0.16 (1.72)
Estonia	−0.797*** (3.92)	1.14*** (5.64)	−1.067*** (6.02)	−0.24 (1.44)	0.01 (0.03)	0.212** (2.78)
Slovenia	−0.801*** (4.34)	0.832*** (4.95)	−1.458*** (8.18)	−0.42 (2.69)	−0.391* (1.98)	−0.540*** (4.49)
Mediterranean (EU) Ref Italy Spain	0.09 (0.38)	0.06 (0.32)	0.22 (1.29)	1.17 (7.30)	0.24 (0.83)	−0.01 (0.12)
Greece	0.42	−0.11	0.466*	0.16	0.07	−0.08

	GLS (Gaussian)	GLS (Gaussian)	GLS (Gaussian)	Ordered Logit	GLS (Gaussian)	Binary Probit
(leading z-value)	(1.59)	(0.55)	(2.04)	(0.93)	(0.26)	(0.57)
Mediterranean — Cyprus (Non-EU)	-1.149** (3.37)	-0.23 (1.04)	-1.266** (2.72)	1.74 (4.64)	0.11 (0.38)	0.01 (0.05)
Ref Turkey — Israel	0.21 (0.66)	0.03 (0.12)	-0.780** (2.90)	1.70 (7.63)	0.647* (2.53)	0.17 (1.73)
Turkish Cyprus	2.15*** (3.71)	-1.06 (1.89)	0.942** (2.84)	0.47 (2.84)	0.882* (2.02)	-0.629* (2.25)
Liberal — US	0.569** (2.99)	-0.453** (3.22)	0.390** (2.72)	-0.53 (4.64)	0.04 (0.24)	-0.17 (1.84)
Ref UK — Canada	0.32 (1.90)	-0.15 (1.10)	0.07 (0.55)	0.26 (2.30)	0.08 (1.02)	-0.227** (2.07)
Australia	0.52 (1.35)	0.18 (1.10)	0.385* (2.32)	0.44 (3.10)	0.09 (1.09)	-0.508** (3.36)
New Zealand	0.53 (1.49)	-0.38 (1.41)	0.30 (1.14)	-0.18 (0.83)	0.09 (0.97)	-0.37* (1.73)
Employees (000s)	-0.02 (1.51)	-0.088*** (6.12)	-0.01 (0.84)	0.04 (3.80)	-0.09 (5.99)	-0.01 (0.77)
Public sector	0.01* (2.60)	0.06 (1.31)	-0.04 (0.78)	0.00 (0.03)	-0.254*** (4.31)	-0.187*** (5.65)
GDP per capital (bn)	0.00 (0.31)	-0.02 (1.35)	0.03 (1.72)	-0.01 (0.92)	0.01 (1.02)	-0.023* (2.36)
Industry Dummies	YES	YES	YES	YES	YES	YES
Estimator	GLS (Gaussian)	GLS (Gaussian)	GLS (Gaussian)	Ordered Logit	GLS (Gaussian)	Binary Probit
N	3,335	3,691	2,880	5,736	1,853	1,770
Log pseudo likelihood	-4742	-5190	-3451	-8082	-2320	-815
Pseudo R^2	0.0732*	0.0961*	0.105	0.062	0.1438*	0.189

Three estimation strategies are employed reflecting the structure of the survey questions. With each estimator z-statistics with robust standard errors are reported. *p<0.05; **p<0.01; ***p<0.001 (two-tailed tests).

For probit estimations, coefficients are estimated marginal effects ($\partial F / \partial \chi_k$), i.e., the marginal effect of $\Pr(y = 1)$ given a unit increase in the value of the relevant continuous regressor (χ_k) holding all other regressors at their sample means. The discrete change in probability is reported for binary regressors. z-statistics are reported and are derived using robust standard errors. The GLS estimations assume a Gaussian (normal) distribution. Ordered logit reports odds ratio. Approximate likelihood-ratio test of proportionality of odds across response categories supporting an ordered estimation (Prob $> \chi^2 = 0.7615$). The R^2 in the GLS estimated columns are derived via OLS and are purely an indicative means to compare goodness of fit across estimations.

effect of size on HRM. We know that larger organizations are more likely to formalize relationships and to recognize trade unions. Hence it is no surprise to find that size is a significant factor for formalized communication. Size has an impact on the use of stock options as a form of compensation. This makes sense given the greater likelihood of larger organizations having shareholder ownership. Size impacts on the organization's use of FIXED TERM CONTRACTS. The results indicate that firm size has a negative impact on the degree to which organizations outsource their training (% EXTERNAL TRAINING) and on the two variables related to the stability of the relationship between employee and firm (PROPORTION OF REDUNDANCY). Larger firms are more likely to have the capacity to operate in-house training, and also have greater resources to absorb temporary shocks. However, neither the amount spent on training (TRAINING EXPENDITURE) nor the form of redundancy (COMPULSORY REDUNDANCY) were significantly influenced by organizational size.

Apart from size, being in the public sector is also a significant control variable. It influences the log likelihood of six of the ten estimations. Industry dummies, whose coefficients are not provided here, were jointly significant in all estimations.

GDP per capita is significant at the 5% level in five cases, indicating that controlling for differences in levels of development matters, as these could be conflated with nationality or VoC.

We tested whether or not employment practices of organizations differ between 'varieties' of capitalism, as represented by country clusters (*Hypothesis 1*) by examining whether or not Varieties of Capitalism are statistically indistinguishable. The findings would show that each of the five other specific 'capitalist varieties' does not differ statistically from zero relative to the LIBERAL economies, if there were no differences between them. The data reveal that this is certainly not the case, with no single HRM practice being identical across VoCs. Hence, we are unequivocally able to reject the hypothesis that employment practices do not statistically differ between VoCs. In fact there are at least two significant coefficients on one of the five alternative capitalist varieties in all the estimations. If we consider the Co-ordinated Market Economies, the regulated, collaborative or stakeholder economies in our CONTINENTAL EUROPEAN group, there are significant differences from the LIBERAL market economies on every single employment practice. Indeed, relative to the LIBERAL economy benchmark, across the full spectrum of labour market practices more than 75% of the coefficients differ statistically from the LIBERAL benchmark reference group. When we exclude country differences, omitting the full array of country-specific effects, we find that around 80% of the coefficients differed significantly from the LIBERAL benchmark. The lower proportion of significant coefficients undoubtedly reflects some multi-collinearly associated with the incorporation of a full set of country effects. The implication is that the results provided, despite being quite provocative, actually underestimate the extent of differences between VoC.

There are a number of clearly discernable patterns in the data. For example, it is apparent that the countries in the Nordic SOCIAL DEMOCRATIC cluster have a robust preference for more group-oriented COMMUNICATION METHODS with management. This would reflect the relative strength of unions in such contexts, and the tendency for different forms of voice to be complementary (Brewster et al. 2007a; Brewster et al. 2007b). The magnitude of the coefficients is estimated marginal effects, so we are able to also comment on the extent of the differences between VOCs. The coefficients for the SOCIAL DEMOCRATIC VoC's communication methods show a variation ranging from 12% for TEAM BRIEFING to more than 50% for WORK COUNCILS between the SOCIAL DEMOCRATIC economies and the LIBERAL benchmark cluster. Works councils are particularly likely to be associated with established collective bargaining, underscoring the complementarity of practices in such contexts (Brewster et al. 2007b). FINANCIAL incentives are found much less commonly in the SOCIAL DEMOCRATIC cluster, which could reflect the fact that financial participation and output based reward schemes are often used by management as a mechanism for building consensus (Gollan et al. 2006: 501) which is not so much of a problem in these societies, or as part of a calculative HRM agenda (Gooderham et al. 1999) which is much less appropriate in the Nordic economies.

We have focused on performance based pay for managerial and professional employees, since this is often used as a mechanism for solving the agency problem and is most likely, therefore, to be associated with a culture of maximizing shareholder value. However, such schemes have made little headway in most of the TRANSITIONAL economies of Europe, which provides something of a challenge to the received wisdom that they, or many of them, are aping the policies and practices of the LMEs (c.f. Lane 2007). In contrast, it is clear that there is an entrenchment of the works council model in countries such as Slovenia. Table 8.3 also shows that the Nordic SOCIAL DEMOCRATIC nations utilize STOCK OPTIONS three times less for managers relative to the benchmark LIBERAL economies. They also use them less for professional and technical employees although this group is only 3% less likely to be provided with options by firms in the Nordic states than by firms in LIBERAL economies. Again, this would reflect the concern with aligning management with the interests of owners, marginalizing other stakeholders, a feature of liberal market capitalism (Dore 2000).

As another illustration, if we look at the coefficients from the first column on Table 8.4 that analyses Communication with Management via WORKFORCE MEETINGS, we can see that both the SOCIAL DEMOCRATIC and CONTINENTAL EUROPEAN VoCs differ at the 0.1% level from the LME benchmark. The TRANSITION economies differ at the 1% level of significance from the LIBERAL economies.

Nor can we reject the fact that either of the Mediterranean varieties differs from the LIBERAL benchmark. The employment practices of organizations differ between 'varieties' of capitalism (as represented by country clusters) in Communication with Management via WORKFORCE MEETINGS. We indicate that they statistically differ using the short hand DIFFER. As with the test of all varieties, we will be able to reject the hypothesis that two forms of capitalisms are equivalent to each other but differ from the LIBERAL reference group. We find that across all labour market practices that there are significant differences between two or more VoCs compared to the liberal market economy benchmark. The findings provide unambiguous evidence supporting *Hypothesis 1*: the employment practices of organizations differ between varieties of capitalism (as represented by country clusters). The findings could not be more definitive: different VoCs exist and they are reflected in differences in human resource management policies and practices and employment practices between the varieties.

The clusters are not, of course, uniform and there are divergent practices occurring amongst particular firms within each VoC cluster. However, we are able to show that, on average, there is strong evidence within the data for the differences between the varieties of capitalism.

Having established that alternative VoCs differ from the LIBERAL economy benchmark (the Hall and Soskice 2001 thesis), we next test those estimates on a pair-wise basis between the five 'varieties of capitalism' (broadly those suggested by Amable 2003) to ascertain whether or not there are differences between other VoCs across each of the labour market practices analyzed. So, for example, we can test whether the data support the null hypothesis that SOCIAL DEMOCRATIC = CONTINENTAL EUROPEAN against the alternative hypothesis SOCIAL DEMOCRATIC ≠ CONTINENTAL EUROPEAN; and we do this for each of the labour market practices we analyze. Hypothesis testing between pairs of VoCs tests whether the groupings we are analyzing do differ and, if so, would provide further support for the validity of demarcating between VoC country clusters on the Amable (2003) model. For example, if we were to find that SOCIAL DEMOCRATIC and CONTINENTAL EUROPEAN VoCs were not statistically different across the multiple HRM dimensions examined we could collapse these groups into a common 'COORDINATED MARKET CLUSTER' that would characterize labour market practices across that wider region, as suggested by Hall and Soskice (2001).

Our findings are summarized in Table 8.5. This captures the extent that the employment practices of organizations in any one variety of capitalism are distinctly different from those operating in any other specific variety (or cluster). Where the two members of bilateral capitalist economy pairs are statically indistinguishable from both the reference group and each other they are denoted as SIMILAR. The table distinguishes between

1 clear differences (DIFFER) i.e. where there is a statistical difference between the pairs; and
2 clear similarities (SIMILAR) where there is no distinguishable statistical difference between the pairs.

In either case we can infer statistical difference directly. In cases where differences cannot be inferred directly formal testing is required.

As an example we take the communication practice of VIA WORKFORCE MEETINGS. Table 8.4 shows that MED (EU) and MED (non-EU) coefficients are similar and cannot be distinguished from the LIBERAL benchmark or each other. We can directly infer that they are SIMILAR. However, it is clear that the MED (EU) and MED (non-EU) differ from the SOCIAL DEMOCRATIC, CONTINENTAL EUROPEAN and TRANSITIONAL clusters which all differ from the LIBERAL benchmark. We can directly infer that they DIFFER because it is not clear, a priori, whether there are statistically identifiable differences between SOCIAL DEMOCRATIC,

CONTINENTAL EUROPEAN and TRANSITIONAL clusters. To establish whether or not this is the case we provide formal tests at the conventional 5% level.

In all three cases the tests support the null hypothesis that the coefficients do not statistically differ. However, in instances where the coefficients are statistically significant for more than one variety of capitalism, we formally test whether these are statistically jointly equivalent between the pair. If we look at the top line of Table 8.5, for example, we can see whether the Nordic (SOCIAL DEMOCRATIC) and CME (CONTINENTAL EUROPEAN) varieties of capitalism differ statistically in their use of WORKFORCE MEETINGS to communicate with management. We can see that both VoCs share a taste for WORKFORCE MEETINGS with the SOCIAL DEMOCRATIC VoC having a 19% higher preference for that form of organizational communication than the LIBERAL benchmark while the CONTINENTAL EUROPEAN score is 13% higher. Testing these two coefficients we find that we cannot reject the hypothesis at any level of significance below 6.96%. Similarly, both SOCIAL DEMOCRATIC and CONTINENTAL EUROPEAN varieties have a much greater use of communication via WORK COUNCILS – being 52% and 56% more likely to use these than firms in LIBERAL capitalist firms – and we find that we cannot reject the hypothesis at any level of significance below the 8.44% level. This would reflect the greater embeddedness of collective representation in such contexts (Hall and Soskice 2001; Brewster et al. 2007a). These findings are summarized in Panel A of Table 8.5 where we can see that there are a total of four cluster pairings that we cannot distinguish between.

We can summarize the degree to which that equivalence exists between clusters. Tracing the row along the Table illustrates that equivalence between SOCIAL DEMOCRATIC and CONTINENTAL EUROPEAN varieties is supported in four further instances (or for 37% of the employment practices examined) between the two capitalism varieties. It can be seen there are a number of instances where neither member of a pair of countries is statistically different from the LME (LIBERAL) reference group and where, therefore, we are able to state that these varieties of capitalism are similar to the LIBERAL group (i.e. SIMILAR) on those aspects of human resource management.

To clarify our findings, the number of instances where there are pair-wise equivalences between capitalism varieties is summarized in the final column of Table 8.5. Panel A shows there are considerably more similarities between varieties of capitalism when examined pair-wise. Indeed, on average there are slightly more pairings that are statistically significant (32 of the 130 cells), where the conceptual boundaries between forms of capitalism may be said to blur. It is clear that there is considerable diversity between varieties of capitalism. At one extreme, five of the ten employment elements are statistically equivalent i.e. between the MEDITERRANEAN (EU) and CONTINENTAL EUROPEAN varieties, however, this is the case for none of the thirteen employment practices between the SOCIAL DEMOCRATIC and MEDITERRANEAN (EU) clusters, only one between the SOCIAL DEMOCRATIC and MEDITERRANEAN (non-EU) clusters, and four of TRANSITIONAL and the Mediterranean countries with EU membership, and three of the MEDITERRANEAN (EU) compared to their non-EU counterparts. The number of overlapping categories by VoC can be calculated by summing the equivalence for the pairings from Table 8.4

Table 8.5 Testing Difference Within and Between Varieties of Capitalism

| | | Financial Incentives | |
		Manage-ment Stock Options	Prof/ Techni-cal Stock Options
PANEL A	Varieties of Capitalism	DIFFER	DIFFER
Between	Social Democratic–Continental European	0.0696	0.0000
Capitalisms	Social Democratic–Transition	0.9866	0.0000
	Social Democratic–Mediterranean (EU)	DIFFER	0.0000
	Social Democratic–Mediterranean (Non–EU)	DIFFER	0.0000
	Continental Europe–Transition	0.3687	0.1780
	Continental Europe–Mediterranean (EU)	DIFFER	0.8397
	Continental Europe–Mediterranean (Non–EU)	DIFFER	0.0130
	Mediterranean (EU)–Transition	DIFFER	0.1019
	Mediterranean (non–EU)–Transition	DIFFER	0.0018
	Mediterranean (EU)–Mediterranean (Non–EU)	SIMILAR	0.0035
	Summary	4	3
PANEL B	Liberal	DIFFER	DIFFER
Within	Social Democratic	DIFFER	DIFFER
Capitalisms	Continental Europe	DIFFER	DIFFER
	Mediterranean (EU)	DIFFER	DIFFER
	Mediterranean (Non–EU)	DIFFER	DIFFER
	Transition	DIFFER	DIFFER
	Summary	0	0

Note: p–statistic reported. Where statistics are in bold they are significant at p>0.05 or better using two-tailed testing. DIFFER refers to statistical differences at the p = 0.05 or greater. SIMILAR reflects all co-efficients within a chester being insignificantly different from the reference group.

Table 8.5 Testing Difference Within and Between Varieties of Capitalism (Continued)

| | | Training | |
		log(Training Expenditure)	log(% External)
PANEL A	Varieties of Capitalism	DIFFER	DIFFER
Between	Social Democratic–Continental European	0.0272	DIFFER
Capitalisms	Social Democratic–Transition	0.0117	DIFFER
	Social Democratic–Mediterranean (EU)	DIFFER	DIFFER
	Social Democratic–Mediterranean (Non–EU)	DIFFER	DIFFER
	Continental Europe–Transition	0.0012	0.0136
	Continental Europe–Mediterranean (EU)	SIMILAR	0.346

Management Performance Pay	Prof/Technical Performance Pay	Communication with Management			
		Via Workforce Meetings	Via Team Briefings	Via Attitude Surveys	Via Work Councils
DIFFER	DIFFER	DIFFER	DIFFER	DIFFER	DIFFER
0.0844	DIFFER	0.0996	0.7525	0.0000	0.0000
0.0711	DIFFER	DIFFER	DIFFER	0.0026	0.0000
0.0000	DIFFER	0.0000	DIFFER	0.0000	0.0000
0.0965	DIFFER	DIFFER	0.0007	DIFFER	DIFFER
0.0003	SIMILAR	DIFFER	DIFFER	0.1510	0.0038
0.0000	SIMILAR	0.0153	DIFFER	0.5686	0.1487
0.0034	SIMILAR	DIFFER	0.0033	DIFFER	DIFFER
0.0001	SIMILAR	DIFFER	DIFFER	0.0067	0.0042
0.4962	SIMILAR	DIFFER	DIFFER	DIFFER	DIFFER
0.0214	SIMILAR	DIFFER	DIFFER	DIFFER	DIFFER
4	6	1	1	2	1
DIFFER	SIMILAR	DIFFER	DIFFER	DIFFER	DIFFER
DIFFER	DIFFER	DIFFER	DIFFER	DIFFER	DIFFER
DIFFER	DIFFER	DIFFER	DIFFER	DIFFER	DIFFER
DIFFER	DIFFER	DIFFER	DIFFER	DIFFER	SIMILAR
SIMILAR	DIFFER	DIFFER	DIFFER	DIFFER	DIFFER
DIFFER	DIFFER	DIFFER	DIFFER	DIFFER	DIFFER
1	2	0	0	2	1

Training Days (Manual)	Contractual & Redundancy Arrangements			Equivalence Summary
	Proportion on Fixed Term Contract	log(Proportion of Redundancy)	Compulsory Redundancy	
DIFFER	DIFFER	DIFFER	DIFFER	0
DIFFER	DIFFER	DIFFER	DIFFER	4
0.0529	DIFFER	DIFFER	DIFFER	3
DIFFER	DIFFER	DIFFER	DIFFER	0
DIFFER	DIFFER	DIFFER	DIFFER	1
DIFFER	0.2959	DIFFER	0.0935	6
DIFFER	DIFFER	0.4502	0.0712	7

	Continental Europe–Mediterranean (Non–EU)	SIMILAR	0.090
	Mediterranean (EU)–Transition	DIFFER	0.0167
	Mediterranean (Non–EU)–Transition	DIFFER	0.0287
	Mediterranean (EU)–Mediterranean (Non–EU)	SIMILAR	0.1289
	Summary	3	3
PANEL B	Liberal	DIFFER	SIMILAR
Within	Social Democratic	0.0908	DIFFER
Capitalisms	Continental Europe	DIFFER	DIFFER
	Mediterranean (EU)	SIMILAR	SIMILAR
	Mediterranean (Non–EU)	DIFFER	DIFFER
	Transition	0.0637	0.4657
	Summary	3	4

*p–statistics reported with results in bold being significant at the 5% level or below.

and adding the number of equivalent instances to the LIBERAL benchmark from Table 8.3. For example, there are four instances where SOCIAL DEMOCRATIC practices are equivalent to the LIBERAL case (i.e. PROPORTION OF TRAINING, TRAINING DAYS, PROPORTION OF REDUNDANCY and COMPULSORY REDUN-DANCY) and a further 12 instances where there is overlap with VoCs other than the LIBERAL benchmark (i.e. four instances with CONTINENTAL EUROPE, three with TRANSITIONAL, and one with non-EU MEDITERRANEAN EUROPE), hence a total of 12 equivalences. CONTINENTAL EUROPE has 21.

This understanding of which VoCs have most overlap with other VoCs enables us to gauge the relative coherence and distinctiveness of each capitalist model. There are similarities – they are, after all, each forms of capitalism – and the extent of overlap is captured by the equivalence summaries at the end of each row. Perhaps not surprisingly, particularly since these VOCs are often conceived in the literature as forming a coherent block, the largest overlap is between CON-TINENTAL EUROPEAN and southern European countries in the EU. The CON-TINENTAL EUROPEAN and TRANSITIONAL, and CONTINENTAL EUROPEAN and SOCIAL DEMOCRATIC VoCs are the next most closely aligned. The VoC with the greatest overlap is the CONTINENTAL EUROPEAN, CME, model and the Nordic, SOCIAL DEMOCRATIC, model is the most distinctive. CONTINENTAL EUROPEAN and MEDITERRANEAN (EU) nations have a greater degree of overlap than the LIBERAL economies. This may reflect the persistence of a corporatist tradition in larger Mediterranean firms, even in smaller firms (including the SMEs that are not covered by this survey). Hence, treating CMEs as a single 'non-LME' model may have minimal impact if the heartland 'Germanic' model is conflated with some of the Amable categories, but will have substantial distorting effects when combined with others. The findings emphasize that the globalizing force of liberal market economies is by no means dominant.

The bottom row of Panel A summarizes the number of instances in which employment practices are statistically significantly equivalent (at conventional

0.0121	0.0900	DIFFER	DIFFER	3
DIFFER	0.0000	DIFFER	0.2182	2
DIFFER	0.0284	DIFFER	DIFFER	1
0.0063	0.0718	DIFFER	DIFFER	5
1	5	1	3	
SIMILAR	DIFFER	SIMILAR	DIFFER	4
SIMILAR	DIFFER	SIMILAR	DIFFER	3
DIFFER	DIFFER	SIMILAR	DIFFER	1
DIFFER	DIFFER	SIMILAR	SIMILAR	6
DIFFER	DIFFER	DIFFER	DIFFER	2
DIFFER	DIFFER	DIFFER	DIFFER	2
2	0	4	1	

levels). The variables are clearly distinct and diverge. For instance, the PROPOR-TION OF TEMPORARY CONTRACTS is the most similar employment practice across VoCs with five of the ten pairings being equivalent; by contrast, there is not a single instance where training is equivalent. Overall, between the different varieties of capitalism we find that a quarter (24.6%) of the employment practices are similar between nations within clusters, and hence that there is categorical evidence of substantial differences between VoCs.

Panel B of Table 8.5 addresses *Hypothesis 2*: exploring the differences *within* varieties of capitalism.[1] To assess this we test whether the coefficients for each country within a cluster are equivalent, having accounted for VoC. Within each VoC we include in the estimation country dummies. In each case the largest economy in the cluster is used as the reference group. Hence, the coefficients represent deviations from VoCs relative to the largest country within each VoC. We then test whether the other countries in the same cluster differ from each other statistically. For example, having controlled for Norway being a SOCIAL DEMOCRATIC country, relative to Sweden (the reference), do Norwegian firms on average use the same labour market practices as other members of that VoC (i.e. NORWAY = FINLAND = DENMARK against the alternative hypothesis that NORWAY ≠ FINLAND ≠ DENMARK)?

Overall, the results indicate that there is almost as much diversity within varieties of capitalism as between them; with almost a quarter (23.1%) of the coefficients indicating no statistical difference between varietal pairs (30 of the 130), and almost a fifth (19.0% or 16 of 84) of coefficients within capitalist varieties being statistically indistinguishable. Hence a key finding from this research is that although it confirms persistent differences between the various capitalist market archetypes, we need a more complicated, complex and nuanced picture of the relationships within and between varieties of capitalism than has been captured in the literature up to now.

The research provides evidence about several important differences between capitalist archetypes. First, it is clear that a number of alternative types of capitalism persist, with crucial differences in firm practices in areas such as share incentives for managers, job security and the usage of redundancies, in collective representation and the need and ability to provide training. However, these differences are more complex than might at first seem. For example, security of tenure is not a universal feature of coordinated European capitalism. In Denmark and Norway, for example, flexicurity policies mean that workers have relatively weak legal job protection, but this is compensated for by strong provision for externally marketable skills. There can also be 'internal flexicurity' so that, in Germany for example, short-time working for companies in trouble is supported by state subsidies for 'non-working time' of 67%: in 2009 over a million workers were supported through this route and 56% of them took advantage of the additional training subsidy. Moreover, whilst it has been suggested that transitional economies are moving toward the LME model, the narrow, managerial share incentives model has made little headway there (Le et al. 2013).

The results confirm *Hypotheses 1 and 1.1*. The simple dichotomous models of capitalist diversity (c.f. Hall and Soskice 2001) fail to capture the reality, and indeed, challenge approaches that suggest that core areas of firm practice are coalescing around a common liberal market model (Hansmann and Kraakman 2004). As examples, whilst the social democratic and continental European countries both incorporate strong collaborative features, specifically in terms of *delegation* to employees, they differ fundamentally in terms of aspects of *interdependence* (c.f. Whitley 1999). Although there are similar levels of firm level spending on training and development (and see Goergen et al. 2012), in the former, security of tenure is much weaker (Croucher et al. 2012). Flexicurity systems in operation in countries such as Norway and Denmark allow workers ongoing access to training for employment relevant skills, to compensate for weaker occupational security (Madsen 2004; c.f. Lind et al. 2004) and whilst this may reduce the incremental development of firm specific human capital, it allows workers to top up industry relevant or generic skills. In the CMEs the opposite applies: even with 'internal flexibility' the incremental development of firm specific capital assumes a greater importance than further training and development in more externally relevant skills (c.f. Mueller 1992). These differences will strengthen different dimensions of organizational flexibility in different locations (c.f. Burgoon and Raess 2009), but may also yield specific advantages within particular sectors and associated dominant production models.

Second, we are able to confirm *Hypothesis 2*. We have shown that no variety of capitalism is a uniform monolithic bloc. Within every category of varieties of capitalism, there are significant differences between the countries: amongst the countries in the transitional economies Variety of Capitalism, for instance, Slovenia is close to continental European capitalism, and Estonia to the liberal model, in many areas, as suggested by the existing literature on the subject (Buchen 2007). Meanwhile, whilst firms in liberal markets may not always spend a great deal of time per employee in training, high job turnover rates necessitate relatively high training spends. In each category, there is a significant minority of firms doing something quite different to the dominant paradigm. Some of this may be a reflection of organization size, or it could relate to sector (certain institutional environments may be more conducive to some sectors than others, see Deeg 2005). Equally, a case has been made for the importance of sub-national regions (Almond 2011), although in each case these will explain only some of the diversity. Much of it may, indeed, evidence the uneven and experimental nature of systemic change (Lane and Wood 2009).

Theoretical Implications

The VoC literature has provided a broad analytical framework for understanding what firms do in different contexts, based on a linking of extra-firm and intra-firm relations to a dominant mode of corporate governance (see Lincoln and Kalleberg 1990; Dore 2000; Hall and Soskice 2001; Whitley 1999). The various authorities in this field all explore corporate behaviour in the context of corporate governance. They argue that this, in turn, is moulded – and remoulds – conventions and relationships between the firm and core stakeholder groupings. Our evidence shows that there is considerable explanatory power in the predictions in this literature of continued institutional diversity, and that the homogenizing pressures of globalization and hegemonic neo-liberal ideologies may have been over-stated (Streeck 2005: 580). This does not mean that there are no persuasive critiques that can be leveled at this literature, reflecting the inherent limitations of the structuralist tradition and its placing of the firm as the primary level of analysis within nation-specific institutional frameworks (c.f. Hall and Soskice 2001; Whitley 1999). Not only do these theories neglect structural changes in the global capitalist ecosystem, but they have very little ability, as presently propounded, to explain change in any particular type of capitalist market economy. Furthermore, they understate and lack any model for explaining internal diversity within specific national contexts (Lane and Wood 2009; Jessop 2001), although Amable's focus on societal features and compromises implicitly allows for firm level diversity. Indeed, the uneven and contested process of liberalization would suggest significant diversity in more coordinated capitalist systems (c.f. Amable 2003: 256–57).

The country typologies presented in the literature do not fit that closely with the data, and it is worth reiterating the fact that Amable's analysis of industrial relations yields some differences to his overall country classification, although there is a broad correspondence (see Amable 2003: 104–06). Existing research based on the Cranet surveys confirms that bounded diversity exists within national contexts (Brewster et al. 2006a; c.f. Streeck 2008). However, no new or better fitting country categorizations emerged from the data, so that we feel safe to argue that different ways of doing things persist within national settings, however, without 'diffuse' diversity or even converging divergences (c.f. Katz and Darbishire 2000).

This does not mean that institutions 'work' in different ways for different players within national settings, nor that regional and/or industry specific institutions do not play an important role (Crouch and Voelzkow 2004; Lane and Wood 2009), and/ or that clusters of firms may innovate or hold on to past ways of doing things, even if an evaluation of formal institutional frameworks would suggest this is sub-optimal (Streeck 2008). This research leaves us a long way from suggesting the abandonment of the categorization of countries according to capitalist archetypes. Rather, we found that there were important differences in ways of doing things that accord with the broad framework suggested by Amable (2003); what we did find, however, was that each of these categories incorporated specific variations in internal diversity that was distinct to it.

Conclusions

Our results illuminate national economic development and the extent to which a range of different combinations of institutions and practices may yield benefits to key actors. We also show, by discriminating between a number of European 'capitalisms', that the varieties of capitalism are more complex than has been discussed heretofore, and certainly cannot be neatly classified as a homogeneous Continental European or European Union (EU) group. These findings suggest that work that centers on regional blocks, such as the European Union, as a unit of analysis is likely to omit important institutional variation and may provide misleading policy implications. More generally, by examining how firm behaviour is affected by the institutional environment this chapter contributes to a more nuanced understanding of business systems.

This paper has provided empirical evidence testing the assumption that there are varieties of capitalism and that there is more difference between them than within them. We did find that distinct varieties of capitalism can be identified, but we also found that the picture needs to be significantly more nuanced if it is to reflect reality. We have argued that this may be because the differences between nations within any cluster have been underestimated or that the differences within each nation state may be the key factor. It is clear that particular clusters of HRM practices are particularly likely to be encountered in specific national contexts. Whilst not always what might be initially expected, these reflect underlying complementarities, and are aimed at building on systemic strengths or compensating for systemic weaknesses (Crouch 2005). We did find that whilst the transitional European economies have some distinct features, this category does appear to be diverging into distinct trajectories, as suggested by Lane (2007).

More generally speaking, large numbers of firms in each context were doing very different things, in seeking to reap complementarities specific to region and firm type, and/or in innovating. A fertile area of future enquiry would be to examine more closely the specific nature of internal diversity, identifying the principle "minority" clusters of practices in each context. Whilst the varieties of capitalism literature provides a useful starting point, highlighting the persistence of different sets of human resource management practices in different national contexts, and emphasizing the differences between these types, it only provides the broad framework of a complete picture. Organizational level HRM practices are likely to vary considerably within national contexts, reflecting specific firm characteristics, and related to size and sector. Key issues for future research would encompass a closer look at the specific sets of practices that are likely to emerge and persist within particular varieties of capitalism, building on more descriptive case study work in the area (c.f. Crouch and Voelzkow 2004). Furthermore, the relationship between diversity and change needs considerably more analysis. We need to understand the extent to which diversity within specific contexts might reflect, for example, the emergence and diffusion of new paradigms, or might be part of a process of hybridization with other existing ones (see Boyer 2006). A Polyanian 'double movement' (Kalleberg 2008: 4) progress may be at work, with periodic swings between an emphasis on market mechanisms and uncertainty, and social contracts and certainty, in line with long term economic fluctuations. In recent years, with the collapse of growth from the neo-liberal movement and the plunge into governmental austerity in some developed countries, there are pressures for LMEs to become less neo-liberal, in the same manner that there were pressures on coordinated markets to become more neo-liberal in the 1980s. Such process will be uneven and hotly contested, reinforcing diversity within varieties of capitalism. This will occur simultaneously with the persistence of different trajectories.

Finally, it should be borne in mind that the literature on comparative capitalisms is an emerging one; much of the work up to now has been conceptual or has drawn evidence eclectically from existing national or international databases. Thus it has been hard to analyze the data at anything other than a broad general level. In this chapter we have been able to use organization level data across a range of countries and types of capitalism to get a more fine-grained look at these issues. This has enabled us to provide more empirical evidence both on the nature of diversity and what types of firm level practices are likely to be encountered in a broad range of economies.

Practically the chapter demonstrates both the persistence of national difference and, indeed, highlights the viability of a range of alternative practices, the latter of great relevance given the current global economic crisis, and the ongoing search for policy alternatives. The fact that firms within geographical contexts tend to have many similarities in practices has highlighted the importance not only of mediation, but also of associated inter-firm relationships; current pressures towards greater protectionism on national lines and nationally specific support for firms is likely to impact on such relations.

Note

1 With both VoC and country-specific dummies holding explanatory power the results confirm the need to incorporate VoCs into cross-country in order to avoid misspecification.

References

Ahmadjian, C.L. and Robbins, G.E. (2005) 'A clash of capitalisms: Foreign shareholders and corporate restructuring in 1990s Japan', *American Sociological Review* 70: 451–71.
Albert, M. (1991) 'Capitalisme contra Capitalisme,' Paris, Editions du Seuil
Almond, P. (2011) 'The sub-national embeddedness of international HRM', *Human Relations* 64(4): 531–51
Amable, B. (2003) *The Diversity of Modern Capitalism*. Oxford: Oxford University Press.
Aoki, M. (2010) *Corporations in Evolving Diversity*. Oxford: Oxford University Press.
Bandelj, N. (2009) 'The global economy as an instituted process: The case of Eastern and Central Europe', *American Sociological Review* 74: 128–49.

Boyer, R. (2005) 'How and why capitalism differ', *Economy and Society*, 34(4): 509–57.

Boyer, R. (2006) 'How do institutions cohere and change?', pp. 13–61 in G. Wood and P. James (eds) *Institutions, Production and Working Life*. Oxford: Oxford University Press.

Boyer, R. and Hollingsworth, J. Rogers (1997) 'From national embeddedness to spatial and institutional nestedness', pp. 433–84 in J.R. Hollingsworth and R. Boyer (eds) *Contemporary Capitalism: The Embeddedness of Institutions*. Cambridge and New York: Cambridge University Press.

Brewster, C., Brookes, M., Croucher, R. and Wood, G. (2007a) 'Collective and individual voice: Convergence in Europe?', *International Journal of Human Resource Management* 18: 1246–62.

Brewster, C., Brookes, M. and Wood, G. (2006a) 'Varieties of capitalism and varieties of firm', pp. 217–34 in G. Wood and P. James (eds) *Institutions, Production and Working Life*. Oxford: Oxford University Press.

Brewster, C., Wood, G., Brookes, M. and van Ommeren, J. (2006b) 'What determines the size of the HR function?: a cross-national analysis', *Human Resource Management* 45(1): 3–21.

Brewster, C., Wood., G., Croucher, C. and Brookes, M. (2007b) 'Are works councils and joint consultative committees a threat to trade unions? A comparative analysis', *Economic and Industrial Democracy* 28(1): 53–81.

Buchen, C. (2007) 'Estonia and Slovenia as antipodes', pp. 65–89 in D. Lane and M. Myant *Varieties of Capitalism in Post Communist Countries*. London: Palgrave.

Burgoon, B. and Raess, D. (2009) 'Flexibility and working time', *Politics and Society* 37(4): 554–75.

Crouch, C. (2005) 'Three meanings of complementarity', *Socio-Economic Review* 3: 359–63.

Crouch, C. and Voelzkow, T.H. (2004) 'Introduction', pp. 1–10 in C. Crouch, P. Le Galès, C. Trigilia and T.H. Voelzkow (eds) *Changing Governance of Local Economies*. Oxford: Oxford University Press.

Croucher, R., Wood, G., Brookes, M. and Brewster, C. (2012) 'Employee turnover, HRM and institutional contexts', *Economic and Industrial Democracy* 33(4): 605–20.

Deeg, R. (2005) 'Complementarity and institutional change: How useful a concept', Discussion Paper SP II – 2005 – 21. Berlin: Social Science Research Centre.

Deeg, R. and Jackson, G. (2007) 'Towards a more dynamic theory of capitalist diversity', *Socio-Economic Review* 5(1): 149–80.

Dore, R. (2000) *Stock Market Capitalism: Welfare Capitalism*. Cambridge: Cambridge University Press.

Edwards, T. and Kuruvilla, S. (2005) 'International HRM: national business systems, organizational politics and the international division of labour in MNC's', *The International Journal of Human Resource Management*, 16 (1): 1–21.

Goergen, M., Brewster, C. and Wood, G. (2009) 'Corporate governance and training', *Journal of Industrial Relations* 51: 459–87.

Goergen, M., Brewster, C., Wood, G. and Wilkinson, A. (2012) 'Varieties of capitalism and investments in human capital', *Industrial Relations* 51(2): 501–27.

Gollan, P.J., Poutsma, E. and Veersma, U. (2006) 'Editors' introduction: New roads in organizational participation?', *Industrial Relations* 45: 499–512.

Gooderham, P., Nordhaug, O. and Ringdal, K. (1999) 'Institutional and rational determinants of organizational practices: Human resource management in European firms', *Administrative Science Quarterly* 44: 507–31.

Hall, P.A. and Soskice, D. (2001) 'An introduction to the varieties of capitalism', pp. 1–70 in P. Hall and D. Soskice (eds) *Varieties of Capitalism: The Institutional Basis of Competitive Advantage*. Oxford: Oxford University Press.

Hall, P.A., and Thelen, K. (2009) 'Institutional change in varieties of capitalism', *Socio-Economic Review* 7: 7–35.

Hansmann, H. and Kraakman, R. (2004) 'The end of history for corporate law', in J. Gordon and M. Roe (eds) *Convergence and Persistence in Corporate Governance*. Cambridge: Cambridge University Press.

Hollingsworth, R.J. (2006) 'Advancing our understanding of capitalism with Niels Bohr's thinking about complementarity', pp. 62–82 in P. James and G. Wood (eds) *Institutions and Working Life*. Oxford: Oxford University Press.

Hudson, R. (2006) 'The production of institutional complementarity: The case of north east England', pp. 104–22 in P. James and G. Wood (eds) *Institutions, Production and Working Life*. Oxford: Oxford University Press.

Jacoby, S., *Employing Bureaucracy: Managers, Unions, and the Transformation of the Workplace in the Twentieth Century* (Erlbaum, 2004).

Jessop, B. (2001) 'Series preface', in B. Jessop (ed.) *Regulation Theory and the Crisis of Capitalism Volume 5 – Developments and Extensions*. London: Edward Elgar.

Kajzer, A. and Brezigar-Masten, A. (2008) 'Labour market developments, flexibility and the search for flexicurity model in Slovenia', *CEEOL Journal of Economics* 2: 154–68.

Kalleberg, A.L. (2008) 'Precarious work, insecure workers: Employment relations in transition', *American Sociological Review* 7: 1–22.

Katz, H.C. (2005) 'The causes and consequences of increased within-country variance in employment practices', *British Journal of Industrial Relations* 43: 577–83.

Katz, H. and Darbishire, O. (2000) *Converging Divergences: Worldwide Changes in Employment Systems*. New York: Cornell University Press.

Lane, D. (2007) 'Post state socialism: A diversity of capitalisms?', pp. 13–39 in D. Lane and M. Myant (eds) *Varieties of Capitalism in Post Communist Countries*. London: Palgrave.

Lane, C. and Wood, G. (2009) 'Introducing diversity in capitalism and capitalist diversity', *Economy and Society* 38: 531–51.

La Porta, R., Lopez-de-Silanes, F. and Shleifer, A. (1999) 'Corporate ownership around the world', *The Journal of Finance* 54: 471–517.

Le, H., Demirbag, M., Wood G. and Brewster, C. (2013) 'Management compensation In MNCs: Some empirical evidence', *Management International Review* (in print).

Lincoln, J.R. and Kalleberg, A.L. (1990) *Culture, Control and Commitment: A Study of Work Organization in the United States and Japan*. Cambridge: Cambridge University Press.

Lind, J., Knudsen, J. and Jorgenson, H. (2004) *Labour and Employment Regulation in Europe*. Brussels: Presses Interuniversitaires Europeennes.

Madsen, P. (2004) 'The Danish model of flexicurity: experiences and lessons', *Transfer* 10(2): 187–207.

Morgan, G. (2007) 'National business systems research: Process and prospects', *Scandinavian Journal of Management* 23: 127–45.

Morgan, G., Campbell, J., Crouch, C., Pedersen, O. and Whitley, R. (2010) *The Oxford Handbook of Comparative Institutional Analysis*. Oxford: Oxford University Press.

Mueller, F. (1992) 'Flexible working practices in engine plants', *Industrial Relations Journal* 23(3): 191–204.

Pagano, M. and Volpin, P. (2005) 'The political economy of corporate governance', *American Economic Review* 95: 1005–30.

Roe, M. (2003) *Political Determinants of Corporate Governance*. Oxford: Oxford University Press.

Streeck, W. (2005) 'Rejoinder: On terminology, functionalism, (historical) institutionalism and liberalization', *Socio-Economic Review* 5: 577–87.

Streeck, W. (2008) *Reforming Capitalism: Institutional Change in the German Political Economy*. Oxford: Oxford University Press.

Streeck, W. and Thelen, K. (2005) 'Introduction: Institutional change in advanced political economies', pp. 1–39 in W. Streeck and K. Thelen (eds) *Beyond Continuity. Institutional Change in Advanced Political Economies*. Oxford: Oxford University Press.

Whitley, R. (1999) *Divergent Capitalisms: The Social Structuring and Change of Business Systems*. Oxford: Oxford University Press.

Appendix A Survey Questions (Cranet Survey, 2004)

Area	Variable	Survey Question
Compensation	Managers offered stock options	Do you offer any stock options to [**management employees**]? Yes or no.
	Prof/tech offered stock options	Do you offer any stock options to [**professional/technical employees**]? Yes or no.
	Managers offered performance related pay	Do you offer variable pay (pay that varies at intervals, eg. annually/monthly/weekly) to [prof/tech employees] based on [**individual performance**]? Yes or no.
	Managers offered performance related pay	Do you offer variable pay (pay that varies at intervals, eg. annually/monthly/weekly) to [**management**] based on [**individual performance**]? Yes or no.
HRM Activity in the Organization	Communicate to management through regular workforce meetings	Has there been a change in the way employees communicate their views to management in the past three years? Via [**regular workforce meetings**]. Yes or no.
	Communicate to management through team briefings	Has there been a change in the way employees communicate their views to management in the past three years? Via [**team briefings**]. Yes or no.
	Communicate to management through Work Councils	Has there been a change in the way employees communicate their views to management in the past three years? Via [**work councils**]. Yes or no.
Employee Development	Spend on training	Approximately what proportion of the annual payroll costs is currently spent on training?
	% employees receiving external training	Approximately what percentage of employees have received [**training (external)**] within the last year?
	No of days of training for manual workers	How many days training per year does each employee in [**manual**] employment receive on average?
Staffing Practice	Proportion temporary/casual	Indicate the approximate proportion of those employed by your organization who are on [**temporary or casual**] working arrangements?
	Proportion on temporary contract	Please indicate the approximate proportion of those employed by your organization on [**temporary contractual**] working arrangements? (0–5% 6–10% 11–20% 21–50% >50%)
	Proportion of redundancy within an organization	How has the total number of employees (full time equivalents) in your organization changed in the last three years? **Decreased (percentage)**
	Compulsory redundancy	If the number of employees has decreased, have any of the following methods been used to reduce the number of people employed? [**Compulsory redundancy**] Yes or no.

Appendix B Descriptive Statistics (Cranet Survey, 2004)

		Number of Observations	Mean	Std Dev.	Minimum	Maximum
Compensation	Management Stock Options	6,503	0.16	0.36	0	1
	Prof/Technical Stock Options	6,503	0.06	0.23	0	1
	Management Performance Pay	6,503	0.42	0.49	0	1
	Prof/Technical Performance Pay	6,503	0.36	0.48	0	1
Communication within the Organization	log(Training Expenditure)	6,503	0.81	0.39	0	1
	log(% External Training)	6,503	0.83	0.38	0	1
	log(Training Days (Manual)	1,990	0.75	0.43	0	1
Development	Proportion on Fixed Term Contract	3,997	2.70	1.05	-4.61	4.61
	log(Proportion of Redundancy)	3,813	1.63	0.64	-2.30	3.91
	Compulsory Redundancy	3,917	1.53	0.74	-0.69	3.91
Staffing Practice	Workforce Meetings	6,503	2.11	1.16	0	6
	Team Briefings	2,066	2.40	0.93	-0.22	6.91
Size	Worker Councils	5,736	6.103295	1.40912	0.69	13.12
Public/Private	Public Sector	6,503	0.34338	0.474874	0	1
Development	GDP per capita	6,503	29,368.58	12,014.68	2,760	51,810
Industry	Agriculture	6,503	0.019683	0.13892	0	1
	Energy and Water	6,503	0.038444	0.19228	0	1
	Chemical Products, Extraction and Processing	6,503	0.036599	0.187788	0	1
	Metal Manufacturing, Mechancial, Electrical Engineering	6,503	0.130555	0.336939	0	1
	Other Manufacturing	6,503	0.147317	0.354449	0	1
	Building and Civil Engineering	6,503	0.036445	0.187408	0	1
	Retil and Distribution, Hotels and Catering	6,503	0.075042	0.26348	0	1

Transport and Communication	6,503	0.048439	0.214709	0	1
Banking, Finance, Insurance, Business Services	6,503	0.083654	0.276889	0	1
Personal, Domestic and Recreational Services	6,503	0.008919	0.094025	0	1
Health Services	6,503	0.06966	0.254593	0	1
Other Services	6,503	0.027987	0.164948	0	1
Education	6,503	0.061818	0.240843	0	1
Social Services	6,503	0.04521	0.20778	0	1
Public Administration	6,503	0.075504	0.264223	0	1
Other	6,503	0.094726	0.292858	0	1

	Financial Incentives				Communication with Management		
	Management Stock Options	Prof/Technical Stock Options	Management Performance Pay	Prof/Technical Performance Pay	Via Workforce Meetings	Via Team Briefings	Via Work Councils
Management Stock Options	1						
Prof/Technical Stock Options	0.5761	1					
Management Performance Pay	0.1882	0.0955	1				
Prof/Technical Performance Pay	0.1711	0.1088	0.6563	1			
log(Training Expenditure)	0.0672	0.0606	0.0500	0.0463	1		
log(% External Training)	0.0203	0.0230	0.0419	0.0449	0.1907	1	
log(TRAINING DAYS (MANAGEMENT))	0.0043	0.0382	-0.0132	0.0267	0.1414	0.1252	1
Proportion on Fixed Term Contract	-0.0295	-0.0198	-0.0100	-0.0121	-0.0023	0.0189	0.0469
log(Proportion of Redundancy)	0.0649	0.0697	0.0263	0.0231	0.0760	-0.0219	0.0248
Compulsory Redundancy	0.0750	0.0651	-0.0150	0.0036	0.0568	0.0690	0.0285
Workforce Meetings	0.0043	-0.0038	0.0168	0.0115	0.0724	0.073	0.031
Team Briefings	0.0537	0.0184	0.0610	0.0525	0.0462	0.0796	0.0367
Worker Councils	-0.0017	-0.0397	0.1165	0.1312	0.0425	0.0258	-0.0076

	Training		
	log(Training Expenditure)	log(% External)	Training Days (Manual)
Management Stock Options			
Prof/Technical Stock Options			
Management Performance Pay			
Prof/Technical Performance Pay			

	Contractual & Redundancy Arrangements		
	Proportion on Fixed Term Contract	log(Proportion of Redundancy)	Compulsory Redundancy
Management Stock Options			
Prof/Technical Stock Options			
Management Performance Pay			
Prof/Technical Performance Pay			

	Proportion on Fixed Term Contract	log(Proportion of Redundancy)	Compulsory Redundancy	Workforce Meetings	Team Briefings	Worker Councils
log(Training Expenditure)						
log(% External Training)						
log(TRAINING DAYS (MANAGEMENT))						
Proportion on Fixed Term Contract	1					
log(Proportion of Redundancy)	−0.034	1				
Compulsory Redundancy	−0.0272	0.2271	1			
Workforce Meetings	0.0183	−0.0024	0.0151	1		
Team Briefings	0.0245	0.0072	−0.0150	0.1194	1	
Worker Councils	−0.0062	0.0463	−0.0126	−0.022	0.1194	1

9 Institutions, Labour Management Practices and Firm Performance in Europe

RICHARD CROUCHER AND MARIAN RIZOV

Introduction

In this chapter we test how different institutional environments and associated collaborative types of labour management practices (LMPs) at firm level improve firm performance in European countries. The European 'social model' suggests that the existence of a collaborative approach to companies' relations with employees has historic political origins (Martens, 1999). In the German case, arguably at the centre of the European model, a political consensus that aspects of 'liberalisation' are required has long been developing (Lane, 2000). Equally, at the European level, it has been argued that the European Employment Strategy, now in place for over ten years, threatens to crowd out the EU's more traditional rights-based approach to employment regulation in the name of job creation (Fredman, 2006). It is therefore important to evaluate the argument that the efficiency benefits of collaborative practices encouraged by rights-based approaches are inextricably linked to the benefits that employees derive from them (Akerlof, 1982). In short, there is a need for an evaluation of the traditional emphasis on employment rights and related supportive institutional structures that constitute the European social model.

Many previous studies have attempted to establish a link between LMPs in general and profitability, but these have been criticised for omitting employee relations variables (Wright and Haggerty, 2005). We examine two specific types of LMP, characterised by their approaches to employer–employee relations as defined by Gooderham et al. (1999) to establish how effective each type is in enhancing organisational performance in different national contexts. These two forms – 'collaborative' and 'calculative' HRM – are essentially defined by the degree to which employee involvement and participation are emphasised. We augment the analysis of collaborative practices as defined by Gooderham et al. with other indicators that explicitly consider the role of teams and employee consultative committees.

We theoretically elaborate and empirically test the proposition that collaborative forms of LMPs are more likely to enhance the labour extraction process and firm performance than calculative alternatives. For the empirical analysis we use Cranet, a large cross-country dataset providing human resource management (HRM) information at firm level. Our examination of European firms strongly supports the proposition that in those countries where the institutional setting is most conducive, collaborative organisational level practices enhance the labour extraction process and lead to superior firm performance. Calculative practices have a weaker impact on the labour extraction function and firm performance.

The chapter is organised as follows. In the following section, we review literature on the link between institutional settings and LMPs and develop a theoretical framework to analyse relationships in different national institutional environments. We also develop our hypotheses for evaluating relationships between LMPs and institutional settings. We show that resolving the inherent employer–employee conflict of interest by adopting optimal LMPs at organisational level corresponding to the national institutional setting is efficient and ultimately can be welfare-improving. We describe the data used and the scaling procedures employed in order to create LMP measures. We then test our propositions empirically and discuss the results. Conclusions are drawn in a final section, where we draw out our findings' theoretical implications.

Institutional Setting, LMPs and Firm Performance

Different national institutional frameworks support different LMPs. The Varieties of Capitalism (VoC) literature has variants, categorising countries and grouping them either by 'Variety' (Hall and Soskice, 2001) or 'business system' (Whitley, 1999). In the broadest terms, the USA, Britain and Ireland are invariably put into one category ('Liberal Market Economies' [Hall and Soskice, 2001] or 'compartmentalised' [Whitley, 1999]) and those of Western Europe into another ('Coordinated Market Economies' [Hall and Soskice, 2001]; 'collaborative' [Whitley, 1999]). The extent to which institutional complementarities within systems help develop high-trust relations at the organisational level is a defining characteristic of national systems (Whitley, 1999; Hall and Soskice, 2001; Amable, 2003). Whitley (1999) places particular emphasis on the importance of co-operation between employers and employees, as demonstrated in the analytical significance of his 'employer–employee interdependence' concept, described as the degree to which both parties are willing to invest in each other. The implication is that where interdependence is encouraged by the systemic institutional context and is relatively well developed, this will in turn raise levels of mutual investment and efficiency, productivity and quality. Systemic features in the economies categorised by Whitley (1999) as 'co-operative' serve to support the development of high-trust relations, and the converse is also true for his 'compartmentalised' (broadly equivalent to the 'low trust' or liberal market economies [LME]) category (Harcourt and Wood, 2007).

The formal institution of teamwork by management may also both reflect and entail different degrees of delegation and therefore trust to the teams, but the very fact of their institution by management requires a certain minimum level of trust (Tzafrir, 2005). Ackroyd and Thompson (1999) and Tzafrir (2005) show that despite considerable variation, high-trust relations between management and employees are associated with team working and especially with its more autonomous forms. Trust is likely to be further built by collective consultative mechanisms that, again allowing for degrees of variation between them, give employees an opportunity for 'voice'. These mechanisms afford a degree of protection to individuals exercising voice. The collective provides support, encouragement and some protection to individual workers via its capacity to take sanctions against those threatening its members (Brewster et al., 2007). Finally, group payment systems in general also tend to increase workers decision-making latitude and to reinforce employee collectives in relation to management, and are therefore viewed negatively by 'calculative' forms of LMP which stress individual rewards for individual effort (Legge, 1995).

Some forms of LMP emphasise collaboration between employees and employers and others do not (Gooderham et al., 1999). Gooderham et al. (1999: 510) argue that LMPs contain an 'inherent duality' between 'strong economic calculative considerations and ... a more humanistic orientation' and therefore distinguish two types of practice: 'collaborative' and 'calculative', structured by both agency and institutional settings in different countries. The indicators of the two forms that they develop are shown in Table 9.1 below.

Table 9.1 Calculative and Collaborative LMPs

Calculative: **Individual and Formal**	**Collaborative:** **Mission, Briefings, Communication**
Individual performance appraisals for managers	Written ***mission*** statement
Individual performance appraisals for professional/technical staff	Formal ***briefings*** about company strategy for managers
Individual performance appraisals for clerical staff	Formal ***briefings*** about company strategy for professional/technical staff
Individual performance appraisals for manual staff	Formal ***briefings*** about company strategy for clerical staff
Individual reward systems (merit pay and performance related pay) for managers	Formal ***briefings*** about company strategy for manual staff
Individual reward systems (merit pay and performance related pay) for professional/technical staff	Written ***communication*** policy with employees
Individual reward systems (merit pay and performance related pay) for clerical staff	
Individual reward systems (merit pay and performance related pay) for manual staff	
Formal evaluation of personnel training immediately after training	
Formal evaluation of training some months later	

Source: Rizov and Croucher (2000: 253–72).

The calculative–collaborative distinction is useful but should be supplemented if it is fully to capture high-trust relations in the collaborative form. The Gooderham et al. (1999) framework stresses communications practices. While these are revealing of the degree to which employee communications to all grades of employee are viewed as significant by the company, they do not show how far work processes are delegated to employees, how far their views are sought through consultative mechanisms, nor how worker collectives are reinforced by group payment systems. We therefore incorporate three further indicators: one showing the extent of team-working, the second the extent of collective consultative practices and the third the extent of group payment systems.

In the spirit of Bowles (1985), Gordon (1994) and Osterman (1994) we view LMPs as an instrument designed to enhance the 'labour extraction function'. Our first argument is that the labour extraction function should be viewed as endogenously determined by the interaction of institutional environment and firm-specific LMPs (e.g., Bowles, 1985). Our second argument, pursued in parallel with the first, is that collaborative forms of HRM are more likely to enhance the labour extraction process and bring improved performance than calculative alternatives (e.g., Levine and D'Andrea Tyson, 1990). Third, as Gooderham et al. (1999) argue, the different forms of LMP are likely to be differentially supported by different institutional frameworks.

There have been many attempts, especially by American authors, to link LMPs in general and firm performance; we make no attempt to review them all here (for critical reviews, see Guest et al., 2003 and Wright and Haggerty, 2005). Early studies tended to link a limited set of LMPs to outcomes (see, for example, Cutcher-Gershenfeld, 1991). Later studies, inspired by the 'High Performance Work Systems' (HPWS) paradigm, identified extended groups of practices that were linked with superior organisational performance (Huselid, 1995; Becker and Gerhart, 1996; Appelbaum et al., 2000). However, there have also been empirical studies yielding negative results (Cappelli and Neumark, 2001), and the HPWS school of thought has been criticised for failing to recognise that conflicts in the employment relationship are likely to limit HRM effectiveness (Godard, 2004). Godard's (2004) criticism is consistent with that made of the HPWS literature by Wright and Haggerty (2005) who argue that there are missing variables in the discussion (those normally used are typically pay-linked to productivity and promotion possibilities). The missing variables are those linked to employee relations broadly conceived and those relating to collaborative, trust-building practices. We therefore adopt a method that meets these criticisms by testing the links between two types of LMPs encapsulating two different employee–employer relations paradigms and firm performance. These variables are particularly relevant in Europe, where employment relationships (even in the UK) are characterised by a relatively strong collective dimension in comparison to the USA (Hall and Gingerich, 2005).

An alternative, less satisfactory framework for analysing the link between labour use and organisational performance is that of neoclassical efficiency-wage theory. The theory treats workers' motivation as exogenous to the firm and the industrial relations system (note that employee motivation is assumed to depend solely on the real wage rate and intensity of monitoring). Yet, from the lack of trade-off between wages and monitoring shown in studies of 'high- and low-trust' national groupings, it follows that employees' motivation must be treated as endogenous to the nature of labour–management relations (Gordon, 1994; Naastepad and Storm, 2006).

There are other aspects of the labour extraction function (which may not be directly driven by LMPs) that are, by and large, indicators of high-trust relations. A minimum degree of co-operation is a necessary condition of production, but the level of co-operation may be raised if trust is at a high level (Akerlof, 1982). Trust, defined as the supposition by each side that the other will act benevolently, is more fragile and conditional on the perceived solidity of institutional guarantees (Creed and Miles, 1996; Hoff, 2002). Levels of trust may show some consistency across organisations, but are also likely to vary between different work and occupational groups, and employee strata; the difference between different employee strata is reflected in the Gooderham et al. (1999) indicators.

As Buchele and Christiansen (1999: 91) argue, continuous improvements in productivity depend not on individual efforts, but on the effective interaction among workers (team-work), among work groups or departments (co-ordination), and between management and workers (co-operation). Baldamus (1961) argued that effort cannot be measured, and therefore management monitoring of employees had to be subordinated to motivational methods; the extent to which employee ideas of trust and team-work were influenced by management were of vital importance to superior company performance. Because no contract can be complete, a degree of control will always remain with employees, necessitating management efforts to build trust, reflected in efforts to influence employees' underlying emotions (Baldamus 1961: 41).

Akerlof (1982) similarly shows that individuals' productive behaviour is determined by the social definition of the situation adopted by the relevant workers. Akerlof (1982) focuses on the implicit gift-exchange nature of employment arrangements, where exchange is based on reciprocity and trust and relations are endogenously determined.[1] Management has to make constant efforts to influence these norms (MacInnes et al., 1985). Further, employees' willingness to give up the protection offered by rigid work rules, disclose their proprietary (tacit) knowledge, and initiate changes in the production process that raise labour productivity and the firm's capacity for innovation, depends, to a large extent, on management committing to 'high-trust' work practices (Buchele and Christiansen, 1999; Naastepad and Storm, 2006). The (Taylorist) alternative is high levels of employee monitoring, which threaten to undermine trust. The implication is that co-operative and group-based LMPs with strong implicit gift exchanges will tend to enhance firm performance.

However, national systems do not determine LMPs. At firm level, systemic options present managements, even in highly co-ordinated systems such as the German system, with considerable room for practices that differ from the clusters of ideal firm types specified by Whitley (Singe and Croucher, 2005). 'High-trust' LMPs may also be attempted in low-trust economies with varying degrees of success (Danford et al., 2005), and may be more supported by legal and institutional arrangements in 'low-trust' economies than sometimes recognised, as UK case studies have indicated (Deakin et al., 2006). On the other hand, perceived breaches of trust by managements in 'high-trust' countries (characterised by low monitoring intensity and high real wage growth) may also occur. In these countries, an increase in monitoring intensity, *ceteris paribus*, may lead to a reduction in employees' effort and productivity (Drago and Perlman, 1989; Naastepad and Storm, 2006).

In summary, our hypotheses on the optimality of LMPs and their synergies within various institutional settings are as follows:

H1: Collaborative forms of LMP are more strongly associated with superior firm performance than calculative forms
H2: These associations are strongest where national institutional and normative settings support them
H3: Employer–employee consultative committees and collective payment methods are associated with superior firm performance.

Data and variables

We econometrically test the hypotheses derived from our theoretical analysis. Data used for the tests are extracted from Cranet, an international survey of LMPs conducted at regular intervals since 1989. The most senior HRM manager in each firm is asked a comprehensive set of questions about the firm and its LMPs. Our data are derived from the 1999–2000 round of surveys, while the study by Gooderham et al. (1999) which we extend uses the previous round of surveys in 1995–96. Full technical details of the survey are provided in Tregaskis et al. (2004).

Since a central issue in our analysis is the importance of institutional factors and organisational practices for the labour extraction function, and thus for firm performance, we use data from several countries exhibiting diverse institutional settings and diverse LMPs. Following this line of reasoning we also control for and compare results from samples with and without firms that are foreign subsidiaries.[2] The rationale is that such firms' LMPs may have been at least influenced by different country-of-origin institutional environments albeit in a complex way, as argued by Gooderham et al. (1998).

The main dependent variable in our analysis is firm performance (*perf*) measured as a composite index comprised of five partial measures: service quality, level of productivity, profitability, product to market time and rate of innovation. Each partial measure is an ordinal categorical variable.[3] We apply Mokken's nonparametric scaling approach to produce our synthetic performance measure (Mokken and Lewis, 1982). The unweighted sum of item scores has to be monotonously related to the latent true scores as demonstrated by Sijtsma et al. (1990). This implies that Mokken's model provides estimates of the scale scores only at ordinal level. As in other studies, the primary scaling criterion is Loevinger's H-coefficient of homogeneity. A set of items constitute a scale if the total scale has a H-value exceeding 0.30; values above 0.50 indicate strong scales. The details of the items included in the performance scale, results of the scaling procedure and reliability analysis are reported in Table 9.2.

Table 9.2 Performance and LMPs Scales

Scale/Variable	MSP		Alpha
	Mean	H	
Performance scale (*perf*)	—	0.45	0.76
Profitability between 3 and 1 (high–low)	2.13	0.43	0.71
Productivity between 3 and 1 (high–low)	2.21	0.49	0.69
Service quality between 3 and 1 (high–low)	2.45	0.44	0.74
Product to market between 3 and 1 (high–low)	2.06	0.50	0.68
Innovation between 3 and 1 (high–low)	2.10	0.40	0.73
Calculative scale (*calc*)	—	0.64	0.71
Individual rewards: manual	0.15	0.84	0.69
Individual rewards: clerical	0.28	0.87	0.68
Individual rewards: professionals	0.41	0.87	0.69
Individual rewards: managers	0.66	0.82	0.71
Performance appraisal: manual	0.47	0.46	0.68
Performance appraisal: clerical	0.60	0.62	0.65
Performance appraisal: professionals	0.65	0.66	0.65
Performance appraisal: managers	0.67	0.56	0.67
Formal evaluation: immediate	0.52	0.36	0.70
Formal evaluation: later	0.32	0.43	0.71
Collaborative scale (*coll*)	—	0.63	0.70
Strategy briefings: manual	0.36	0.88	0.57
Strategy briefings: clerical	0.47	0.84	0.54
Strategy briefings: professionals	0.62	0.76	0.59
Strategy briefings: managers	0.96	0.67	0.71
Written mission statement	0.80	0.36	0.71
Communication policy	0.77	0.30	0.73
Group practices scale (*grpr*)	—	0.57	0.71
Joint consultative committee	0.56	0.30	0.75
Employee share options: manual	0.15	0.56	0.68
Employee share options: clerical	0.16	0.53	0.68
Employee share options: professionals	0.19	0.49	0.68
Profit sharing: manual	0.20	0.58	0.66
Profit sharing: clerical	0.24	0.63	0.66
Profit sharing: professionals	0.29	0.65	0.66
Group bonus: manual	0.21	0.61	0.70
Group bonus: clerical	0.20	0.66	0.69
Group bonus: professionals	0.21	0.68	0.69

Source: Rizov and Croucher (2009: 253–72).

Notes: MSP denotes Mokken Scaling Program. H is Loevinger's coefficient of homogeneity (weighted); all H-coefficients are significantly different from zero at the 0.001 level. Alpha is Cronbach's alpha measure of reliability.

Furthermore, for the impact of work organisation on firm performance, Levine and D'Andrea Tyson (1990) amongst others report that substantial shop floor participation leads to some combination of an increase in satisfaction, commitment, quality and productivity, and a reduction in labour turnover and absenteeism. Therefore, we further extend our analysis of performance by relating labour extraction measures: absenteeism (*abse*) and turnover (*turn*) to various factors affecting the extraction function. Low turnover has been shown to have a considerable affect on the effectiveness of HPWSs in generating improved results in the US context (Guthrie et al., 2004). Absenteeism is measured as average days per employee per year. Turnover is the annual staff turnover in percent. Both measures of labour extraction are approximate and are affected by various economic and institutional country-specific factors in addition to the main determinants of the labour extraction function. With this caveat, linking absenteeism and turnover to LMPs in regressions where major economic and institutional factors are controlled for represents a useful empirical representation of our theoretical framework.

Next, to formulate measures of the LMPs within firms that approximate aspects of institutional environment at firm level as well, we refer to the strategic HRM model following Gooderham et al. (1999). They identify two types of practices: calculative (*calc*) and collaborative (*coll*) LMPs. Subsumed under the former are practices that aim at securing a fit between strategy and human resources, while the latter category captures practices designed to enhance mutuality, consensus and trust.

The calculative approach aims at ensuring that production activities are at all times efficiently (which in this context implies profitably) supplied with the necessary input of human resources (including monitoring personnel). Associated with this model are a range of efficiency-seeking devices aimed at ensuring that each employee's contribution to the firm is assessed and thereafter rewarded accordingly through performance appraisals and individually oriented reward systems. Investment in employee development is also carefully monitored to evaluate its benefits for the business strategy. Importantly, any such calculative approach is dependent upon the feasibility of treating each employee as an individual rather than a member of a collective entity protected by collectively bargained contracts and unions. Furthermore, if calculative practices are adopted it is reasonable to expect that management will possess substantial autonomy within the firm. Such autonomy will require power not be curtailed by strong regulative pressure at firm level by law and norms nor by influential unions.

The collaborative approach has a distinctly more developmental and humanistic focus often expressed in explicit statements about the value of the employees to the firm. Employees are viewed as active partners and core assets, including in terms of creativity and innovation. The collaborative emphasis is characterised by efforts to create and communicate a culture of partnership between employer and employees as well as among employees. Management attempts to formulate a strategic direction communicated to the firm's employees in the form of mission, goals or strategy statements via an explicit employee communication policy. Sources of collaborative practices can be found in the support of unions or other collective bodies representing employee interests. Furthermore, the introduction of collaborative practices is highly dependent on the degree of autonomous action enjoyed by HRM departments. A minimum amount of freedom of action is necessary if there is to be sufficient space for a communicative style of operation of the HRM function. Clearly, strong nationally specific influences will be present.

The two sets of LMPs considered characterise, in general, two distinct forms of labour extraction as discussed above, although as asserted by Harrison (1993), the two types of practices should not be conceived of as representing two ends of a continuum but should rather be viewed as orthogonal. Gooderham et al. (1999) demonstrate that the two sets of practices may be clearly differentiated in this way whilst acknowledging that elements of both may be present in organisations. A key reason for this, in international terms, is that the specific management practices are supported or undermined by institutional constraints in different countries, a point that Gooderham and Nordhaug (2003) elaborate in later work. In our empirical analysis we test for the relationship between calculative and collaborative practices and their joint impact on performance.

Next, we extend the Gooderham et al. (1999) LMP typology with a third measure explicitly reflecting the existence of joint consultative committees and group payment systems, which we designate group-based practices (*grpr*). In this index we include features at firm level reflecting the existence of joint employee consultative committees and profit-sharing schemes applied to different segments of the labour force. We expect that the index will capture some aspects of the impact of Akerlof's (1982) implicit gift exchange mechanism on labour extraction and ultimately on firm performance.

To develop measures for LMPs, we use Mokken's nonparametric latent trial model for unidimensional scaling (Mokken and Lewis, 1982). Thus, we follow the methodology used by Gooderham et al. (1999) which allows us to compare the measures of interest estimated with data from two consecutive rounds of surveys. Mokken's approach does not make overly restrictive assumptions and provides an internal scaling criterion that ensures a unidimensional scale. This is an important advantage in this case where dichotomous items are used and do not satisfy the assumption of interval scale items. Details of the items included in the scales, results of the scaling procedure and reliability analysis are reported in Table 9.2.

Besides variables of interest related to LMPs, the determinants of the labour extraction function – cost of job loss at firm level (w^d) and intensity of monitoring (s) – are the main variables in our performance regression specifications. The w^d variable is measured as the percentage of labour cost in the operating costs which when controlled for firm size and external market conditions (see below) would approximate to the potential cost of job loss at firm level. The s variable is measured by the proportion of the firm's employees that are managers. In the Cranet dataset there are three other categories of employees reported: manual, clerical and professional (technical) employees. As Gordon (1994) argues, the proportion of managers in the firm's employment approximates to the intensity of monitoring.

Finally, we control for several other firm characteristics affecting performance. These are log of firm size (*lfsize*) and log of firm age (*lfage*), qualitative characteristics of the labour force such as dummy variable indicating employees 45 years of age or older (*eage45*) and dummy variable indicating employees with at least higher education (*eedugr*). Market conditions are controlled for by a three-step ordinal scale (*market*) indicating whether the firm's market is booming, steady or stagnating. Industrial sector information – a set of industry dummy variables – is included in all regression specifications (except the base one). In all regressions a control dummy variable for foreign-subsidiary status of firms is also included. Country dummy variables are used in all extended regression specifications to control for important variations in institutional settings. In selected specifications also cross-effects of the country dummies and HRM variables of interest are included in addition. Summary statistics and short definitions of all regression variables are reported in Table 9.3.[4]

Table 9.3 Summary Statistics of Regression Variables

Variable	Description	Mean	S.d.
perf	Performance composite index ranging between 5 and 15 (low–high)	10.97	2.30
abse	Average number of days of absence per employee per year	7.95	6.52
turn	Employee turnover at firm level in per cent per year	8.24	10.58
w^d	Percentage of labour cost in total operating cost	38.98	21.36
s	Ratio of managers to employees in per cent	9.10	9.20
lfsize	Log of firm size (total labour force)	6.05	1.20
lfage	Log of firm age (years)	3.66	0.91
eage45	Percentage of labour force 45 years of age or older	32.87	18.76
eedugr	Percentage of labour force with graduate or postgraduate education	23.11	16.77
market	Index of market conditions and business cycle development ranging between 1 and 3 (recession–expansion)	1.61	0.70
calc	Calculative LMPs composite index ranging between 0 and 10	4.65	2.23
coll	Collaborative LMPs composite index ranging between 0 and 6	3.97	1.62
grpr	Group-based LMPs composite index ranging between 0 and 10	4.24	2.05
Manufacturing	Manufacturing industries dummy variable	0.50	0.79
Construction	Construction industries dummy variable	0.04	0.20
Transportation	Transportation industries dummy variable	0.06	0.24
Bank and finance	Banking and finance services industries dummy variable	0.09	0.29
Personal services	Personal services industries dummy variable	0.01	0.11
Other industries	Other industries dummy variable	0.30	0.46

Foreign subsidiary	Dummy variable which is 1 if the firm is a foreign subsidiary and 0 otherwise	0.30	0.46
UK	UK dummy variable	0.14	0.34
France	France dummy variable	0.08	0.26
Germany	Germany dummy variable	0.15	0.35
Sweden	Sweden dummy variable	0.04	0.21
Spain	Spain dummy variable	0.06	0.23
Denmark	Denmark dummy variable	0.08	0.27
Norway	Norway dummy variable	0.13	0.34
Ireland	Ireland dummy variable	0.11	0.31
Finland	Finland dummy variable	0.11	0.31
Austria	Austria dummy variable	0.05	0.23
Belgium	Belgium dummy variable	0.05	0.22

Source: Rizov and Croucher (2009: 253–72).

Note: Number of observations used in calculating summery statistics is 1,045 except for *absc* and *turn* where number of observations is 779 and 965, respectively.

Results

We estimate three sets of OLS regressions. First, we estimate a set of equations where firm performance is directly linked to the HRM variables of interest while controlling for institutional context and several other important determinants of performance such as firm size and age, qualitative characteristics of the labour force, market conditions and industry specificity. The results of this analysis are reported in Tables 9.4a and 9.4b. We start with a base specification where only variables corresponding to the neoclassical efficiency-wage model are included. Then we extend the specification by introducing a richer set of controls and LMPs variables. Second, we consider a direct empirical approximation of the labour extraction function, using two dependent variables, labour force turnover and absenteeism. We extend the specifications in a manner similar to the performance regressions. The results are reported in Table 9.5a and Table 9.5b, respectively.[5]

Table 9.4a Regression Analysis of Firm Performance

Variable	(1)	(2)	(3)	(4)
w^d	**−0.019 (0.003)**	**−0.018 (0.004)**	**−0.017 (0.004)**	**−0.015 (0.004)**
s	0.006 (0.008)	0.006 (0.009)	0.006 (0.009)	0.007 (0.009)
lfsize	0.025 (0.059)	0.077 (0.064)	0.0049 (0.064)	0.016 (0.065)
lfage	**−0.204 (0.082)**	**−0.167 (0.084)**	**−0.153 (0.084)**	**−0.155 (0.084)**
eage45	−0.004 (0.004)	−0.003 (0.004)	−0.003 (0.004)	−0.003 (0.004)
eedugr	0.004 (0.003)	**0.006 (0.003)**	**0.005 (0.003)**	0.004 (0.003)
market	**0.182 (0.102)**	**0.206 (0.103)**	**0.202 (0.103)**	**0.194 (0.102)**
calc	—	—	**0.063 (0.032)**	**0.056 (0.032)**
coll	—	—	**0.075 (0.045)**	0.066 (0.047)
grpr	—	—	—	**0.102 (0.039)**
Construction	—	0.329 (0.361)	0.402 (0.361)	0.445 (0.360)

Transportation	—	−0.187 (0.309)	−0.129 (0.361)	−0.080 (0.308)
Bank and finance	—	−0.229 (0.274)	−0.261 (0.273)	−0.249 (0.272)
Personal services	—	0.455 (0.632)	0.427 (0.631)	0.436 (0.629)
Other industries	—	**−0.300 (0.182)**	−0.278 (0.182)	−0.202 (0.184)
France	—	**−0.709 (0.360)**	**−0.635 (0.328)**	**−0.727 (0.338)**
Germany	—	0.297 (0.272)	0.145 (0.277)	0.077 (0.277)
Sweden	—	−0.500 (0.380)	−0.581 (0.380)	−0.526 (0.379)
Spain	—	−0.260 (0.353)	−0.158 (0.355)	−0.188 (0.357)
Denmark	—	0.014 (0.322)	0.075 (0.324)	0.167 (0.325)
Norway	—	−0.134 (0.279)	−0.020 (0.285)	−0.041 (0.285)
Ireland	—	0.023 (0.302)	0.087 (0.302)	0.158 (0.302)
Finland	—	−0.001 (0.289)	0.036 (0.302)	0.063 (0.302)
Austria	—	**0.802 (0.355)**	**0.885 (0.356)**	**0.943 (0.355)**
Belgium	—	0.315 (0.364)	0.281 (0.363)	0.355 (0.364)
Control for subsidiary	Yes	Yes	Yes	Yes
Controls for reporter	Yes	Yes	Yes	Yes
$\bar{R}^2$	0.24	0.28	0.32	0.35
Number observations	1045	1045	1045	1045

Source: Rizov and Croucher (2009: 253–72).

Note: In the table each column shows coefficients and standard errors in parenthesis. Coefficients in bold denote significance at 10% level or better. Reference country is the UK and reference industry is manufacturing.

Tables 9.4a and 9.4b contain several general findings of interest. The LMP variables have positive and, in general, statistically significant impacts on firm performance. When the LMP variables are interacted with country dummies (Table 9.4b), thus controlling for the specific link between LMPs and countries' institutional settings, we find differential effects of the variables of interest on firm

Table 9.4b Regression Analysis of Firm Performance: Cross Effects

Variable	(5)	(6)
w^d	**−0.017 (0.004)**	**−0.015 (0.004)**
s	0.005 (0.009)	0.004 (0.009)
lfsize	0.057 (0.065)	0.047 (0.066)
lfage	**−0.172 (0.085)**	**−0.168 (0.085)**
eage45	−0.003 (0.004)	−0.002 (0.004)
eedugr	**0.005 (0.003)**	0.004 (0.003)
market	**0.198 (0.104)**	**0.199 (0.104)**
calc	0.032 (0.084)	0.032 (0.084)
coll	0.030 (0.118)	0.040 (0.118)
grpr	—	**0.111 (0.059)**
France	−1.540 (1.036)	−1.415 (1.127)
Germany	0.981 (0.781)	1.063 (0.824)
Sweden	−0.968 (0.631)	−1.046 (0.853)

Spain	−1.280 (1.080)	**−1.841 (1.117)**
Denmark	−0.969 (0.992)	−0.711 (0.914)
Norway	−0.796 (0.844)	−0.773 (0.862)
Ireland	0.576 (0.926)	0.796 (0.940)
Finland	0.199 (0.994)	0.183 (0.901)
Austria	0.610 (0.892)	0.482 (0.588)
Belgium	−0.693 (0.452)	−0.572 (0.413)
France*calc	0.031 (0.134)	0.036 (0.138)
Germany*calc	0.166 (0.122)	0.163 (0.122)
Sweden*calc	0.190 (0.189)	0.200 (0.188)
Spain*calc	0.133 (0.176)	0.167 (0.178)
Denmark*calc	**−0.410 (0.137)**	**−0.314 (0.143)**
Norway*calc	−0.046 (0.117)	−0.052 (0.119)
Ireland*calc	−0.093 (0.129)	−0.099 (0.130)
Finland*calc	0.018 (0.126)	0.010 (0.126)
Austria*calc	0.062 (0.156)	0.074 (0.155)
Belgium*calc	0.096 (0.162)	0.064 (0.170)
France*coll	**0.291 (0.129)**	**0.322 (0.159)**
Germany*coll	**0.201 (0.133)**	**0.203 (0.132)**
Sweden*coll	**0.146 (0.083)**	**0.130 (0.083)**
Spain*coll	**0.380 (0.224)**	**0.373 (0.223)**
Denmark*coll	**0.272 (0.155)**	**0.269 (0.154)**
Norway*coll	0.172 (0.174)	0.154 (0.175)
Ireland*coll	−0.027 (0.180)	−0.034 (0.184)
Finland*coll	−0.051 (0.193)	−0.072 (0.194)
Austria*coll	0.042 (0.158)	−0.037 (0.157)
Belgium*coll	**0.334 (0.201)**	0.328 (0.206)
France*grpr	—	**0.226 (0.135)**
Germany*grpr	—	0.081 (0.136)
Sweden*grpr	—	−0.012 (0.165)
Spain*grpr	—	0.289 (0.225)
Denmark*grpr	—	−0.196 (0.219)
Norway*grpr	—	−0.126 (0.129)
Ireland*grpr	—	−0.035 (0.131)
Finland*grpr	—	0.061 (0.126)
Austria*grpr	—	0.133 (0.148)
Belgium*grpr	—	0.088 (0.132)
Control for subsidiary	Yes	Yes
Controls for reporter	Yes	Yes
$\bar{R}^2$	0.39	0.43
Number observations	1045	1045

Source: Rizov and Croucher (2009: 253–72).

Note: In the table each column shows coefficients and standard errors in parenthesis. Coefficients in bold denote significance at 10% level or better. Industry dummies are included in all regressions but results are not reported. Reference country is the UK and reference industry is manufacturing.

performance. Overall, the effect of collaborative practices is positive and significant in countries that fall in the 'high-trust' category. The group-based practices variable significantly impacts performance of firms in both 'low-trust' and 'intermediate' categories of countries. In most countries it seems that the different types of LMPs coexist; however, there usually is one dominant (or more important) type of practice affecting firm performance.

Thus, the results related to the interaction between LMPs and country-specific (institutional) conditions are of particular interest. Specifically, Table 9.4b shows that calculative practices affect performance positively (but not statistically significantly) in most countries analysed, compared to the reference country (the UK). The only country where calculative practices have a negative and statistically significant impact on performance is Denmark. This may be related to the very specific evolution of Danish industrial relations (Due et al., 1994). Collaborative practices seem to have stronger economic and statistically significant positive impacts on performance in several countries variously categorised in VoC literature as 'co-operative', 'co-ordinated' and so on. These are France, Germany, Sweden, Denmark, Belgium and Spain. With respect to group-based practices, UK firms appear to perform well as only firms in France outperform British firms. Group-based practices also have a positive but not statistically significant impact on performance in several other 'co-operative' or 'co-ordinated' countries.

The results in Table 9.5a and Table 9.5b confirm our main findings as the largest impact derives from collaborative and group-based practices. Absenteeism (Table 9.5a) is lower in firms that employ any of the three types of practices, controlling for industry and country effects. Turnover (Table 9.5b) is also minimised by applying LMPs. These results suggest that the labour extraction function is improved by systematic application of LMPs at firm level. It is evident that collaborative and group-based practices have a stronger impact in both sets of regressions. When the link between LMPs and country-specific institutions is explored, we again find differential effects across countries and types of practice, in line with the different institutional contexts. These findings confirm our proposition that the labour extraction function should be viewed as endogenously determined by the interaction of the institutional environment and firm-specific LMPs

Table 9.5a Analysis of Labour Extraction Function: Absenteeism

Variable	(1)	(2)	(3)	(4)
w^d	0.009 (0.012)	0.008 (0.012)	0.006 (0.012)	0.007 (0.013)
s	−0.035 (0.027)	**−0.056 (0.029)**	**−0.054 (0.029)**	**−0.058 (0.030)**
lfsize	**0.423 (0.194)**	**0.370 (0.204)**	**0.458 (0.211)**	**0.402 (0.214)**
lfage	−0.029 (0.265)	−0.218 (0.268)	−0.195 (0.269)	−0.123 (0.274)
eage45	**0.039 (0.012)**	**0.039 (0.012)**	**0.040 (0.013)**	**0.036 (0.013)**
eedugr	**−0.030 (0.009)**	**−0.025 (0.009)**	**−0.024 (0.009)**	**−0.023 (0.009)**
market	−0.234 (0.340)	−0.133 (0.336)	−0.094 (0.337)	−0.111 (0.342)
calc	—	—	−0.042 (0.104)	−0.027 (0.253)
coll	—	—	**−0.172 (0.103)**	—0.114 (0.360)
grpr	—	—	**−0.200 (0.108)**	−0.068 (0.242)
France	—	**3.159 (1.048)**	**3.354 (1.100)**	**4.583 (2.801)**

Germany	—	**2.262 (0.821)**	**2.022 (0.842)**	3.341 (2.569)
Sweden	—	**6.043 (1.354)**	**6.037 (1.358)**	6.308 (4.023)
Spain	—	**2.374 (1.098)**	**1.983 (1.120)**	3.820 (2.507)
Denmark	—	**−1.842 (1.074)**	**−1.914 (1.093)**	−1.835 (1.330)
Norway	—	**3.046 (0.846)**	**3.028 (0.877)**	2.377 (2.669)
Ireland	—	0.251 (0.969)	0.116 (0.981)	0.695 (1.118)
Finland	—	−1.335 (0.928)	−1.186 (0.950)	−2.396 (2.339)
Austria	—	**2.683 (1.114)**	**2.502 (1.118)**	**4.926 (2.181)**
Belgium	—	0.060 (0.203)	−0.020 (0.205)	1.440 (2.064)
France*calc	—	—	—	−0.478 (0.430)
Germany*calc	—	—	—	−0.030 (0.077)
Sweden*calc	—	—	—	1.111 (0.780)
Spain*calc	—	—	—	−0.695 (0.562)
Denmark*calc	—	—	—	0.224 (0.477)
Norway*calc	—	—	—	0.191 (0.358)
Ireland*calc	—	—	—	0.095 (0.212)
Finland*calc	—	—	—	0.523 (0.407)
Austria*calc	—	—	—	−0.206 (0.511)
Belgium*calc	—	—	—	−0.080 (0.525)
France*coll	—	—	—	−0.014 (0.087)
Germany*coll	—	—	—	**−0.397 (0.218)**
Sweden*coll	—	—	—	**−1.153 (0.703)**
Spain*coll	—	—	—	0.092 (0.590)
Denmark*coll	—	—	—	**−0.270 (0.137)**
Norway*coll	—	—	—	−0.739 (0.532)
Ireland*coll	—	—	—	−0.260 (0.412)
Finland*coll	—	—	—	−0.326 (0.324)
Austria*coll	—	—	—	**−1.326 (0.705)**
Belgium*coll	—	—	—	−0.253 (0.347)
France*grpr	—	—	—	−0.116 (0.099)
Germany*grpr	—	—	—	−0.056 (0.117)
Sweden*grpr	—	—	—	**−2.146 (0.572)**
Spain*grpr	—	—	—	0.351 (0.837)
Denmark*grpr	—	—	—	**−0.141 (0.076)**
Norway*grpr	—	—	—	**−0.372 (0.210)**
Ireland*grpr	—	—	—	−0.002 (0.159)
Finland*grpr	—	—	—	**−0.585 (0.349)**
Austria*grpr	—	—	—	−0.174 (0.186)
Belgium*grpr	—	—	—	−0.034 (0.074)
Control for subsidiary	Yes	Yes	Yes	Yes
$\bar{R}^2$	0.23	0.30	0.34	0.41
Number observations	779	779	779	779

Source: Rizov and Croucher (2009: 253–72).

Note: In the table each column shows coefficients and standard errors in parenthesis. Coefficients in bold denote significance at 10% level or better. Industry dummies are included in all regressions but results are not reported. Reference country is the UK and reference industry is manufacturing.

rather than as simply an exogenous trade-off between wages and monitoring as neoclassical efficiency-wage theory asserts.

Specifically, in Table 9.5a, column (4), the interaction terms of collaborative practices measure are negative for all countries and are statistically significant for Germany, Sweden, Denmark and Austria. This suggests that collaborative practices improve labour extraction in every country. However, the impact is strongest in the four countries mentioned. The relationships depicted by the interaction terms of group-based practices measure are also negative everywhere, implying less absenteeism, except in Spain where the coefficient is positive but statistically insignificant. Interestingly, the impact of group-based practices on absenteeism is most statistically significant in the Scandinavian countries.

Table 9.5b Analysis of Labour Extraction Function: Turnover

Variable	(1)	(2)	(3)	(4)
w^d	**0.032 (0.016)**	0.016 (0.017)	0.016 (0.017)	0.016 (0.017)
s	**0.095 (0.040)**	0.045 (0.044)	0.036 (0.044)	0.050 (0.045)
lfsize	**0.432 (0.255)**	0.264 (0.290)	0.295 (0.300)	0.296 (0.302)
lfage	**−1.505 (0.378)**	**−1.098 (0.379)**	**−0.996 (0.380)**	**−0.919 (0.385)**
eage45	**−0.075 (0.018)**	**−0.080 (0.018)**	**−0.076 (0.018)**	**−0.082 (0.018)**
eedugr	−0.019 (0.012)	**−0.027 (0.012)**	**−0.027 (0.013)**	**−0.028 (0.013)**
market	0.766 (0.482)	0.698 (0.472)	0.718 (0.473)	0.651 (0.479)
calc	—	—	−0.128 (0.094)	−0.138 (0.386)
coll	—	—	**−0.394 (0.151)**	−0.658 (0.536)
grpr	—	—	**−0.315 (0.183)**	**−0.622 (0.364)**
France	—	**−7.178 (1.484)**	**−6.780 (1.542)**	−2.209 (3.394)
Germany	—	**−8.239 (1.227)**	**−8.133 (1.252)**	**−9.006 (3.808)**
Sweden	—	**−8.064 (1.700)**	**−8.342 (1.703)**	−8.996 (7.491)
Spain	—	**−5.269 (1.672)**	**−5.639 (1.697)**	−2.591 (3.609)
Denmark	—	**−3.951 (1.495)**	**−3.656 (1.518)**	**−6.549 (3.952)**
Norway	—	**−6.720 (1.244)**	**−6.139 (1.278)**	**−8.298 (3.927)**
Ireland	—	**−5.879 (1.380)**	**−5.785 (1.390)**	**−8.737 (4.318)**
Finland	—	**−7.712 (1.358)**	**−7.323 (1.377)**	−6.735 (4.719)
Austria	—	**−7.847 (1.628)**	**−7.393 (1.634)**	**−9.596 (5.145)**
Belgium	—	**−7.558 (1.629)**	**−7.899 (1.630)**	**−9.689 (5.131)**
France*calc	—	—	—	−0.570 (0.640)
Germany*calc	—	—	—	0.7757 (0.560)
Sweden*calc	—	—	—	0.537 (0.836)
Spain*calc	—	—	—	−0.839 (0.885)
Denmark*calc	—	—	—	**1.182 (0.661)**
Norway*calc	—	—	—	0.248 (0.539)
Ireland*calc	—	—	—	0.862 (0.604)
Finland*calc	—	—	—	**1.488 (0.590)**
Austria*calc	—	—	—	**0.813 (0.424)**
Belgium*calc	—	—	—	**0.773 (0.355)**
France*coll	—	—	—	**−1.790 (0.938)**
Germany*coll	—	—	—	**−0.824 (0.497)**

Sweden*coll	—	—	—	**−0.732 (0.442)**
Spain*coll	—	—	—	−1.921 (1.233)
Denmark*coll	—	—	—	**−1.277 (0.729)**
Norway*coll	—	—	—	−0.157 (0.591)
Ireland*coll	—	—	—	−0.999 (0.855)
Finland*coll	—	—	—	**−1.618 (0.904)**
Austria*coll	—	—	—	−0.638 (1.205)
Belgium*coll	—	—	—	−0.351 (0.974)
France*grpr	—	—	—	−0.280 (0.733)
Germany*grpr	—	—	—	−0.041 (0.420)
Sweden*grpr	—	—	—	0.258 (0.745)
Spain*grpr	—	—	—	**1.712 (1.008)**
Denmark*grpr	—	—	—	−1.429 (1.090)
Norway*grpr	—	—	—	−0.215 (0.664)
Ireland*grpr	—	—	—	**1.234 (0.622)**
Finland*grpr	—	—	—	−0.138 (0.595)
Austria*grpr	—	—	—	0.366 (0.858)
Belgium*grpr	—	—	—	−0.250 (1.013)
Control for subsidiary	Yes	Yes	Yes	Yes
$\bar{R}^2$	0.25	0.32	0.36	0.42
Number observations	965	965	965	965

Source: Rizov and Croucher (2009: 253–72).

Note: In the table each column shows coefficients and standard errors in parenthesis. Coefficients in bold denote significance at 10% level or better. Industry dummies are included in all regressions but results are not reported. Reference country is the UK and reference industry is manufacturing.

The results in Table 9.5b, column (4) where the dependent variable is employee turnover also support the general proposition that both collaborative and group-based LMPs positively impact the labour extraction process. It is important to note, however, that when the cross-effects of calculative practices measure are considered, for several countries (Denmark, Finland, Austria and Belgium) the effects are positive, suggesting that there is more employee turnover in firms that use calculative LMPs. The results for the cross-effects of collaborative practices measure are the opposite and show that the impact on labour extraction is positive (as demonstrated by low turnover) in all countries, as the effect is statistically significant in France, Germany, Sweden, Denmark and Finland. The results for cross-effects of group-based practices measure are mixed as the labour extraction function appears to be adversely (reflected in high turnover) and statistically significantly affected in Spain and Ireland.

Conclusion and Discussion

The chapter has tested the theoretically derived hypothesis (H1) that collaborative forms of LMPs are more likely to enhance the labour extraction process and firm performance than calculative alternatives. The proposition was strongly supported in those countries where the institutional setting was most conducive to these organisational level practices (H2), which are essentially related to strong communication with employees. The countries concerned are the strongest versions of the 'Co-ordinated Market Economies' (CME) of Western Europe. This supplements and is consistent with other studies' findings in relation to forms of employee voice. Within these national contexts, different forms of voice are encouraged by the institutional framework and therefore co-exist, mutually reinforcing each other, optimising employee wages and working conditions, productivity and organisational performance (Hubler and Jirjahn, 2003). In the UK context, inherent tensions between different forms of practice exist, with particularly strong pressures towards individualisation and direct forms of expression (Bryson, 2004).

Calculative practices had a weaker impact on the labour extraction function and firm performance. In the case of Denmark, where calculative practices existed, these were negatively associated with performance and negatively associated with absenteeism and turnover. Denmark has an institutional framework providing especially strong support for collaborative practices, and has been categorised as an unambiguously 'Co-ordinated Market Economy' (Hall and Soskice, 2001; Hall and Gingerich, 2005). It is distinctive within the CME category for its high degree of employer–union consensual decision taking, requiring relatively little state intervention for its maintenance (Due et al., 1994 and 2000). This suggests that in a country with an especially strong institutional and normative disposition towards collaborative practices, the contrast between calculative practices and these contextual factors is so acute as to generate a counterproductive employee reaction and weaker firm performance.

We also tested the hypothesis (H3) that group-based practices might also generate improved employee–employer relationships and performance. The findings here are more mixed, but confirm and extend to other countries analyses, specifically to the German case (Addison et al., 2004; Singe and Croucher, 2005). Other strongly collaborative national contexts gave similar results. The mixed nature of findings concerning group-based practices is to be expected given the wide range of contents subsumed under this heading. They also interact with other arrangements; their effectiveness is conditional on a wide range of factors, including how they are combined with other complementary approaches such as quality circles (Becker and Gerhart, 1996). Group-based practices were expected to give positive results in countries where they were strongly supported by the context and again, this was the case. In Sweden, such practices had a strong effect on absenteeism in relation to the UK reference group, possibly because of their content but equally possibly because of the way that they act in line with the particularly strong collaborative institutional framework (Whitley, 1999).

The limitations of this study are first, that employee attitudes have not been directly tested and second, that self-reported (subjective) measures of all the indicators are used. In the latter case, it would have been ideal to combine these with more objective measures as recommended by Wall et al. (2004). No international data set at organisational level currently allows this, but future research could usefully address both of these limitations. In the first case, that of employee attitudes, there is a particular need not only to approach the issue by survey data but also to combine survey data with other data (which might helpfully be observationally derived) that could demonstrate the mechanisms at work at organisational level.

Nevertheless, our findings have significant implications for political economy. First, they provide underpinning for the utility of the 'CME' concept itself, which has been criticised for a lack of differentiation (Allen, 2004), but which in respect of the employment practice–performance link appears to have some justification. On the other hand, the finding has a second consequence for the significance of the Varieties of Capitalism conceptualisation. Central to the Varieties of Capitalism formulation in its original form is the argument that particular national institutional configurations cannot be considered 'superior' to others. Rather, it is a question of the 'fit' between labour market practices, the mode of production ('Fordist' or 'flexible specialisation') at organisational level and the requirements of the markets being sold into that determine success in specific markets (Hall and Soskice, 2001). Becker (2007) has criticised the theory, suggesting that practices may be quite different from those envisaged by Hall and Soskice, but may nevertheless be 'equi-functional'. In this view, LMEs can perform as well as CMEs even in 'flexible specialisation' types of production if companies adopt 'equi-functional' practices. In short, companies operating in LMEs can succeed even in markets demanding high quality where they compensate for a lack of contextual support.

Our findings demonstrate that the CME model is superior in supporting productive efficiency at the organisational level. This is consistent with Panic (2007), who demonstrates that there are no macro-economic performance grounds for 'liberalising' European economies since the Scandinavian economies have performed comparatively well, especially in relation to LMEs. Our evidence supplements his by showing that the ways that CMEs encourage company level communications appear central to raising efficiency. All of this supports the EU policy of attempting to extend industrial communications policies across the EU, including to the LMEs (Britain and Ireland) and the new entrant countries via such measures as the Information and Consultation Directive. It also tends to support an argument that the weak transposition of the Directive into English law is inadequate and unlikely to foster the diffusion of collaborative practices (Hall, 2005).

Notes

1 More specifically, Akerlof's (1982) model posits that monitoring is performed by employee groups. Excess remuneration to some members of the employee group and leniency of work rules constitute the major gifts by the employer to employees. Employees' gift to the employer – effort in excess of formal work standards – is linked to the employer's gift to employees. The key assumption in this mechanism is reciprocity as a major feature of gift exchange, as well as of market exchange. In gift exchanges, however, effort norms are established according to the 'fair day's work' concept rather than by market forces. In return employees expect to be treated fairly by the employer. The concept of fair treatment is not based on absolute standards, rather on comparisons of one's own situation with that of other

individuals. Individuals use comparison with others as a guide to how they ought to behave or how they ought to be treated

2 We report here results for samples where we do not exclude but control for the status of a firm being a foreign subsidiary. Using Wald tests of differences between coefficients estimated from the full and the restricted sample shows that the coefficients do not significantly differ. We report here results from the full sample with a control for foreign subsidiary status which does not appears to be statistically significant in any specification.

3 We recognise a potential bias in the construction of the dependent variable. The dependent variable is a composite index of five measures, including service quality and innovation. Arguably, it might favour a collaborative view, since service quality and innovation are theoretically both, when effective, dependent more strongly upon collaborative processes. Further, in order to investigate the issue empirically, we run regressions with only narrowly defined, and neutral to HRM, measures of performance, specifically level of productivity and profitability. The results of these regressions are qualitatively very similar to the results reported in the paper, suggesting that the formulation of the dependent variable as a composite index does not bias our main findings. The auxiliary regression results are available from the authors upon request.

4 In all regressions we have included as controls for measurement error, due to self-reporting, variables describing important characteristics of individuals that filled out the questionnaires. These individual-level control variables are gender, education, years of service in the organization and we assume that they are not correlated with the firm-level variables.

5 All regressions contain a dummy variable controlling for the foreign-subsidiary status of firms, and individual-reporter controls which were all found not to be statistically significant in any regression and therefore their coefficients were not reported. Furthermore, the stepwise introduction of explanatory variables and the stability of coefficients in all regressions suggest minimal problems with endogeneity.

References

Ackroyd, S. and Thompson, P. (1999) *Organizational Misbehaviour*. London: Sage.

Addison, J., Schnabel, C. and Wagner, J. (2004) 'The course of research into the economic consequences of German works councils', *British Journal of Industrial Relations* 42(2): 255–81.

Akerlof, G. (1982) 'Labor contracts as partial gift exchange', *Quarterly Journal of Economics* 97(4): 543–69.

Allen, M. (2004) 'Varieties of capitalism: not enough variety', *Socio-Economic Review* 2(1): 87–108.

Amable, B. (2003) *The Diversity of Modern Capitalism*. Oxford: Oxford University Press.

Appelbaum, E., Bailey, T., Berg, P. and Kallenberg, A.L. (2000) *Manufacturing Advantage: Why High Performance Work Systems Pay Off*. Ithaca, NY: Cornell University Press.

Baldamus, W.G. (1961) *Efficiency and Effort: An Analysis of Industrial Administration*. London: Tavistock.

Becker, U. (2007) 'Open systemness and contested reference frames and change. A reformulation of the varieties of capitalism theory', *Socio-Economic Review* 5(2): 261–86.

Becker, G. and Gerhart, B. (1996) 'The impact of HRM on organizational performance', *Academy of Management Journal* 39: 779–801.

Bowles, S. (1985) 'The production process in a competitive economy: Walrasian, Neo-Hobbesian and Marxian models', *American Economic Review* 75(1): 16–36.

Brewster, C., Wood, G., Croucher, R. and Brookes, M. (2007) 'Are works councils a threat to trade unions? A comparative analysis', *Economic and Industrial Democracy* 28(1): 49–77.

Bryson, A. (2004) 'Managerial responsiveness to union and nonunion worker voice in Britain', *Industrial Relations* 43(1): 213–41.

Buchele, R. and Christiansen, J. (1999) 'Labor relations and productivity growth in advanced capitalist economies', *Review of Radical Political Economies* 31(1): 87–110.

Cappelli, P. and Neumark, D. (2001) 'Do high performance work systems improve establishment level outcomes?', *Industrial and Labor Relations Review* 54(4): 737–75.

Creed, W.E.D. and Miles, R.E. (1996) 'Trust in organizations: A conceptual framework linking organizational forms, managerial philosophies, and the opportunity costs of controls', pp.16–38 in R.M. Kramer and T.R. Tyler (eds) *Trust in Organizations: Frontiers of Theory and Research*. Thousand Oaks, CA: Sage.

Cutcher-Gershenfeld, J. (1991) 'The impact on economic performance of a transformation in workplace relations', *Industrial and Labor Relations Review* 44(2): 241–60.

Danford, A., Richardson, M., Stewart, P., Tailby, S. and Upchurch, M. (2005) *Partnership and the High Performance Workplace: Work and Employment Relations in the Aerospace Industry*. Basingstoke: Palgrave Macmillan.

Deakin, S., Hobbs, R., Konzelmann, S. and Wilkinson, F. (2006) 'Anglo American corporate governance and the employment relationship: A case to answer?' *Socio-Economic Review* 4: 155–74.

Drago, R. and Perlman, R. (1989) 'Supervision and high wages as competing incentives: A basis for labour segmentation theory', in R. Drago and R. Perlman (eds) *Microeconomic Issues in Labour Economics: New Approaches*. New York: Harvester Press.

Due, J., Madsen, J.S. and Jensen, C.S. (2000) 'The "September Compromise": A strategic choice by Danish employers in 1899', *Historical Studies in Industrial Relations* 10: 43–70.

Due, J., Madsen, J.S., Jensen, C.S. and Petersen, L.K. (1994) *The Survival of the Danish Model*. Copenhagen: DJØF.

Fredman, S. (2006) 'Transformation or dilution: Fundamental rights in the European social space', *European Law Journal* 12: 41–60.

Godard, J. (2004) 'A critical assessment of the high-performance paradigm', *British Journal of Industrial Relations* 42(2): 349–78.

Gooderham, P. and Nordhaug, O. (2003) *International Management: Cross-Boundary Challenges*. Oxford: Blackwell.

Gooderham, P., Nordhaug, O. and Ringdal, K. (1998) 'When in Rome, do they do as Romans? HRM practices of US subsidiaries in Europe', *Management International Review* 38: 47–63.

Gooderham, P., Nordhaug, O. and Ringdal, K. (1999) 'Institutional and rational determinants of organizational practices: Human resource management in European firms', *Administrative Science Quarterly* 44: 507–31.

Gordon, D. (1994) 'Bosses of different stripes: A cross-national perspective on monitoring and supervision', *American Economic Review* 84(2): 375–79.

Guest, D., Mitchie, J., Sheehan, M. and Conway, N. (2003) 'A UK study of the relationship between human resource management and corporate performance', *British Journal of Industrial Relations* 41(2): 291–314.

Guthrie, J.P., Datta, D.K. and Wright, P.M. (2004) 'Peeling back the onion. Competitive advantage through people and test of a causal model', Cornell Centre for Advanced HR Studies, Working Paper 04–09, Cornell University, New York

Hall, M. (2005) 'Assessing the information and consultation of employees regulations', *Industrial Law Journal* 34(2): 103–26.

Hall, P.A. and Gingerich, D.W. (2005) 'Varieties of capitalism and institutional complementarities in the macroeconomy', MPifG Discussion Paper 04/5. Cologne: Max Planck Institute.

Hall, P.A. and Soskice, D. (eds) (2001) *Varieties of Capitalism: The Institutional Foundations of Competitive Advantage*. Oxford: Oxford University Press.

Harcourt, M. and Wood, G. (2007) 'The importance of employment protection for skill development in coordinated market economies', *European Journal of Industrial Relations* 13(2): 141–60.

Harrison, R. (1993) 'Concepts and issues in human resource management', pp. 35–66 in R. Harrison (ed.) *Human Resource Management: Issues and Strategies*. Wokingham: Addison-Wesley.

Hoff, A. (2002) *Vertrauensarbeitszeit: Einfach Flexible Arbeiten*. Wiesbaden: Gabler Verlag.

Hubler, O. and Jirjahn, U. (2003) 'Works councils and collective bargaining in Germany: The impact on productivity and wages', *Scottish Journal of Political Economy* 50(4): 471–92.

Huselid, M.A. (1995) 'The impact of human resource management practices on turnover, productivity, and corporate financial performance', *The Academy of Management Journal* 38(3): 635–72.

Lane, C. (2000) 'Globalization and the German model of capitalism – erosion or survival?', *British Journal of Sociology* 51(3): 207–34.

Legge, K. (1995) *Human Resource Management: Rhetorics and Reality*. Basingstoke: MacMillan Business.

Legge, K. (2005) *Human Resource Management: Rhetoric and Realities*. London: Macmillan.

Levine, D.I. and D'Andrea Tyson, L. (1990) 'Participation, productivity and the firm's environment', in A.S. Blinder (ed.) *Paying for Productivity: A Look at the Evidence*. Washington, DC: Brookings Institution.

MacInnes, J., Cressey, P. and Eldridge, J. (1985) *Just Managing: Authority and Democracy in Industry*. Milton Keynes, Open University Press.

Martens, H. (1999) 'Auslaufmodell oder Reformkonzept für die Teilhabegesellschaft?', *Soziale Welt* 1/1999: 67–86.

Mokken, R. and Lewis, C. (1982) 'A nonparametric approach to the analysis of dichotomous item responses', *Applied Psychological Measurement* 6: 417–30.

Naastepad C.W.M. and Storm, S. (2006) 'The innovating firm in a societal context: Labor-management relations and labor productivity', pp. 170–91 in R.M. Verburg, J.R. Ortt and W.M. Dicke (eds) *Managing Technology and Innovation*. London: Routledge.

Osterman, P. (1994) 'Supervision, discretion, and work organization', *American Economic Review* 84(2): 380–84.

Panic, M. (2007) 'Does Europe need neoliberal reforms?', *Cambridge Journal of Economics* 31(1): 145–69.

Rizov, R. and Croucher, R. (2009) 'Human resource management and performance in European firms', *Cambridge Journal of Economics* 33(2): 253–72.

Sijtsma, K., Debets, P. and Molenaar, I.W. (1990) 'Mokken scale analysis for polytomous items: Theory, a computer program and an empirical application', *Quality and Quantity* 24: 173–88.

Singe, I. and Croucher, R. (2005) 'US multi-nationals and the German industrial relations system', *Management Review* 16(1): 123–37.

Tregaskis, O., Mahoney, C. and Atterbury, S. (2004) 'International survey methodology: Experiences from the Cranet network', pp. 437–50 in C. Brewster, W. Mayrhofer and M. Morley (eds) *Human Resource Management in Europe*. Amsterdam: Elsevier.

Tzafrir, S. (2005) 'The relationship between trust, HRM practices and firm performance', *International Journal of Human Resource Management* 16(9): 1600–22.

Wall, T.D., Mitchie, J., Patterson, M., Wood, S.J., Sheenhan, N., Clegg, C.W. and West, M. (2004) 'On the validity of subjective measures of company performance', *Personnel Psychology* 57: 95–118.

Whitley, R. (1999) *Divergent Capitalisms*. Oxford: Oxford University Press

Wright, P.M. and Haggerty, J.J. (2005) 'Missing variables in theories of strategic HRM', *Management Revue* 16(2): 164–73.

10 What Role do MNCs Play in Different Market Economies?

CHRIS BREWSTER, GEOFFREY WOOD AND
MICHAEL BROOKES

A key issue in understanding human resource management across different national and economic market systems concerns the role of multinational corporations (MNCs). They are often seen, and usually see themselves, as being 'carriers' of global best practice. Other strands of literature see the MNC as reflecting and enforcing home based policies and practices in their subsidiary locations. Much of the institutional literature, the business systems or comparative capitalisms literature is concerned with differences between systems and pays little attention to the role of the MNC, implying perhaps that they just have to adapt to the local environment. This chapter explores the role of MNCs within different forms of market economy.

In recent years the impact of multinational corporations (MNCs) on employment practices within different countries and different market economies has been gathering pace rapidly. Less attention has been paid to whether and how different national institutions may restrict the autonomy of MNCs. There are existing studies of the impact of MNCs on HRM in different national settings that examine the difference between foreign-owned firms and domestic organisations (see, for example: Almond et al., 2003; Ferner, 1997; Gooderham et al., 1999; c.f. Ferner et al. 2012). Firms can therefore be characterised by whether they operate in a single country (domestic firms) or internationally (MNCs) and whether or not they are foreign owned or domestic owned. So there are three types of organisation that may be relevant here: foreign-owned MNCs – firms which are subsidiaries of an international group operating in a country other than the home country of the group; domestic-owned MNCs – firms which are part of an international group but operating in the home country of that group; and domestic organisations – single country firms.

We ask to what extent do MNCs import their own approaches to host countries, to what extent do they adopt those of the host country or, perhaps, where do they fall between these two extremes? How different are they from their local indigenous counterparts and how are we to explain these positions? We explore the three schools of thought indicated above, and add a fourth, to reflect the likelihood that this is a complex area with different pressures operating in a complex and inter-related way. Then we focus on the human resource management implications of these debates. We outline some of the ways that the Cranet data have been used to examine the empirical evidence; show what findings that research has uncovered and then draw conclusions about the extent of similarity, isomorphism and duality.

The Debates

These issues have been widely debated. In summary, we can identify four different responses. First, there are theories that suggest that MNCs will tend to follow common practices whichever country they are in, either because of *global homogeneity* – these are global organisations applying best practice around the world. Second, they may do the same thing because of *ethnocentricity* – despite all the attempts to move such organisations towards being 'trans-national' or 'global', firms operating across national boundaries remain stubbornly rooted in the culture and institutions of their home base. Third, there are theories of *local isomorphism* which either explicitly or by implication argue that firms adjust their policies to reflect the culture or the institutions of the host countries in which they have subsidiaries. This may be done in policy terms at a global level or it may be done through practice at a local level, with the local managers simply 'adapting' or 'bending' their own management approaches to fit the local exigencies. Fourth, *duality theories* suggest that firms face conflicting pressures both towards and away from the local practices, with complex inter-actions and complex results such that the subsidiaries of MNCs operate neither like their parent nor like the other businesses in the host country. HRM, as the practice most commonly 'localised' (Rosenzweig and Nohria, 1994), is a useful test-bed for such theories. We explore each one in turn.

Global Homogeneity

Globalisation is a widely used term (and one that often used to mean rather different things). However, it generally implies a relatively recent process of unification that has taken place in markets and consumer tastes, facilitated by an increasingly mobile investor capital and rapid technological change. Within and between firms, it is assumed that they operate as if they are nationless and borderless (Ohmae, 1990, 1996). The growth in the number, reach and power of MNCs is seen as key to the growth of this process (Moody, 1997, 2002; Meyer, 2000). Much attention is currently being focused on how multinationals are changing local HRM practices by importing successful practices across national borders.

Globalisation theories hold that, whilst it is true that business is at least originally based on geographically limited economic systems, economies are increasingly becoming globally integrated, resulting in a proliferation of global management structures and the convergence of management techniques around shared notions of 'best practice' (Sera, 1992). The theory states that in order to enhance their competitiveness as their power to set prices is eroded in the face of competition, profitability increasingly depends on cutting the costs of inputs and enhancing productivity. Firms that operate across national boundaries are most exposed to the forces of globalisation, and hence, are most likely to fall in line with dominant worldwide practices aimed at enhancing competitiveness in world markets.

The role of the multinational firm, and its ability to promote integrated international standards has in the literature been contrasted with the pressures that such firms face to be locally responsive (Ashkenas et al., 1995; Hamel and Prahalad, 1985; Kim and Gray, 2005; Yip, 1995). Applying similar organisational practices worldwide is argued as favouring the effective utilisation of the total capacities of the entire firm and being more efficient (Kostova and Roth, 2002; Zeira and Harari, 1977) on the assumption that firms pursue economic advantage through choices 'guided by unambiguous preferences and bounded rationality' (Gooderham et al., 1999: 507). Practices that promote the maximisation of economic goals will be identified and the 'best practices' spread across the company's operations worldwide. Eventually, although the diffusion process may be slow and uneven, international practices will develop that are, to a large degree, uniform. Global markets create new homogeneous environments where the conditions in which companies operate become similar in terms of products, competition and the rate of technological change (Duysters and Hagedoorn, 2001). Global competition places greater demands on the co-ordination of resources, equipment, finance and people. It becomes necessary, to take one example, to co-ordinate pricing, service and product support across the world once international customers have the ability to compare these things in different regions and source from the cheapest. In response, the global enterprise adopts a global business strategy transcending both internal (people, processes and structure) and external (time and country) factors (Parker, 1998). In terms of human resource management, firms will either try to enforce their own view of the most efficient ways of handling HRM in other countries; or these other countries will through market pressures be forced towards policies that mirror the most efficient economy – widely assumed to be the USA (Jain et al., 1998; McDonough, 2003; Smith and Meiksins, 1995). It is argued that there is evidence of the increasingly significant effects of MNCs on HRM policies and practices (see, for example, Almond et al., 2003; Ferner and Quintanilla, 1998; Gooderham et al., 1999; Poutsma et al., 2005).

Ethnocentricity

MNCs are not of course all the same. A typical categorisation is by country of origin of ownership. Country of origin is by no means a simple concept given the way that such a notion has become increasingly indistinct with share ownership spread amongst funds from different countries and with the growth of international joint ventures. However, many studies in international business (Buckley and Casson, 2010; Buckley et al., 2007; Dunning, 2001) and bodies such as the United Nations Conference on Trade and Development (various dates) have concluded that in practice the transcendent, nation-less, global firm is very rare indeed: the country of origin of firms is usually in practice fairly obvious. Multinational firms are mostly extremely local: 85 per cent of multinationals produce more than two-thirds of their output in their home market, with two-thirds of their employees being nationals of their home country (*Economist*, 2000). Indeed, most MNCs cannot easily be defined as stateless (Hu, 1992); the United Nations Conference on Trade and Development (UNCTAD) index of transnationality lists only six organisations scoring above 90 out of 100.[1] Hence, one stream of research argues that MNCs tend towards ethnocentricity, that is, they mirror the dominant practices of the country of origin (Zeira and Harari, 1977) and apply them wherever they operate (see, for example, Bae et al., 1998; Ferner, 1997; Ngo et al., 1998). MNCs therefore might adopt different approaches towards human resource management in such circumstances. In the classic texts, Perlmutter (1969) and Heenan and Perlmutter (1979) argued that MNCs tend to adopt one of four main approaches towards human resource management: ethnocentric; polycentric; regional; and geocentric. Later writers such as Mayrhofer and Brewster (1996) argued that, in practice, the vast majority of firms are ethnocentric. Similarly, Lao and Ngo (2001) suggest that the country of origin of MNCs is likely to have a significant impact on their practices in other countries.

Local isomorphism

However, these theories of globalisation for reasons of either market forces or ethnocentricity have not gone unchallenged. Both the 'cultural' authors and the 'institutional' authors argue that nation states remain crucial to international business (Brewster, 2004; Sorge 2004).

The cultural tradition tends to see culture as an integrative, normative device (Bacharach, 1989: 499). Most of these culturalist accounts have conflated cultural distinctions with country distinctions (see e.g. Hofstede, 1980, 2001; House et al., 2004). Cultural theories vary but may be seen as reflected in the often different and often squabbling writings of specialists who have tried to identify integrated social system differences (Giddens, 1990; Parsons, 1951) and those such as Hofstede (1980, 2001), House et al., (2004) who have researched different dimensions within national cultures. However, what all these approaches have in common is that they treat culture as a given: it will be very difficult for a society to depart in any radical way from established rules and norms (Fukuyama, 1995; Lane, 1998). Culture provides a persistent boundary, limit to or 'segment' within which individuals and groups understand their situation (Weber, 2000: 207) and individual and group cultural orientations reflect specific cultural characteristics, whilst firms will vary within specific cultures according to institutional realities (Giacobbe-Miller et al., 2003).

The institutionalist theories, of more immediate interest in this book, argue that organisations sharing the same environment will, over time, adopt similar characteristics. They become 'isomorphic' with each other (DiMaggio and Powell, 1983; Kostova and Roth, 2002), because of coercive effects (the firm is forced to adopt specific practices); mimetic effects (firms copy practices they believe to be associated with success) or normative effects (firms behave in ways considered appropriate to the environment) (DiMaggio and Powell, 1983). Firms conform – to formal rules and unwritten norms – for reasons of efficiency and legitimacy

(Haveman, 1993; Kostova and Roth, 2002; Marsden, 1999). In most cases social transactions are embedded in specific contexts (Boyer and Hollingsworth, 1997). Of course, these complex institutional pressures are nested at different levels (Hollingsworth and Boyer, 1997), but a primary concern of contemporary institutional accounts focuses on the country level (Guler et al., 2002). This reflects the formal regulatory structures, the manner in which the socialisation process is framed by nation-specific formal and informal patterns of behaviour – and, perhaps, the greater ease of researching within one national context. At the country level, following local norms gives advantages in terms of achieving local legitimacy, leading to lower costs to the organisation through following such norms. The national embeddedness of employment and labour practices is part of a long tradition within the industrial relations literature (Goddard, 2002; Jacoby, 2005), but this has been less explored in the HRM literature. It is clear that there is considerable variation between countries in the way that markets and other institutional arrangements operate (Hollingsworth and Boyer, 1997; Whitley, 1999, 2000).

However, whilst patterns of characteristics tend to occur within countries, all countries are not equally distinct. The varieties of capitalism literature (Hall and Soskice, 2001) suggests that there is a contrast between co-ordinated market economies (CMEs), which have a higher level of regulation and institutionalisation of HRM activities, and liberal market economies (LMEs) which show lower levels of regulation. This will impact MNCs. In CMEs, multinational firms may be encouraged to adopt particular sets of practices in line with national government policies and industrial strategies whilst in LMEs they may be granted a relatively free rein in an attempt to attract investment. The responses of key interests in society are likely to mould the practices adopted by MNCs' subsidiaries (Guillen, 2000).

Both cultural and institutional theories would suggest the need for MNCs to obtain legitimacy or adapt their activities in specific contexts. This is what causes isomorphism within a country (Kostova and Roth, 2002). This applies to human resource management as well and is reflected in the HRM literature (Croucher et al., 2010; Croucher et al., 2012; De Cieri and Dowling, 1999; Ferner and Quintanilla, 1998; Goergen et al. 2012).

Duality theories

Duality theories take different forms but all suggest that MNCs face conflicting pressures towards global integration and local adaptation (Evans et al., 2002; Gooderham et al., 1998; Kostova and Roth, 2002; Rosenzweig and Singh, 1991). For MNCs this is reflected in the classic integration/differentiation debate (Birkinshaw et al., 1995; Lawrence and Lorsch, 1969; Roth and Morrison, 1990). Firms look for integration because it allows them to spread best practice around their subsidiaries so that their policies can be cost-effective and fairly, equally, adopted across the organisation worldwide (Pfeffer, 1994). Applying HRM systems uniformly within a company across the globe creates cross-border equity and comparability. Alignment of systems internationally facilitates an internal, international labour market (Almond et al., 2003). The differentiation approach focuses on the need to fit HRM practices to local conditions, rejecting the notion of one best way of doing things in all contexts (Brewster and Mayrhofer, 2012; Delery and Doty, 1996). MNCs are under continual pressure to achieve both integration and differentiation at the same time – duality theory (Evans et al., 2002; Kostova and Roth, 2002). This has been widely discussed in the strategy literature (Ashkenas et al., 1995; Hamel and Prahalad, 1985; Kim and Gray, 2005; Yip, 1995) and, but with different terminology – best practice vs best external fit – in the HRM literature (Farndale and Paauwe, 2007).

Where any particular practice will align itself at any particular time and in any particular location is likely to be a matter of, on the location side, the extent of the constraints on firms and, on the company side, a matter of company policy and, within the notion of bounded rationality, the corporate strategic choice of the MNC (Gooderham and Nordhaug, 2003; Taylor et al., 1996).

Some also note that the speed at which different sets of practices are diffused is likely to vary between practices and from context to context (Guler et al., 2002; and, with specific reference to HRM, Hannon et al., 1995; McGaughey and De Cieri, 1999; Schuler et al., 1993). Institutions are nested at a range of levels – supra-national, national, and sub-national – leading to simultaneous pressures towards convergence and difference (Boyer and Hollingsworth, 1997). Firms may try to homogenise activities from country to country in accordance with a global strategy, but they will also be compelled to take account of local difference; the outcome will therefore be a tension between the two tendencies. Comaroff and Comaroff (2001) note that globalisation processes do not have simple homogenising effects; rather they are reshaped, resisted and redeployed by the socially embedded processes of people in the host country, so that each host country operation retains a certain distinctiveness (see also D'Aunno et al., 2000; Ferner, 1997; Ferner and Quintanilla, 1998). The result is that within each MNC there is a differentiation between countries (Bartlett and Ghoshal, 1989). Some organisations may be more sensitive to pressures of local adaptation, while others may be more prone to internal consistency, depending on ownership structures, size, importance and the degree of integration of processes. And hence, even within the same subsidiary, some management practices might closely follow the parent company ones, while others may more resemble those of the host country. In some situations compliance with the 'ways of the country' may make for greater operational efficiency (Lee and Yarwood, 1983: 657) that outweighs the value of global integration. In some cases, adherence to legal or fiscal rules for example, the subsidiary may have no choice. The result is that in most MNCs the duality of global integration and local differentiation will be a continuous tension (Evans et al., 2002).

These general tensions are inevitably included in specific areas of management such as HRM (see Edwards and Ferner, 2002, for a review). The same pressures towards a greater homogeneity and the application of corporate-wide policies occur simultaneously with pressures to localise HRM practice to deal with local educational standards, labour markets, legislation, trade unions, and so on. Again these pressures and responses are uneven and episodic, making for variation in practice within and between MNCs and within and between locations.

Defining Features of Employment Practices

Empirical exploration of these issues is limited and patchy, partly because there is little agreement as to what should be included in the HRM systems to be explored. Two core features were identified by Whitley (1999): employer–employee interdependence and delegation to employees. The degree of employer–employee interdependence has two sub-dimensions: the willingness of the organisation to invest in its people through training and development; and the relative security of tenure enjoyed by employees (Whitley, 1999: 38; see also Marsden, 1999; Storey, 2007), measured by the dominant contractual forms used by the firm (e.g. permanent, temporary or fixed term), the regularity with which the firm makes use of redundancies, the methods employed to reduce staff numbers, and the use of subcontractors. The second feature identified by Whitley, the extent of delegation to employees, is shown in the degree to which managers are willing to allow employees discretion in the performance of tasks, their willingness to bargain with employee representatives, and mechanisms for involvement and feedback.

Are these constant within a society (i.e. do MNCs adopt the same practices as the indigenous companies) or do MNCs operate similarly across a range of countries *and* differently from the dominant ways of managing people in those countries? If MNCs practice HRM in similar ways worldwide, this would reflect the effects of globalisation. If they do not, this would reflect the importance of the local business system. Rosenzweig and Nohria (1994) argued that HRM is the management practice most likely to be found at the localisation end of the scale and this chapter presents evidence of a test of the globalisation, ethnocentricity, local isomorphism and duality accounts. We offer the following hypotheses:

H1: HRM practices will mirror those of the country in which they are domiciled, reflecting the effects of local institutional configurations and/or culture.
H2: HRM practices in MNC subsidiaries will mirror the HRM practices in their country of origin.
H3: HRM practices in MNCs exemplify a common model, reflecting the effects of globalisation, to which transnational organisations are the most exposed.
H4: HRM practices in MNC subsidiaries vary from context to context, reflecting the relative strengths of home country versus host country institutions.

Methodology

In this chapter we use the results from the 1999–2000 survey in 19 European countries,[2] and Japan, a country that is often, together with Scandinavia and Germany, seen as a typical example of a CME (Hall and Soskice, 2001). The data for all these countries includes at least 100 observations; in total there are 6,939 private sector companies in our sample.

To determine the balance between the impact of host country, country of origin and MNC status on the HRM practices of MNCs, we tested the proposition that different types of firm are similar in terms of their interdependence and delegation, thus allowing us to examine our hypotheses.

For each of the relevant sub-dimensions an empirical model is estimated with variables from the Cranet survey representing each of the sub-dimensions being used as the dependent variable of a model and estimated as a function of size (cf. Marginson et al., 1993), industrial sector and country in which the establishment is located. If the dependent variable is a continuous variable the model was estimated using ordinary least squares[3] and where the dependent variable is binary a logit model was used.[4]

These models were then re-estimated for the domestic firms and foreign-owned MNC samples and a straightforward structural test applied. If there is no real difference in the behaviour of the two groups of firms there should be no statistically significant difference between the estimated results from the individual sub-samples and overall sample when the two sub-samples are pooled together.[5]

The explanatory variables used were drawn from the literature and included size (measured by the number of employees in the establishment), sectoral differences (controlled for by using the 16 NACE category sectoral dummies) and country differences (via a dummy variable for each of the 20 countries). As the empirical analysis requires estimating 45 different models, i.e. each of the 15 sub-dimensions for the pooled, domestic and foreign samples, a large number of results is generated. Consequently, not all can be reproduced here.

Findings

The analysis depends on whether the HRM practices of MNCs' subsidiaries are similar to or different from those of their host nation. Indicators of interdependence and delegation are used to categorise the behaviour of the organisations sampled. Table 10.1 records the means, standard deviations and numbers of observations of these variables for the 20 countries included in the analysis, but separated into domestic firms (including local MNCs) and foreign-owned MNCs.

A first view suggests, indeed, that foreign-owned MNCs behave differently to locally owned firms: for example, they appear to spend more on training and to train more people, they are more likely to evaluate training needs, etc. However, from the raw data it is difficult to establish whether these differences are significant and whether they reflect the differing circumstances facing the firms that are included in the sample. Consequently, multivariate analysis is applied and the various models outlined in the method section are estimated and then tested for structural differences.

Table 10.2 shows the method of estimation, the calculated test statistic and whether the null hypothesis of domestic and foreign firms behaving the same way can be accepted, for each of the 15 models. The null hypothesis is rejected in all cases except one (reductions in number of employees), indicating that foreign-owned MNCs generally behave in a different fashion to domestic firms. So, the

Table 10.1 Interdependence and Delegation: Descriptive Statistics

Variable	Domestic Firms			Foreign-owned MNCs		
	Mean	St. Dev.	No. Obs.	Mean	St. Dev.	No. Obs.
Interdependence						
Proportion of wage bill spent on training	2.8	2.89	3772	3.29	2.83	747
Proportion of employees having training in the last year	42.42	31.06	4583	53.98	31.47	922
Formal analysis of training needs (yes/no)	0.643	0.48	5837	0.8	0.4	1102
Number of employees has decreased in last 3 years (yes/no)	0.08	0.26	5837	0.05	0.21	1102
% decrease in employees	16.54	18.58	4231	21.85	22.38	808
Harsher methods employed to decrease workforce (yes/no)	0.55	0.49	5837	0.62	0.48	1102
Greater use of more numerically flexible employment {i.e. an ability to rapidly upsize or downsize} (yes/no)	0.57	0.49	5837	0.69	0.46	1102
Proportion of workforce temporary	2.58	1.34	5349	2.84	1.32	1027
Proportion of workforce with fixed term contracts	2.8	1.41	5421	2.81	1.35	1025
Delegation						
Pay bargaining above the establishment level (yes/no)	0.76	0.42	5837	0.7	0.46	1102
Financial participation (yes/no)	0.58	0.49	5837	0.71	0.45	1102
Union penetration	4.36	2.02	5712	3.9	2.12	1084
Non-bargaining representation (yes/no)	0.68	0.46	5837	0.61	0.49	1102
Change in upward communication in last 3 years (yes/no)	0.66	0.47	5837	0.76	0.43	1102
Change in downward formal communication in last 3 years (yes/no)	0.81	0.39	5837	0.89	0.32	1102

Source: Brewster, Wood and Brookes (2008).

Table 10.2 Structural Tests: Domestic Firms (MNCs and non-MNCs) vs. Foreign MNCs

Dependent Variable	Model Type	Test Stat	Accept/Reject
Interdependence			
Proportion of wage bill spent on training	OLS	1.46	Reject at 5%
Proportion of employees having training in the last year	OLS	4.86	Reject at 1%
Formal analysis of training needs	Logit	104.9	Reject at 1%
Number of employees has decreased in last 3 years	Logit	25.3	Accept
% decrease in employees	OLS	2.7	Reject at 1%
Methods employed to decrease workforce	Logit	65.5	Reject at 1%
Greater use of more flexible employment	Logit	83.1	Reject at 1%
Proportion of workforce temporary	OLS	2.52	Reject at 1%
Proportion of workforce with fixed term contracts	OLS	1.81	Reject at 1%
Delegation			
Pay bargaining above the establishment level	Logit	62.5	Reject at 1%
Financial participation	Logit	96.6	Reject at 1%
Union penetration	OLS	3.69	Reject at 1%
Non-bargaining representation	Logit	58.9	Reject at 1%
Change in upward communication in last 3 years	Logit	51.9	Reject at 1%
Change in downward formal communication in last 3 years	Logit	77.3	Reject at 1%

Source: Brewster, Wood and Brookes (2008).

effects of country of domicile isomorphism seem limited: it seems that MNCs act differently in the host country from their indigenous counterparts. Hyphothesis 1 is therefore rejected. Host country institutions or culture do not seem to be generally effective in forcing MNCs to adapt to more 'local' ways of operating. Either a common model of practice amongst MNCs worldwide is being developed, or the institutional pressures in their country of origin are greater pressures than the host country institutional restraints.

However, the predictive power of the models is rather low, generally in the region of 10–20%. And differences in size and sector account for about 2% of the variation in the dependent variables. So these only have a small effect upon interdependence and delegation, whilst host country has a larger effect though still relatively small.[6] The majority of the variation in delegation and interdependence results from factors not covered in the data set. Since these unobserved differences appear to affect domestic firms and foreign-owned MNCs in a different way, and since the models are already controlled for at the country level, the influences must either be forces operating at a range of levels or primarily at an international level. The former would suggest the presence of duality and the latter would indicate similarities cutting across national boundaries: in other words, Hypotheses 2, 3 or 4 may be correct.

Since the domestic samples actually include home-based MNCs these alternative hypotheses could be, and were, also tested. If the unobserved factors affect local MNCs and non-local MNCs similarly, it can be assumed that the dominant pressures operate at the international level. So the process was repeated but with domestic-owned MNCs and foreign-owned MNCs as the two sub-samples. Table 10.3 records the statistics from the raw data and Table 10.4 reports the structural test results.

Table 10.3 Interdependence and Delegation: Domestic MNCs and Foreign MNCs

Variable	Domestic-owned MNCs			Foreign-owned MNCs		
	Mean	St. Dev.	No. Obs.	Mean	St. Dev.	No. Obs.
Interdependence						
Proportion of wage bill spent on training	3.21	2.83	660	3.29	2.83	747
Proportion of employees having training in the last year	44.94	29.28	794	53.98	31.5	922
Formal analysis of training needs (yes/no)	0.75	0.43	1004	0.8	0.4	1102
Number of employees has decreased in last 3 years (yes/no)	0.06	0.23	1004	0.05	0.21	1102
% decrease in employees	18.22	19.79	772	21.85	22.4	808
Harsher methods employed to decrease workforce (yes/no)	0.59	0.49	1004	0.62	0.48	1102
Greater use of more flexible employment (yes/no)	0.66	0.47	1004	0.69	0.46	1102
Proportion of workforce temporary	2.75	1.27	934	2.84	1.32	1027
Proportion of workforce with fixed term contracts	2.75	1.22	946	2.81	1.35	1025
Delegation						
Pay bargaining above the establishment level (yes/no)	0.74	0.44	1004	0.7	0.46	1102

Financial participation (yes/no)	0.78	0.42	1004	0.71	0.45	1102
Union penetration	4.14	2.06	981	3.9	2.12	1084
Non-bargaining representation (yes/no)	0.75	0.43	1004	0.61	0.49	1102
Change in upward communication in last 3 years (yes/no)	0.71	0.46	1004	0.76	0.43	1102
Change in downward formal communication in last 3 years (yes/no)	0.88	0.32	1004	0.89	0.32	1102

Source: Brewster, Wood, and Brookes (2008)

Table 10.4 Structural Tests: Domestic MNCs vs. Foreign MNCs

Dependent Variable	**Model Type**	**Test Stat.**	**Accept/Reject**
Interdependence			
Proportion of wage bill spent on training	OLS	1.45	Reject at 5%
Proportion of employees trained in the last year	OLS	1.25	Accept
Formal analysis of training needs	Logit	32.9	Accept
Number of employees has decreased in last 3 years	Logit	24	Accept
% decrease in employees	OLS	1.12	Accept
Methods employed to decrease workforce	Logit	22.4	Accept
Greater use of more flexible employment	Logit	33.0	Accept
Proportion of workforce temporary	OLS	0.75	Accept
Proportion of workforce with fixed term contracts	OLS	1.38	Accept
Delegation			
Pay bargaining above the establishment level	Logit	36.3	Accept
Financial participation	Logit	44.2	Reject at 5%
Union penetration	OLS	1.60	Reject at 5%
Non-bargaining representation	Logit	7.2	Accept
Change in upward communication in last 3 years	Logit	21.1	Accept
Change in downward communication in last 3 years	Logit	23.7	Accept

Source: Brewster, Wood and Brookes (2008).

With only a limited number of exceptions (financial participation and union penetration), the evidence shows that MNCs pursue similar HRM practices within a specific locale regardless of whether they are foreign subsidiaries or indigenous home operations: in other words, it does not seem that country of origin effects are of overriding importance, other than in a limited number of areas. So Hypothesis 2 is rejected; MNCs' HRM practices are not driven by the country of origin effect but by the fact that they are MNCs: generally they behave differently to their country-specific counterparts, in both home and host countries.

Hypothesis 3 suggests that there is a tendency for MNCs to behave in a similar way in the manner in which they manage their people. There is some evidence for this, as we have shown, but some differences were apparent. These show differences in three areas. First, there is the use of training: indigenous firms are likely to be more fully aware of the limitations and possibilities of local training systems – particularly those operating at sub-national level – resulting in different approaches towards skills development, whilst foreign-owned firms may seek to replicate the dominant approaches to training in their country of origin for the sake of familiarity or for other reasons (Marsden, 1999). Second, union penetration varies from country to country with the trade unions tending to be stronger in collaborative market economies and in certain types of emerging market than in mature liberal market economies and in less developed countries. Third, the varying use of financial participation will reflect particular ownership structures and/or company or sectoral specific ways of doing things (Pendleton et al., 2003). Hence, whilst we cannot reject Hypothesis 3 outright, enough differences remain to suggest that HRM in MNCs is a contested domain, with the pressures of institutions operating at a range of levels and/or combining with specific local conditions impacting managers' strategic choices.

On the basis of this survey evidence, Hypothesis 4 seems the most plausible. The way that MNC subsidiaries manage their human resources clearly varies from context to context, and is likely to be the result of tensions between the relative strengths of the globalisation philosophy, home country pressures and host country institutions, reflecting the contradictory effects of national regulation and/or the uneven diffusion of emerging transnational best practices (Pendleton et al., 2003).

Discussion: MNCs and Host Country HRM Practices

In the international business literature it has been assumed since the early days (Caves, 1974) that MNCs will have a competitive advantage over indigenous firms and will be distinct from them (Buckley and Casson, 1985; Chung, 2001; Dunning and Lundan, 2008; Rugman and Verbeke, 2003; Wright et al., 2001). However, previous research has tended to identify similarities between foreign-owned and local firms. Some authors (Amante, 1995; Rosenzweig and Nohria, 1994; Turner et al., 1997) argued that this was evidence of MNCs adapting to local circumstances. There is no doubt that local subsidiaries will by and large have to accept the limitations of local labour markets and local legislation.

Although Colling et al. (2006) found that US multinationals tend to circumvent the collective bargaining and representation arrangements in Germany, there is usually enough scrutiny of foreign MNCs from trade unions and other pressure groups to ensure that they do not drift too far from careful compliance with coercive factors such as legislation and government regulation. Other authors who identified such similarities (Geary and Roche, 2001) argued that this was evidence of local firms emulating foreign MNCs and it seems likely that, to some extent, that would happen also. Our findings are more complex. There was some evidence of national recipes – in other words, most firms tend to do broadly similar things in particular places – though not fully on the lines of the business systems model suggested by Whitley (1999); this would reflect inherent difficulties in categorising different models of capitalism (Boyer, 2006), as well as the nature of internal systemic diversity.

In fact, different patterns and different types of ownership make for different sets of practices within national business systems, echoing some of the most recent critiques of business systems theory (Brewster et al., 2006; Streeck and Thelen, 2005). In other words, MNCs appear to do things differently to other firms within a specific national context, be the latter an MNC's country of origin or of domicile. This is something of a challenge to the varieties of capitalism literature's relative neglect of the nature of internal systemic diversity. It seems that within any country there are numbers of alternative approaches (not diffuse diversity or incoherence) with a minority of firms – in this particular case MNCs – doing things a little differently from the majority.

MNCs respond to differing forces and their response represents a product of the relative strength of competing forces regulating their behaviour – formal laws, informal norms and practices, ownership structures and relations with stakeholders – and the firm's own policies and processes. The research challenges many previous assumptions. It raises significant questions about the cultural explanations: how a firm operates does not seem invariably to reflect either the effects of the dominant culture in their country of origin (ethnocentricity) or in their country of operation (localisation). The research highlights the limitations of any more extreme assumptions of path dependence: MNCs are engaged in continual, multiple compromises and trade-offs between competing pressures and influences. Country of origin effects do not override practice in a wide range of areas as attested to by the common ground in MNC practices within specific national locales irrespective of whether they are indigenous or foreign owned. A similar argument was advanced in another study using the Cranet data – but with different methodology and looking at a smaller number of countries and somewhat different aspects of HRM (Farndale et al., 2008). They critiqued the country of origin assumptions in e.g. Gooderham and colleagues (1999). The fact that the subsidiaries of US MNCs in LMEs were more like what they believed to be their US headquarters operation, than were their subsidiaries in CMEs, might not mean, as suggested, that US MNCs have more scope in the LME economy: it could just as easily be interpreted to mean that they have adjusted their practices to the local environment in both cases.

Positively, the evidence most strongly supports the duality perspective: providing a good fit with the expectations of authors such as Davis et al. (2000), Evans et al. (2002), Gooderham et al. (1998) and Kostova and Roth (2002) and, indeed, with contemporary regulationist theories of institutional nestedness from local and regional to national and supra-national (Boyer, 2006; Boyer and Hollingsworth, 1997), thus making for alternative clusters of practices, with some elements of uniformity and predictability that operate to lower transaction costs between actors (Boyer, 2006; c.f. Marsden, 1999). Similar conclusions were reached on the basis of a study of a single MNC conducted by Almond et al. (2005).

Farndale et al. (2008) had similar findings to this research. Using a wider range of HRM practices they identified significant differences between domestic organisations and MNCs in all areas except for the number of days training provided. But they found differences between foreign-owned and domestic-owned MNCs in four areas: the use of profit sharing and share options, strategy briefings, and individual-level pay bargaining.

Furthermore, they found that there was generally less variation in HRM practices between local companies and MNCs in CMEs than in LMEs. But in some areas, such as pay bargaining and fixed term contracts, there was more variation in the CMEs. They concluded that support for the assumption that CMEs offer more variety than LMEs was mixed. They argued that the differences between LMEs and CMEs may be exaggerated. Given that the UK was their only example of an LME, the employment legislation there has been influenced by increasing levels of regulation arising both from the UK government and from membership of the European Union (EU). They also argued that the differences between the CME countries in their sample (Sweden, the Netherlands and Germany) may also be significant (Amable, 2003).

Conclusions

It is clear that managers in MNCs do not determine their HRM strategies on 'best practice' rational choice lines: rather they respond to a range of institutionally embedded opportunities and constraints operating at a range of levels, to create appropriate policies and practices. Neither the isomorphic pressures operating at their subsidiaries' host location nor those at the country of origin are sufficiently strong enough to cause the MNCs to mimic the HRM practices of their local counterparts or to operate entirely differently from them. They neither act independently of context nor are they bound by context. Furthermore, whilst MNCs generally behaved differently from the indigenous companies in each territory, there was no evidence of 'diffuse diversity'. A limited number of combinations of firm level practices readily coexist in any one country. The duality thesis best reflects the persistent effects of institutional realities: MNCs operate within a nesting of institutions that moulds the practices of firms at supra-, national and sub-national levels (Boyer and Hollingsworth, 1997).

There are other factors to take into account. Some of the differences between national-specific organisations and MNCs may represent a direct product of size (see also Farndale et al., 2008). Larger organisations generally may have more resources to enable them to develop more sophisticated HRM systems where and when these may be useful (Brewster et al., 2008). International firms, specifically, may need to be more sophisticated than those concentrating on local markets; environments are in a constant stage of flux and evolution necessitating sophisticated and strategic responses (Kim and Gray, 2005: 823–4). But on the other hand, whilst they may not be able to easily ignore local norms, larger MNCs may be in a stronger position to depart a little from them, owing to their ability to exert pressure on national governments. This may apply particularly in poorer and transitional economies that are desperate for the foreign investment.

Future research could usefully explore these issues and how the effect of different contexts on MNCs is changing over time and whether there is, indeed, evidence in the other direction – of MNCs creating emerging trends of the Anglo-Saxonisation of HRM practices across national boundaries (Gooderham et al., 1999; Smith and Meiksins, 1995).

Notes

1 See also Dunning, 1997; Gray, 1998; Hirst and Thompson, 1999; Prakash and Hart, 2000; Rugman, 2001; Whitley, 1999) for sceptical views on globalisation.
2 Including Turkey, a country that straddles two continents.
3 The ordinary least squares models are of the usual form; $y_i = \alpha + \beta'x_i + u_i$ with y_i being the dependent variable, α the intercept term, u_i a normally distributed error term, x_i the vector of explanatory variables and β' their estimated coefficients.
4 The logit models are estimated from $L_i = \ln(\frac{P_i}{1-P_i}) = \alpha + \beta'x_i + u_i$ where P_i is the probability that the dependent variable equals 1, $1-P_i$ is the probability of it being zero and L_i is the log of the odds ratio. Since the log of the odds ratio is linear in the parameters the logit model can be estimated in the linear form (Gujarati, 1995).
5 For the OLS models the structural test is a version of the Chow test where F statistic = $\frac{(RSS_{pooled} - RSS_{domestic} - RSS_{foreignmnc's})/k}{(RSS_{domestic} + RSS_{foreignmnc's})/(n_1 + n_2 - 2k)}$ and RSS is the residual sum of squares from the pooled model, the domestic firm model and the foreign MNCs respectively, n_1 is the number of observations from the domestic firm sub-sample and n_2 the same from the foreign-owned MNC sub-sample, finally k is the number of parameters. The F statistic follows an F distribution with degrees of freedom $(k, n_1 + n_2 - 2k)$ (Gujarati, 1995). For the logit models the structural test is a likelihood ratio test of the form; LR $= 2(LL_{domestic} + LL_{foreignmnc's} - LL_{pooled}$ where LR is the likelihood ratio and LL is the maximization of the log-likelihood function from the domestic, foreign MNC and pooled models respectively. LR follows a chi-squared distribution with k degrees of freedom, where k is the number of estimated parameters (Greene, 2000).
6 An analysis examining just the flexible working practices elements of HRM, using a longitudinal sub-set of this data, found that country differences persist over time (Tregaskis and Brewster, 2006).

References

Almond, P., Edwards, T. and Clark, I. (2003) 'Multinationals and changing national business systems in Europe: Towards the "shareholder value" model?', *Industrial Relations Journal* 34(5): 430–45.

Almond, P., Edwards, T., Colling, T., Ferner, A., Gunnigle, P., Muller-Camen, M., Quintanilla, J. and Wachter, H. (2005). 'Unraveling home and host country effects: An investigation of the HR policies of an American multinational in four European countries', *Industrial Relations* 44(2): 267–306.

Amable, B. (2003) *The Diversity of Modern Capitalism*. Oxford: Oxford University Press.

Amante, M. (1993) 'Tensions in industrial democracy and HRM: A case study of a Japanese enterprise in the Phillipines', *International Journal of Human Resource Management* 4(1): 129–58.

Amante, M.S.V. (1995) 'Employment and wage practices of Japanese firms in the Philippines: Convergence with Filipino Chinese and Western owned firms', *International Journal of Human Resource Management* 6(3): 642–55.

Ashkenas, R., Ulrich, D., Jick, T. and Kerr, S. (1995) *The Boundaryless Organization*. San Francisco, CA: Jossey-Bass.

Bacharach, S. (1989) 'Organisational theories: Some criteria for evaluation', *Academy of Management Review* 14(4): 496–515.

Bae, J., Chen, S.-J. and Lawler, J. J. (1998) 'Variations in human resource management in Asian countries: MNC home-country and host-country effects', *International Journal of Human Resource Management* 9(4): 653–7.

Bartlett, C.A. and Ghoshal, S. (1989). *Managing across Boundaries: The Transnational Solution*. Boston, MA: Harvard Business School.

Birkinshaw, J., Morrison, A. and Hulland, J. (1995) 'Structural and competitive determinants of a global integration strategy', *Strategic Management Journal* 16(8): 637–55.

Boyer, R. (2006). 'How do institutions cohere and change?', in P. James and G. Wood (eds), *Institutions and Working Life*. Oxford: Oxford University Press.

Boyer, R. and Hollingsworth, J.R. (1997) 'From national embeddedness to spatial and institutional nestedness', in J.R. Hollingsworth and R. Boyer (eds), *Contemporary Capitalism: The Embeddedness of Institutions*. Cambridge: Cambridge University Press.

Brewster, C. (2004) 'European perspectives on human resource management', *Human Resource Management Review* 14(4): 365–82.

Brewster, C. and Mayrhofer, W. (eds) (2012) *Handbook of Research on Comparative Human Resource Management*. Cheltenham: Edward Elgar.

Brewster, C., Wood, G. and Brookes, M. (2006) 'Varieties of capitalism and varieties of firm', pp. 217–34 in G. Wood and P. James (eds) *Institutions and Working Life*. Oxford: Oxford University Press.

Brewster, C., Wood, G. and Brookes, M. (2008) 'Similarity, isomorphism or duality: Recent survey evidence on the HRM policies of multinational corporations', *British Journal of Management* 19(4): 320–42.

Buckley, P.J. and Casson, M. (1985) *The Future of the Multinational Enterprise: Twenty-fifth Anniversary Edition*. London: Macmillan.

Buckley, P.J., and Casson, M. (2010) *The Multinational Enterprise Revisited: The Essential Buckley and Casson*. Basingstoke: Palgrave Macmillan.

Buckley, P.J., Clegg, L.J., Cross, A.R., Lui, X., Voss, H. and Zheng, P. (2007) 'The determinants of Chinese outward foreign direct investment', *Journal of International Business Studies* 38(4): 499–518.

Caves, R.E. (1974) 'Multinational firms, competition and productivity in host-country markets', *Economica* 41(2): 176–93.

Chung, W. (2001) 'Identifying technology transfer in foreign direct investment: Influence of industry conditions and investing form motives', *Journal of International Business Studies* 32(2): 211–29.

Colling, T., Gunnigle, P., Quintanilla, J. and Tempel, A. (2006) 'Collective representation and participation', in P. Almond and A. Ferner (eds) *American Multinationals in Europe. Managing Employment Relations across National Borders*. Oxford: Oxford University Press.

Comaroff, J. and Comaroff, J. (2001) 'Millenial capitalism: First thoughts on a second coming', in J. Comaroff and J. Comaroff (eds) *Millenial Capitalism and the Culture of Neoliberalism*. Durham, NC: Duke University Press.

Croucher, R., Brookes, M., Wood, G. and Brewster, C. (2010) 'Context, strategy and financial participation: A comparative analysis', *Human Relations* 63: 835–55.

Croucher, R., Wood, G., Brewster, C. and Brookes, M. (2012) 'Employee turnover, HRM and institutional contexts', *Economic and Industrial Democracy* 33(4): 605–20.

D'Aunno, T., Succi, M. and Alexander, J. (2000) 'The role of institutional and market forces in divergent organizational change', *Administrative Science Quarterly* 45: 679–703.

Davis, P., Desai, A. and Francis, J. (2000) 'Mode of international entry: An isomorphism perspective', *Journal of International Business Studies* 31(2): 239–58.

De Cieri H. and Dowling, P.J. (1999) *Strategic HRM in Multinational Enterprises: Theoretical and Empirical Developments*. Greenwich, CT: JAI Press Inc.

Delery, J.E. and Doty, D.H. (1996) 'Modes of theorizing in strategic human resource management: Tests of universalistic, contingency, and configurational performance predictions', *Academy of Management Journal* 39(4): 802–35.

DiMaggio, P.J., and Powell, W.W. (1983) 'The iron cage revisited: Institutional isomorphism and collective rationality in organizational fields', *American Sociological Review* 48(2): 147–60.

Dunning, J.H. (1997) *Alliance Capitalism and Global Business*. London: Routledge.

Dunning, J.H. (2001) 'The eclectic (OLI) paradigm of international production: past, present and future', *International Journal of the Economics of Business* 8(2): 173–90.

Dunning, J.H. and Lundan, S.M. (2008) *Multinational Enterprises and the Global Economy*. Cheltenham: Edward Elgar.

Duysters, G. and Hagedoorn, J. (2001) 'Do company strategies and structures converge in global markets? Evidence from the computer industry', *Journal of International Business Studies* 32(2): 347–56.

Economist (2000) 'The world's view of multinationals', *The Economist*, 354(8155), 29 January, 21–22.

Edwards, T. and Ferner, A. (2002) 'The renewed "American Challenge": a review of employment practice in US multinationals', *Industrial Relations Journal*, 33(2): 94–111.

Evans, P., Pucik, V. and Barsoux, J.-L. (2002) *The Global Challenge. Frameworks for International HRM*. Chicago: McGraw-Hill/Irwin.

Farndale, E., Brewster, C. and Poutsma, E. (2008) 'Co-ordinated vs liberal market HRM: The impact of institutionalisation on multinational firms', *International Journal of Human Resource Management* 19(11): 2004–23.

Farndale, E. and Paauwe, J. (2007) 'Uncovering competitive and institutional drivers of HRM practices in multinational corporations', *Human Resource Management Journal*, 17(4): 355–75.

Ferner, A. (1997) 'Country of origin effects and HRM in multinational companies', *Human Resource Management Journal* 7(1): 19–37.

Ferner, A. and Quintanilla, J. (1998) 'Multinationals, national business systems and HRM: The enduring influence of national identity or a process of "Anglo-Saxonisation"', *International Journal of Human Resource Management* 9(4): 710–31.

Ferner, A.M., Edwards, T. and Tempel, A. (2012) 'Power, institutions and the cross-national transfer of employment practices in multinationals', *Human Relations* 65(2): 163–87.

Fukuyama, F. (1995) *Trust: Social Virtues and the Creation of Prosperity*. New York: Free Press.

Geary, J. and Roche, W. (2001) 'Multinationals and human resource practices in Ireland: a rejection of the "new conformance" thesis', *International Journal of Human Resource Management* 12(1): 109–27.

Giacobbe-Miller, J., Miller, D., Zhang, W. and Victorov, V. (2003). Cultural and Organizational-Level Adaption to Foreign Workplace Ideologies, *Journal of International Business Studies*, 34 (4): 389–407.

Giddens, A. 1990. *The Consequences of Modernity*. Cambridge:Polity Press.

Goddard, J. (2002) Institutional Environments, Employer Practices and States in Liberal Market Economies, *Industrial Relations*, 41 (2): 249–86.

Goergen, M., Brewster, C., Wood, G., Wilkinson, A. (2012) Varieties of capitalism and investments in human capital and *Industrial Relations* 51 (2): 501–27.

Gooderham, P., Nordhaug, O. and Ringdal, K. (1998) When in Rome, do they do as the Romans? HRM Practices of US Subsidiaries in Europe, *Management International Review*, 38 (2): 47–64.

Gooderham, P.N. and Nordhaug, O. (2003) *International Management: Cross-boundary Challenges*. Oxford: Blackwell Publishing.

Gooderham, P.N., Nordhaug, O. and Ringdal, K. (1999) Institutional and Rational Determinants of Organizational Practices: Human Resource Management in European Firms, *Administrative Science Quarterly*, 44 (3): 507–31.

Gray, J. (1998) *False Dawn: The Delusions of Global Capitalism*. New York: New Press.

Greene, W.H. (2000) *Ecometric Analysis*. Hemel Hempstead: Prentice Hall.

Guillen, M. (2000) Organized Labor's View of Multinational Enterprise, *Industrial and Labor Relations Review*, 53 (3): 419–42.

Gujarati, D.N. (1995) *Basic Ecometrics*. London: McGraw-Hill.

Guler, I., Guillen, M. and Macpherson, M. (2002) Global Competition, Institutions and the Diffusion of Organizational Practices, *Administrative Science Quarterly*, 47: 207–32.

Hall, P. and Soskice, D. (2001) An Introduction to the Varieties of Capitalism, in Hall, P. and Soskice, D. (eds.), *Varieties of Capitalism: The Institutional Basis of Competitive Advantage*. Oxford: Oxford University Press.

Hall, P.A. and Soskice, D. (eds) (2001) *Varieties of Capitalism*. Oxford: Oxford University Press.

Hamel, G. and Prahalad, C.K. (1985) 'Do you really have a global strategy?', *Harvard Business Review* July/August: 139–48.

Hannon, J.M., Huang, I.-C. and Jaw, B.-S. (1995) 'International human resource strategy and its determinants: The case of subsidiaries in Taiwan', *Journal of International Business Studies* 26(3): 531–54.

Haveman, H. (1993) 'Follow the leader: Mimetic isomorphism and the entry into new markets', *Administrative Science Quarterly* 38: 593–627.

Heenan, D. and Perlmutter, H. (1979) *Multinational Organisation Development*. Reading, MA: Addison-Wesley.

Hirst, P. and Thompson, G. (1999) 'The future of globalization', *Cooperation and Conflict*, 37(3): 247–65.

Hofstede, G. (1980) *Culture's Consequences: International Differences in Work-Related Values*. Beverly Hills, CA: Sage.

Hofstede, G. (2001) *Culture's Consequences: Comparing Values, Behaviours, Institutions, and Organisations across Nations* (2nd edn) Thousand Oaks, CA: Sage.

Hollingsworth, J.R. and Boyer, R. (1997) 'Coordination of economic actors and social systems of production', in J.R. Hollingsworth and R. Boyer (eds) *Contemporary Capitalism: The Embeddedness of Institutions*. Cambridge: Cambridge University Press.

House, R.J., Hanges, P.J., Javidan, M., Dorfman, P.W. and Gupta, V. (2004) *Culture, Leadership and Organisations: The GLOBE Study of 62 Societies*. New York: Sage.

Hu, Y.S. (1992) 'Global firms are national firms with international operations', *California Management Review*, 34(2): 107–26.

Jacoby, S. (2005) 'Business and society in Japan and the United States', *British Journal of Industrial Relations* 43(4): 617–34.

Jain, H., Lawler, J. and Morishima, M. (1998) 'Multinational corporations, human resource management and host-country nationals', *International Journal of Human Resource Management* 9(4): 533–66.

Kim, Y. and Gray, S.J. (2005) 'Strategic factors influencing international human resource management practices: An empirical study of Australian multinational corporations', *International Journal of Human Resource Management* 16(5): 809–30.

Kostova, T. and Roth, K. (2002) 'Adoption of an organizational practice by subsidiaries of multinational corporations', *Academy of Management Journal* 45(1): 215–33.

Lane, C. (1998) 'Theories and issues in the study of trust', in C. Lane and R. Bachmann (eds) *Trust Within and Between Organizations*. Oxford: Oxford University Press.

Lao, C. and Ngo, H. (2001) 'Organizational development and firm performance: A comparison of multinational and local firms', *Journal of International Business Studies* 32(1): 95–114.

Lawrence, P.R. and Lorsch, J.W. (1969) *Organization and Environment: Managing Differentiation and Integration*. Homewood, IL: Irwin.

Lee, Y. and Yarwood, L. (1983) 'The socialization of expatriate managers in multinational corporations', *Academy of Management Journal*, 26(4): 657–65.

Marginson, P., Armstrong, P., Edwards, P., Purcell, J. and Hubbard, N. (1993) 'The control of industrial relations in large companies: An initial analysis of the second company level industrial relations survey', Warwick Papers in Industrial Relations No. 45, December 1993. Coventry: IRRU.

Marsden, D. (1999) *A Theory of Employment Systems*. Oxford: Oxford University Press.

Mayrhofer, W. and Brewster, C. (1996) 'In praise of ethnocentricity: Expatriate policies in European multinationals', *International Executive* 38(6): 749–78.

McDonough, T. (2003) 'What does long wave theory have to contribute to the debate on globalization?', *Review of Radical Political Economics* 35(3): 280–86.

McGaughey, S.L. and De Cieri, H. (1999) 'Reassessment of convergence and divergence dynamics: Implications for international HRM', *International Journal of Human Resource Management* 10(2): 235–50.

Meyer, J.W. (2000) 'Globalisation – sources and effects on national states and societies', *International Sociology* 15: 133–248.

Moody, K. (1997) *Workers in a Lean World*. London: Verso.

Moody, K. (2002) 'Towards international social movement unionism', in J. Kelly (ed.) *Industrial Relations – Critical Perspectives on Business and Management* Volume 2. London: Routledge.

Ngo, H.Y., Turban, D., Lau, C.M. and Lui, S.Y. (1998) 'Human resource practices and firm performance of multinational corporations: Influences of country origin', *International Journal of Human Resource Management* 9(4):632–52.

Ohmae, K. (1990) *The Borderless World*. New York: Harper Collins.

Ohmae, K. (1996) *The End of the Nation State*. Cambridge, MA: Free Press.

Parker, B. (1998) *Globalization and Business Practice: Managing Across Boundaries*. London: Sage.

Parsons, T. (1951) *The Social System*. Glencoe: Free Press.

Pendleton, A., Poutsma, E., Van Ommeren, J. and Brewster, C. (2003) 'The incidence and determinants of employee share ownership and profit sharing in Europe' in T. Kato and J. Pliskin (eds.). *The determinants of the incidence and the effects of participatory organizations*: 141–72. Amsterdam: JAI Press.

Perlmutter, H. (1969) 'The tortuous evolution of the multinational corporation', *Columbia Journal of World Business* 1: 9–18.

Pfeffer, J. (1994) *Competitive Advantage through People: Unleashing the Power of the Workforce*. Massachusetts: Harvard Business School Press.

Poutsma, E., Ligthart, P.E.M. and Schouteten, R. (2005) 'Employee share schemes in Europe. The influence of US multinationals', *Management Revue* 16(1): 99–122.

Prakash, A. and Hart, J.A. (eds) (2000) *Coping with Globalization*. London: Routledge.

Rosenzweig, P.M. and Nohria, N. (1994) 'Influences on human resource development practices in multinational corporations', *Journal of International Business Studies* 25(2): 229–51.

Rosenzweig, P.M. and Singh, J.V. (1991) 'Organizational environments and the multinational enterprise'. *Academy of Management Review*, 16(2): 240–361.

Roth, K. and Morrison, A.J. (1990) 'An empirical analysis of the integration responsiveness framework in global industries', *Journal of International Business Studies* 21: 541–64.

Rugman, A.M. (2001) 'The myth of global strategy', *International Marketing Review*, 18(6): 583–88.

Rugman, A. and Verbeke, A. (2003) 'Extending the theory of the multinational enterprise: Internationalization and strategic management perspectives', *Journal of International Business Studies* 34(2): 125–37.

Schuler, R.S., Dowling, P.J. and De Cieri, H. (1993) 'An integrative framework of strategic international human resource management', *International Journal of Human Resource Management* 4(4): 717–64.

Sera, K. (1992) 'Corporate globalization: a new trend', *Academy of Management Executive* 6(1): 89–96.

Smith, C. and Meiksins, P. (1995) 'System, society and dominance effects in cross-national organisational analysis', *Work, Employment and Society* 9(2): 241–67.

Sorge, A. (2004) 'Cross-national differences in human resources and organisation', in A.-W. Harzing and J. Van Ruysseveldt (eds) *International Human Resource Management*. London: Sage.

Storey, J. (ed) 2007: *Human Resource Management: A Critical Text* (3rd ed.). London: Thomson.

Streeck, W. and Thelen, K. (eds) (2005) *Beyond Continuity: Institutional Change in Advanced Political Economies*. Oxford: Oxford University Press.

Taylor, S., Beechler, S. and Napier, N. (1996) 'Toward an integrative model of strategic international human resource management', *Academy of Management Review* 21(4): 959–85.

Tregaskis, O. and Brewster, C. (2006) 'Converging or diverging? A comparative analysis of trends in contingent employment practice in Europe over a decade', *Journal of International Business Studies* 37(1): 111–26.

Turner, T., D'Art, D. and Gunnigle, P. (1997) 'Pluralism in retreat: A comparison of Irish and multinational manufacturing companies', *International Journal of Human Resource Management*, 8(6): 825–40.

Weber, M. (2000) 'A science of real individual cultural configurations', in R. Burns and H. Rayment-Pickard (eds) *Philosophies of History*. Oxford: Blackwell.

Whitley, R. (1999) *Divergent Capitalisms: The Social Structuring and Change of Business Systems*. Oxford: Oxford University Press.

Whitley, R. (2000) 'Editorial', *Organization Studies* 21(5): V–X.

Wright, P.M., Dunford, B.B. and Snell, S.A. (2001) 'Human resources and the resource-based view of the firm', *Journal of Management* 27: 701–21.

Yip, G.S. (1995) *Total Global Strategy*. Englewood Cliffs, NJ: Prentice-Hall.

Zeira, Y. and Harari, E. (1977) 'Genuine multinational staffing policy: Expectations and realities', *Academy of Management Journal* 20(2): 327–33.

How Much Does Country Matter? A Cross-national Comparison of HRM Outsourcing Decisions

MICHAEL MOL, CHRIS BREWSTER, GEOFFREY WOOD
AND MICHAEL BROOKES

Introduction

Outsourcing has probably been around for about as long as formal organizations have, but over the past 20 to 30 years there has been a marked increase in the use of outsourcing across a wide range of activities and most industries and countries (Mol, 2007). One such activity is human resources management (HRM). HRM is a container term for a variety of activities and all of these activities in principle could be subject to outsourcing (Gilley et al., 2004; Norman, 2009) although, based on the activity characteristics, some are more likely to be outsourced than others. HRM is a supportive function within organizations that combines routine functions such as basic administration of staff records and payrolls with proactive trouble-shooting such as managing grievances and discipline and negotiation, and/or a more strategic role (Collings and Wood, 2009). When organizations outsource production they, in effect, also outsource the HRM of affected line staff; the effects of this 'hidden form' of HRM outsourcing will be manifested within HRM departments primarily in the form of cutbacks on staffing and capabilities, especially, in unskilled and semi-skilled routine HRM functions. This chapter focuses on the extent to which the HR management of non-outsourced employees may itself be outsourced, and the extent to which it varies according to context.

All the drivers of outsourcing occur at one of four levels (Mol, 2007): the activity characteristics, the firm's characteristics, the competitive environment (industry) in which a firm operates and the wider, national, environment, i.e. the country in which a firm operates. However, in the management literature on outsourcing the latter dimension has not been explored much (cf. Mol and Brewster, 2013), except in work looking at economic liberalization (e.g., Toulan, 2002) and we are not aware of much work looking at the national factors that determine HRM outsourcing. In this chapter our central question is therefore whether and how organizations from different countries differ in their use of HRM outsourcing. This is an interesting question theoretically, as it can tell us whether and how national institutions and cultures affect outsourcing choices. It is also a practically relevant question, particularly to help decision-makers and policy-makers understand how those institutions and cultures enable or constrain outsourcing decisions.

Given the lack of previous analysis of the topic, we take an exploratory approach to answering this question, rather than a strongly hypothesis-driven approach, to get some initial answers. We start by outlining some of the leading conceptual approaches and discussing some known antecedents of (HRM) outsourcing at the activity, firm and industry level. We then turn to the country level to understand how country differences might act as an antecedent to (HRM) outsourcing, exploring conceptually why firms from some countries outsource more or less than their counterparts elsewhere, drawing upon key concepts of the comparative literature. Next, we present empirical evidence from the Cranet survey (see Chapter 2), which tracks a variety of HRM practices, including outsourcing, inside firms operating in dozens of countries. This allows us to test the extent to which firms from these countries differ on the outsourcing of nine HRM tasks and a combined measure of HRM outsourcing and, particularly, which countries outsource significantly more or significantly less than others. We follow this with some discussion and implications for future research. The key contributions of this paper are twofold. Conceptually, we discuss how, on top of activity, firm and industry level accounts, multiple existing theories of cross-national differences in how firms are organized may add to our understanding of outsourcing choices. Empirically, we present some analyses that demonstrate the existence of cross-national differences in HRM outsourcing choices and how pervasive it appears to be.

Drivers of HRM Outsourcing

Activity, Firm, Industry and National Levels

At the activity level, a dominant theory that helps us understand outsourcing choices is transaction cost economics (TCE) (Coase, 1937; Williamson, 1975; 1985). In Williamson's (1985) view, undertaking activities creates two types of costs, production costs and transaction costs. The latter are often defined as the 'costs of running the economy' (Arrow, 1974). While production costs are typically lower in the market (i.e., through outsourcing) owing to specialization and economies of scale, transacting in markets incurs additional transaction costs. Key to understanding whether to outsource an activity is therefore an investigation of the sources of transaction costs. Williamson (1985) sees outsourcing as a governance choice that is determined by three transaction characteristics in particular. Asset specificity refers to the extent to which underlying assets can be redeployed elsewhere (Williamson, 1985). If assets are very specific, ie it is difficult to redeploy them in an alternative context, outsourcing becomes difficult as suppliers will want to have strong guarantees built into contracts before committing to investing in those specific assets, making the contract prohibitively expensive. In other words, the higher the asset specificity, the higher the transaction costs or, very simply, complex activities are likely to attract higher transaction costs. In contrast, standardized activities that are less dependent on implicit understandings between parties will be associated with lower transaction costs; an example of this would be basic payroll administration. Klaas et al. (1999) found people management is an area that is particularly vulnerable to transaction costs. Hence, only areas of HRM that are readily standardized and with low asset specificity, such as payroll administration, are readily outsourceable (cf Chiang et al., 2010: 2764). In the same manner, firms are only likely to outsource if there are clear cost advantages (Chiang et al., 2010: 2764).

In HRM one could consider selection of new employees to be one activity that is likely to be characterized by high asset specificity, as the selection of new employees who will fit the organization requires significant knowledge of the internal working of the organization, its strategy, its culture and so forth. These activities would be hard to outsource. By contrast, some training and development activities could be very low on asset specificity, such as training in the use of specific machinery or technologies, and those activities would typically be outsourced. Galanaki et al. (2008: 2335) argue that when there is a developed external market, transaction costs are reduced. Hence, they argue that training is one of the most outsourced HRM functions. Training is a very diverse function and can range from the bespoke to standardized off the shelf provisions (Galanaki et al., 2008: 2334). Reflecting this, Galanaki et al. (2008: 2334) found that firms may outsource training on either quality or cost grounds; in contrast, many routine areas of HRM, such as payroll administration, tend to be outsourced purely on cost grounds. Chiang et al. (2010: 2796) found that, based on evidence from Hong Kong, the most likely areas to be outsourced include benefits, employee services, payroll administration, staffing and HR information systems. And Gilley et al. (2004) found that training and payroll administration both had some positive effect on performance outcomes, although this was not consistent across measures and models.

At the firm level there are two key observations that have been made by strategic management scholars. One observation is that firms differ in terms of their productive resources and capabilities (Barney, 1991; 1999). The other observation is that when deciding whether to outsource an activity, firms compare the strength of their own productive resources and capabilities to that of outside suppliers (Jacobides and Winter, 2005). Taken together, these observations imply that when making an outsourcing decision we would expect firms to not only have an understanding of their own resources and capabilities but to also make an assessment of how capable outside suppliers are, and to then choose the 'best in world' (Quinn and Hilmer, 1994), highest capability provider.

Whilst the TCE model focuses on costs, the resource based view of the firm emphasizes that competitive advantage is contingent on human capabilities. This point of view suggests that only non-core capabilities should be outsourced; in doing so, HR managers are freed up to concentrate on core capabilities (Chiang et al., 2010: 2764). Hence, the resource based view suggests that firms have capabilities that are not easily replicated, meaning that core capabilities are more likely to be kept in house (Galanaki et al., 2008: 2335).

In HRM firms may over time have gained experience in and developed internal systems for selection, for example, which together could have become an important competitive capability of the firm and could be a cause for that firm to integrate that activity. In the case of low value added areas of economic activity, recruitment and selection systems may be highly formalized, with fixed criteria. An outside provider may add little value here and, even in areas with very high staff turnover (e.g. fast food), demand will be episodic and highly cyclical, making it difficult for outsider providers to reach economies of scale.

Alternatively, there may be outside specialized suppliers in an area like pensions provision that have strong capabilities relative to their potential customers such as deep knowledge of the pension system or specialized information systems, which make it more likely those customers will choose to outsource the activity to those suppliers. Firms may, of course, outsource pensions purely as a mechanism for cutting costs. Given that pensions constitute deferred pay (Lazear, 1990), removing their management from less close scrutiny and offloading the blame for relatively poor performance onto a third party, may reflect both the relatively weak position of employees and, conversely, a reflection of managerial power (cf. Ippolito, 2002).

At the industry level outsourcing decisions are co-determined by various factors. Economists (Shy and Stenbacka, 2003) have paid particular attention to the impact of industry level competition: the more competitive the industry, the more likely firms are to engage in an efficiency drive and as a consequence they will outsource to benefit from low cost outside providers (Kotabe et al., 2012). This is probably especially true if industry competition is primarily based on low cost provision, rather than differentiated products (Mol, 2007; Porter, 1985). The reverse is also true, as outsourcing has actually been shown to increase price competition in an industry (Cachon and Harker, 2002): in that sense outsourcing becomes part of a 'race to the bottom', where firms are ever more disaggregated and customers ever more price conscious. The airline industry is one such example, and it seems to have outsourced a fair share of its HRM practices. By contrast, public sector organizations have probably been much more reluctant to outsource their HRM practices.

An additional explanation can potentially be found at the national level. Two potential explanations for differences at this level are cultural analyses and the institutional ones (Sorge, 2004). Culturally, for instance, it could be that outsourcing is less likely if individuals in countries seek to reduce uncertainty when taking decisions. Two prominent ways of looking at cross-national cultural traits are the Hofstede (1980) and GLOBE (House et al., 2004) studies, both of which propose multiple dimensions of culture, which are partly overlapping. It is not immediately obvious which dimensions of culture would matter the most for outsourcing, although this could be resolved through empirical testing. Smith et al. (2006), based on US and Russian experiences, suggest that national culture may affect relative proclivity towards outsourcing, although they do not provide a comprehensive trans-national comparison of trends in this regard. More importantly, there is some considerable doubt over and criticism of both the Hofstede and GLOBE studies, suggesting they may not accurately reflect cultural distance (e.g., Durvasula et al., 2006; Gerhart and Fang, 2005). And some recent work suggests that among foreign subsidiaries of multinational corporations cross-cultural differences may play less of a role in explaining outsourcing decisions than institutional factors (Mol and Brewster, 2013). Thus, while we do not rule out cultural effects on outsourcing in principle, we look at them with some level of scepticism and devote more attention to the institutional context.

Institutions and Outsourcing: Variations in National Context

Institutional approaches suggest that outsourcing proclivity reflects context (Chiang et al., 2010). The influential Varieties of Capitalism (VoC) literature suggests that, in line with embedded national institutional frameworks, firms will exhibit a tendency towards adopting certain sets of practices according to setting (Hall and Soskice, 2001). The early VoC literature concentrated on the differences between lightly regulated, shareholder orientated, liberal market economies (LMEs), and more regulated, coordinated market economies (CMEs) (Hall and Soskice, 2001; Lincoln and Kalleberg, 1990). The former, generally covering the developed Anglo-Saxon world, are associated with 'arm's length', more impersonal contracting, greater short-termism in contractual relations, deregulated labour markets and adversarial competition. Firms that do well in such settings include, inter alia, those operating in radically innovative high technology industries on account of strong generic skills bases, the ready availability of short term investor capital, spillovers from relatively large defence spending (in the case of the USA) and the stimulation of adversarialism (Thelen, 2001). Low value added service sector firms also prosper in such contexts, benefitting from fluid labour markets and weak worker rights. What both sectors have in common is a tendency towards the use of harder, more calculative, approaches to people management (Gooderham, Nordhaug and Ringdal, 2006).

In CMEs (the Rhineland economies, Scandinavia, Taiwan and Japan), major areas of competitive advantage are incrementally innovative areas of activity, especially in manufacturing (Lincoln and Kalleberg, 1990; Hall and Soskice, 2001). Here, firms rely on good national vocational training systems, patient investor capital and close ties between core firms, suppliers and customers. Again, there are strong intra-industry links. Both unions and employer associations are relatively powerful and encompassing, enabling them to forge meaningful compromises. In CMEs, people management is likely to be softer and more cooperative (Gooderham et al., 2006). In short, in CMEs, ties between an organization and its people (and, indeed, other stakeholders) are likely to be denser and closer than is typically the case in LMEs.

There is a wide range of areas of HRM that firms may choose to outsource. Ongoing payroll administration for many categories of employee is a highly standardized task. Payroll for any job category involves some procedurality and standardization. Hence, it may be an area that readily recommends itself to outsourcing. Firms employing large numbers of unskilled or semi-skilled workers are more likely to make use of standardized forms of reward system (Richbell and Wood, 2009); but equally, as such labour is more readily substitutable, unskilled workers may be more likely to be outsourced themselves. Even the most sophisticated reward package involves some element of routine in terms of physical payment processes. The same goes for the administration of benefits, which may range from simple cash incentives to more sophisticated reward systems. As noted above, the predominant logic behind the outsourcing of pensions may not be to procure better, more expert fund administration, and simply for organizations to rid themselves of the costs and risks of managing pensions internally. At the same time, workers may, as a component of the psychological contract, have some expectations of a basic degree of pension coverage; and managers may be more inclined to breach the psychological contract in contexts where shareholder rights are more entrenched.

The extent to which training and development are outsourced may also be bound up with context. In countries with strong national vocational training systems, firms are likely to concentrate on topping up such skills and capabilities with organization specific 'remedial' training and development, which may be disseminated throughout an individual employee's working life (Goergen et al., 2009; Thelen, 2001). Such training and development is particularly difficult to outsource. In lightly regulated labour markets, typically encountered in liberal markets, where tenure is weak and staff turnover high, firms operating in low skill, low value added areas of the economy may be forced to devote a great deal of resources to basic induction training. At the same time, such training will concentrate on organization-specific standardized production processes (e.g. approved order of food preparation in a fast food chain) which, again, it may be more cost-effective to offer in-house. In contrast, in high technology areas of industry (a prominent sector in liberal markets) where firms rely on graduates with generic skills, there may be advantages accruing from outsourcing training and development to specialist providers who can provide further training closely geared to the needs of the sector.

In more lightly regulated markets firms are more likely to attain numerical flexibility through adjustments in workforce size; in more coordinated markets, firms typically make greater use of softer measures to adjust staffing, such as shortening the working week (Goergen et al., 2013; Harcourt and Wood, 2007). The outplacement of employees to sub-contractors, as part of a broader outsourcing strategy, may be a more prominent feature of liberal markets. Outsourcing the administration of workforce reductions to a specialist HRM provider may provide the firm with access to more sophisticated legal expertise, reducing the prospects for subsequent litigation. In more coordinated markets, labour legislation is very much more extensive than typically encountered in common law/liberal markets which, in turn, are associated with lower levels of litigiousness (see Harcourt et al., 2004). Once more, such outsourcing allows management to disassociate themselves, at least to some extent, from some of the unpleasantness of implementing job cuts; this is more likely in contexts where ties between managers and workers are weaker.

In settings where the relative rights of employees are less rigorously defined by the law, employers may also have incentives to outsource dealing with routine queries; a specialist provider is likely to have developed specialised legal expertise, helping reduce the risk for litigation should a particular concern escalate. In organizations employing highly standardized production processes, it may be easier to outsource the handling of queries to a specialist provider, who has developed generic responses to common concerns.

The use of specialist services for recruitment and selection may be particularly attractive in liberal market contexts where there is a good pool of graduates with generic tertiary skills, but where specific capabilities may be either difficult to resource and/or objectively to certify. Further, any failures in the recruitment process can be remedied more easily in such systems. In contrast, in settings where vocational skills training systems are more developed, firms can rely on more objectively certified measures of industry-relevant skills. In more coordinated settings firms have closer ties to their workforce so recruitment and selection may be more closely bound up with personal and community networks and, hence, more difficult for an outsider organization to perform.

Overall, in settings where firms make use of softer, higher commitment HRM paradigms, closer ties are developed between an organization and its people (Harcourt and Wood, 2007; cf. Hall and Soskice, 2001), possibly making it less attractive to introduce an external third party. The use of specific outsourcing strategies may be bound up with sector and, above all, national realities. Firms in more lightly regulated liberal markets have fewer ties to their workforces, making it more attractive to transfer the management of people to a third party. Hence, it could be argued that outsourcing is likely to be more common in liberal market economies and that organizations there making use of one type of outsourcing are more likely to make use of other types as well.

Hall and Soskice (2001) suggested that only LMEs and CMEs had well developed and mutually supportive complementarities; hence, other economies would face strong pressures to converge towards one or another of these paradigms. In later developments of this literature, it was recognized that many economies did not easily fit into these two categories, and showed little sign of fully converging towards either an LME or a CME. Notable examples are the Mediterranean or Mixed Market Economies (MMEs) and the post-communist Emerging Market Economies (EMEs) (Hancke et al., 2007; cf. Amable, 2003). Although most of the central and eastern European post-state socialist economies can be considered in the separate category of EMEs, some, such as Slovenia and to an extent Slovakia, have moved towards the CME model and others, most notably Estonia, towards the LME model (Lane and Myant, 2007). There is much difference between these two archetypes, reflecting distinct historical legacies; at the same time, they share common ground in terms of weaker institutional coupling, uneven enforcement of the law and greater economic volatility.

Amable (2003) further unpacks the CME category; he suggests that Scandinavia (he means Nordic, 'social democratic capitalism' countries) are sufficiently distinct from the Rhineland economies ('continental European capitalism') to constitute a distinct archetype in their own right. These social democratic economies (SDEs) are not only distinct as a category they are, on some measures, more successful economies than the typically quoted USA liberal market model. Inter alia, these economies are associated with even stronger worker rights than continental European ones, Hence, it could be argued that people management in SDEs will be the 'softest', most cooperative, making HRM outsourcing even less attractive than would be the case in continental Europe.

Institutional Voids

The literature on institutional voids (Delios and Henisz, 2003; Khanna and Palepu, 1999) suggests that the extent to which the institutional set-up of a country is 'complete', i.e. institutions are both present and function well, has a major impact on firm strategy. Much of this work looks at the presence of business groups and effectiveness of business groups (Khanna and Palepu, 1999), but there is some work in the context of outsourcing that suggests the removal of institutional voids leads firms to increase their levels of outsourcing (see Toulan, 2002, for the case of economic liberalization in Argentina). More generally, we would predict that the more such institutional voids are present, the more firms will have to resort to integration, rather than outsourcing, because they cannot rely on the market (i.e. outside suppliers) to supply them with the required inputs at a reasonable cost. In a Williamsonian (1985) sense, institutional voids lead to additional market imperfections, which produce higher transaction costs, which lower the likelihood of outsourcing. These institutional voids in principle can refer to quite a wide variety of country institutions, from basic infrastructure that makes it hard to transport goods or people, through difficulties in obtaining and diffusing information in a country leading to higher costs of searching for and evaluating suppliers (Rangan, 2000), through to a legal system that is deficient because the laws themselves are either not suited to supporting outsourcing arrangements or are not being enforced properly. In short, even if firms may have a strong preference for outsourcing – in line, for example, with the deployment of a low skill/ low value added production paradigm – when institutions are weak, they may not be able to. So although many firms operating in EMEs and MMEs might benefit from outsourcing, institutions may not be fully developed and closely enough coupled to encourage it.

Legal Origin and Outsourcing

Work on the economic impact of legal institutions and their historical origin has been especially prominent in recent times (see Chapter 1) but as far as we are aware has not really been extended to the area of outsourcing. If the argument that outsourcing of HRM is associated with more shareholder orientated approaches is correct, one would expect it to be more widespread in common law countries than in the more diluted forms of civil law (first Scandinavian and then German civil law) and finally least widespread in the countries following the French legal tradition.

In short, our discussion above suggests that differences in HRM outsourcing choices can result not only from activity, firm and industry level explanations, but could well be shaped by national level factors as well. We particularly discussed cultural, varieties of capitalism, institutional voids and legal origin explanations. We acknowledge that these explanations could potentially overlap, because various aspects of institutions and national culture have a tendency to co-evolve, but exploring that overlap is beyond the focus of the current chapter. We now proceed to provide some empirical evidence of cross-national differences in HRM outsourcing choices.

Methods

We use the 2008 version of the Cranet survey. As a data source it provides us with the unique property of collecting HRM outsourcing information across a large number of countries. An overwhelming majority of outsourcing studies occur in a single country, shaping the questions scholars can ask (Mol, 2007), and the potential provided by Cranet to compare outsourcing choices across countries is therefore really useful. Details on the survey methodology are provided in Chapter 2 of this volume.

Outsourcing Variables

For our dependent variables the survey measures for nine individual areas of HRM the extent to which these were outsourced by the firm. Specifically, it asks 'To what extent do you outsource the following areas to external providers?' Respondents answer this question on a scale from 0 (not outsourced) to 4 (completely outsourced) for the nine items: 1) payroll; 2) pensions; 3) benefits; 4) training and development; 5) workforce outplacement/reduction; 6) HR information systems; 7) recruitment; 8) selection; 9) processing routine queries from managers/employees (e.g. HRM call centre). We then additionally create 'HRM outsourcing' that combines all of these items in a single construct. This construct has a Cronbach alpha of 0.73, which is satisfactory, but we note that a principal component analysis suggested there may be a second factor in the data: we could not, however, satisfactorily create that second factor with these items. We therefore retained all items in a single factor but also look at the items separately. In Table 11.1 below we present descriptive data on each of these items as well as the overall HRM outsourcing variable. We observe large differences in the use of these items: while pensions and training and development activities are outsourced relatively often, this is not the case for routine queries and selection procedures. This makes sense in the light of our discussion above about how activity characteristics drive outsourcing decisions: The assets required for some of these activities are highly specific, but for other activities, such as training, outside suppliers can easily redeploy assets for other purposes, such as servicing other customers. We also note that the responses for some of these measures are highly skewed: many firms do not outsource any part of the activity, but there are some that outsource much or all of it.

We proceed with Table 11.2, which contains the correlations between the different types of outsourcing. The table shows that all of the observed correlations are positive (these correlations are all statistically significant at the 5% level as well), suggesting that firms in the sample are more likely to outsource part or all of one of the nine HRM practices if they also outsource part or all of the other eight HRM practices. Furthermore, the outsourcing of each of the nine HRM practices is fairly strongly correlated with our construct of overall outsourcing.

Independent and Control Variables

In our analyses below we use simple dummy variables to represent each of the countries with a value of 1 if the organization is located in that country and 0

Table 11.1 Key Descriptive Values for the Different Types of Outsourcing and the Overall HRM Outsourcing Construct

	Mean	Standard deviation	Skewness	Kurtosis	Observations
1 Payroll	0.82	1.39	1.39	3.32	5,463
2 Pensions	1.38	1.63	0.60	1.67	5,318
3 Benefits	0.71	1.17	1.52	4.16	5,321
4 Training and development	1.30	1.21	0.43	2.11	5,433
5 Outplacement and reduction	0.58	1.11	1.93	5.62	5,275
6 HR information systems	0.88	1.25	1.21	3.24	5,378
7 Recruitment	0.88	1.01	0.95	3.14	5,449
8 Selection	0.48	0.82	1.74	5.58	4,976
9 Routine queries	0.24	0.71	3.50	15.71	5,218
10 HRM outsourcing	7.15	5.99	0.99	3.98	4,446

Table 11.2 Correlations between the Different Types of Outsourcing

	1	2	3	4	5	6	7	8	9
1 Payroll	1								
2 Pensions	0.46	1							
3 Benefits	0.44	0.48	1						
4 Training and development	0.10	0.14	0.21	1					
5 Outplacement and reduction	0.24	0.29	0.29	0.19	1				
6 HR information systems	0.25	0.18	0.25	0.32	0.25	1			
7 Recruitment	0.18	0.17	0.20	0.35	0.22	0.25	1		
8 Selection	0.17	0.14	0.15	0.26	0.28	0.24	0.56	1	
9 Routine queries	0.21	0.16	0.23	0.15	0.22	0.24	0.24	0.27	1
10 HRM outsourcing	0.63	0.65	0.65	0.52	0.57	0.58	0.57	0.52	0.45

otherwise. This provides us with the advantage of being able to understand at a detailed, country-by-country level how outsourcing of each of the practices, and overall outsourcing, differs.

But, given our arguments above that outsourcing is co-determined by factors at the activity, organizational and industry levels, we must apply a further set of control variables. The survey provides us with indicators of the sector in which an organization operates. In our regressions below we use dummies with value of 1 if the organization operates in (and 0 if it does not): 1) 'chemicals'; 2) 'metals manufacturing'; 3) 'other manufacturing'; 4) 'retail'; 5) 'banking and business services'. We use the other sectors (industries) in the survey as a baseline. We control for 'firm size', which could be a proxy for resource strength, by including the logarithm of the number of employees of an organization. It can be argued that smaller firms have lower negotiating power and, hence, are likely to incur higher transaction costs and, consequently, will be less likely to outsource HRM activities (Galanaki et al., 2008: 2335; Klaas et al., 2005). The number of employees is the most easily comparable measure in a very broad cross-section of organizations such as we have here. 'Specialized resources' are measured by the percentage of all of a firm's employees that are professional or technical employees: in line with the theories discussed above we expect this to negatively affect outsourcing. Similarly the variable 'unionization', the percentage of a firm's employees who are members of trade union (coded 1 if 0%, 2 if 1 to 10%, 3 if 11 to 25%, 4 if 26 to 50%, 5 if 51 to 75% and 6 if 76 to 100%), ought to constrain efforts to outsource activities. We then add a 'group' dummy variable with a value of 1 if the organization is part of a larger group, and 0 otherwise. The 'education' variable measures the percentage of the workforce with a college degree. It may be that outsourcing is less prominent in organizations with a highly educated workforce, if workforce education is reflective of the quality of the firm's resources. We also add a dummy called 'HRM department' with value 1 if the organization has a separate department for human resources management. The presence of such a department probably makes it less likely that HRM activities will be outsourced, both because that presence implies HRM activities are seen as important to the organization's competitive success and because the department by nature of its objectives will tend to want to maintain HRM activities in-house and perhaps to draw in more activities. We then add a further dummy, 'HRM board member', with a value of 1 if an individual dedicated to HRM sits on the board of the organization and 0 otherwise. The effect of this variable may be similar to that of the HRM department, although it could also be that a board member has more liberty to outsource HRM activities. The 'geographic scope' of the organization refers to the breadth of the markets an organization operates in. This variable runs from 1 (local), through 2 (regional), 3 (national) and 4 (continent-wide) to 5 (world-wide). Because markets with a wider scope are known to be more competitive, and because exposure to the wider world may increase familiarity of an organization with the practice of outsourcing, we could expect this variable to have a positive effect on outsourcing. Finally, 'market growth' measures changes in organizational sales over time, specifically whether the market the organization currently serves is declining (value of 1), the same (2) or growing (3).

Estimation Methods

Below, we start our analyses with some simple bivariate correlations between the country dummies and the ten measures for outsourcing. Although bivariate correlations fail to account for the possible intervening effects of other variables in observed relationships, they give us some initial insights. We then continue with multivariate analysis. Given the nature of the first nine dependent variables, which run from 0 to 4, an ordinary least squares (OLS) regression is not appropriate due to the limited number of possible outcomes. Because there is a natural hierarchy in the five answers though, we can assume they are 'ordered'. Therefore we apply ordered logit regressions for the nine individual activities. For the overall outsourcing measure it is more reasonable to use OLS regression, although the distribution of the answers is not normal, i.e. as noted above it is fairly heavily skewed. We therefore also apply a double-censored tobit analysis for purposes of robustness.

Results

In Table 11.3 below we present the means for each of the ten dependent variables for each of the countries as well as the grand mean across all the countries. We further show which of these means is significantly different from the grand mean, being either above it, implying organizations in that country outsource more than the average firm in the sample, or below it, outsourcing less. These results seem to demonstrate that there are substantial differences in outsourcing levels between the different countries for each of the variables and that those differences are systematically associated with the country. For instance values for Belgium are above the grand mean for each of the HRM tasks investigated here, whilst those for Taiwan are always below the grand mean. This provides us with an initial answer to part of our research question: It appears that there are indeed differences in HRM outsourcing across the different countries.

We continue by including the various control variables and running multivariate analyses. To do this, we need to use some of our country dummies as the base value in the regressions to avoid problems of multicollinearity – including all the different dummies is impossible as they would then perfectly explain each other. Because we did not want to apply an arbitrary criterion or let Stata decide upon a dummy to exclude, we chose to systematically exclude those countries that displayed a non-significant correlation in Table 11.3 above, as these dummies are least likely to show up as significant in the regressions. Given the exploratory and iterative nature of this chapter and the lack of clearly defined hypotheses about specific countries or sets of countries we think this is an appropriate procedure.

In Table 11.4 below we present these results, which involves ten models (one for every dependent variable; models with control variables only are available upon request). We note that the model statistics for each of the models are solid. We report a pseudo R^2 measure for the ordered logit models, but note that this measure cannot be directly compared to the R^2 measure in the final OLS model. The empirical approach we have taken produces an almost overwhelming amount of evidence and, rather than discussing each variable in every model, we therefore present what we see as the most interesting observations.

First, it appears that firm level variables do not explain much of the variance in the dependent variables, whereas the country dummies pick up quite a lot of variance. Indeed, these results do not appear to correspond to any country categorizations in the existing literature, be they comparative institutional (e.g. Hall and Soskice, 2001; La Porta et al., 2008) or, for that matter, cross cultural approaches, Whilst many CMEs are lower in terms of outsourcing, Germany and Japan are rather at the higher end of the spectrum. It could be argued that the distinctions may not match normal country categorizations (for example, within the CME

Table 11.3 Means for Outsourcing by Country[1]

	1	2	3	4	5	6	7	8	9	10
Grand mean	0.82	1.38	0.71	1.30	0.58	0.88	0.88	0.48	0.24	7.15
Australia	0.49	1.40	0.54	1.46	0.89	0.60	1.15	0.38	0.11	7.01
Austria	0.51	1.29	0.52	1.25	0.22	0.48	0.92	0.50	0.18	5.87
Belgium	*2.21*	*2.31*	*1.54*	*1.46*	*2.30*	*1.51*	*1.20*	*1.15*	*0.62*	*14.31*
Bulgaria	*0.19*	*0.22*	*0.22*	*0.77*	*0.15*	*0.48*	0.79	0.35	0.16	*3.33*
Cyprus	*0.30*	*0.37*	*0.30*	*2.21*	0.36	*1.33*	*1.07*	0.48	*0.42*	6.84
Czech Republic	*0.37*	*0.25*	0.67	*1.65*	*0*	*1.67*	*0.31*	0.48	0.15	*5.56*
Estonia	*0.36*	*0.13*	*0.35*	*2.29*	*0.28*	*1.81*	0.81	0.48	0.14	6.65
Denmark	*0.54*	*1.94*	*0.44*	*0.69*	*0.76*	*0.48*	*0.68*	0.48	*0.12*	*6.13*
Finland	*1.02*	*1.06*	0.62	1.10	*0.25*	0.99	*0.55*	*0.25*	0.25	*6.10*
France	0.88	*0.97*	*0.32*	1.24	0.52	0.89	*1.27*	*0.73*	0.09	6.90
Germany	*1.07*	*1.78*	0.68	0.88	0.57	*0.45*	0.82	n/a	*0.15*	n/a
Greece	0.67	*0.50*	*0.42*	*1.58*	0.32	*1.29*	0.96	*0.73*	0.22	6.68
Hungary	*1.57*	*1.74*	*0.88*	*1.58*	*0.23*	*0.69*	0.74	0.37	0.21	*8.02*
Iceland	*0.59*	1.25	*0.38*	*0.91*	*0.22*	*0.71*	*1.06*	*0.68*	0.14	*5.95*
Israel	0.95	*1.94*	0.51	1.29	*0.05*	*0.59*	0.90	*0.75*	0.18	7.15
Japan	*1.16*	1.43	*1.31*	*1.80*	0.52	1.03	*1.19*	*0.32*	0.27	*9.04*
Lithuania	*0.20*	*0.26*	*0.29*	*2.00*	*0.06*	*0.98*	*1.21*	0.55	0.12	*5.67*
Netherlands	*1.20*	*2.34*	0.67	*1.91*	*0.91*	*1.17*	*1.10*	*0.73*	*1.03*	*11.07*
Norway	0.41	2.16	0.18	0.69	0.08	0.61	0.57	0.43	n/a	n/a
Philippines	0.70	1.33	0.59	1.52	0.56	0.85	0.63	0.33	0.22	6.74
Russia	0.46	*0.32*	*0.30*	1.30	*0.12*	0.66	1.00	0.34	0.16	*4.66*
Serbia	*0.32*	*0.16*	*0.16*	1.18	*0.08*	*0.29*	*0.37*	*0.21*	0.08	*2.84*
Slovakia	0.86	*1.01*	0.59	1.18	*0.33*	0.77	0.90	*0.55*	*0.65*	6.84
Slovenia	*0.22*	*0.81*	*0.29*	1.47	*0.23*	1.06	0.83	*0.32*	0.29	*5.52*
South Africa	*0.33*	*1.68*	*0.95*	1.41	*0.42*	*0.47*	0.80	*0.27*	0.17	6.49
Sweden	0.78	*1.62*	*0.36*	*2.03*	*1.12*	*1.73*	*1.29*	*1.02*	*0.09*	*10.03*
Switzerland	*0.34*	1.69	0.71	1.31	*1.09*	*0.39*	0.72	0.38	*0.09*	*6.72*
Taiwan	*0.02*	*0.05*	*0.13*	*0.79*	*0.07*	0.66	*0.38*	*0.08*	*0.04*	*2.22*
Turkish Cyprus	0.67	*0.59*	*0.35*	*1.67*	*0.28*	0.78	0.89	0.52	0.28	*6.02*
United Kingdom	*1.06*	*1.95*	*1.17*	*0.98*	0.63	0.90	*0.68*	*0.30*	0.14	*7.81*
United States	*1.05*	*1.95*	*1.45*	*0.96*	*0.84*	0.87	*0.56*	*0.14*	0.22	8.02

1 Numbers of variables follow from correlations table. Numbers printed in italics denote that country dummy correlation is significantly different (at 5% significance level) from the grand mean, either above it or below it. Note that significance thresholds may differ from one country to the next due to different subsample sizes.

category, Amable [2003] highlights differences between Scandinavia and continental Europe), but rather specific labour market features. For example, it could be argued that in countries where tenure is weaker (LMEs and the flexicurity economies) firms would be more likely to outsource. However, this would not explain why in one flexicurity country (Netherlands), the extent of outsourcing is high and in another one (Denmark), it is low. Again, whilst LMEs tend to make greater use of outsourcing, in Australia it is rather low.

In looking at central and eastern Europe, in the Czech Republic outsourcing of HRM is low, but in Hungary (a country which is often categorized in the same broad grouping as the Czech Republic) it is high. In other words, the institutional void/underdeveloped institutions explanation does not appear to hold water either. What can explain the lack of validity of normal institutional and cultural categories? This may reflect a number of overlapping factors. First, within some national economies, there may be a more developed group of outsourcing services providers. This development may reflect variations in the type of inter-firm and inter-industry ties. Here, strong inter-industry ties may encourage firms to work together in gaining economies of scale in outsourcing. But, by the same measure, in situations of adversarial competition, firms may desire to make use of outsourcing specialists to gain insights into best practice that would not otherwise be possible in such contexts. Finally, even specialist areas such as training may encompass sophisticated strategic and routine activities (Galanaki et al., 2008); all functional areas of HRM encompass both routine and specialist activities. The only organizational level variable that is significant (and positive) across all models (except model 2) is geographic scope. Being a member of a group also has a positive effect on some forms of HRM outsourcing and on the overall construct. By contrast, sector effects barely seems to play any role here.

Second, there clearly are significant country level effects, both positive and negative, i.e. on the whole, organizations operating in some countries are significantly more (less) likely to outsource part or all of their HRM function.

Third, the country level effects are broadly, but not entirely, consistent across the different activities. For instance, organizations in Taiwan outsource less of all of the activities, while organizations in Belgium outsource more of almost all of the activities (eight out of nine). Having said that, even in Sweden, where organizations outsource more of six out of nine activities, there is one activity (routine queries, in model 9) that gets outsourced less than elsewhere. Other than these three countries, the countries with the most activities that are significantly more or less likely to be outsourced are Bulgaria (less outsourcing of five activities), Cyprus (less outsourcing of four activities, but more of one), the Czech Republic (less outsourcing of three activities, more of one), Denmark (less outsourcing of five activities, more of one), Germany (less outsourcing of four activities, more of two), Greece (more outsourcing of three activities, less of two), Japan (more outsourcing of four activities, less of one), Lithuania (less outsourcing of four activities, more of two), Norway (less outsourcing of four activities, more of one), the Netherlands (more outsourcing of five activities), Slovenia (less outsourcing of five activities) and the United States of America (more outsourcing of four activities, less of three). This would reflect variations in the relative development of markets for outsourced services.

Discussion and Conclusions

How can we explain these findings? We focus especially on what might be possible root causes for the country level effects observed. But we start with the

Table 11.4 Ordered Logit Regression Results for Nine Separate HRM Activities and

	1	2	3	4
Group	0.37(0.09)***	0.19(0.08)*	0.27(0.09)**	0.10(0.07)
Firm size	0.00(0.00)*	0.00(0.00)	0.00(0.00)	0.00(0.00)
Specialized resources	0.00(0.00)	0.00(0.00)	0.00(0.00)	0.00(0.00)
Education	0.00(0.00)	0.00(0.00)	0.00(0.00)	0.00(0.00)
HRM department	−0.73(0.14)***	−0.27(0.14)*	−0.10(0.14)	0.18(0.11)
HRM board member	0.20(0.09)*	0.14(0.08)	0.06(0.09)	0.11(0.07)
Geographic scope	0.18(0.03)***	0.06(0.03)	0.18(0.04)***	0.06(0.03)*
Market growth	0.03(0.06)	−0.05(0.05)	−0.02(0.06)	−0.03(0.05)
Unionization	−0.02(0.02)	−0.06(0.02)*	−0.04(0.03)	0.02(0.02)
Chemicals	−0.33(0.25)	0.08(0.24)	0.10(0.26)	−0.02(0.21)
Metals	−0.28(0.13)*	0.00(0.12)	−0.12(0.13)	0.04(0.11)
Other manufacturing	−0.44(0.15)	−0.08(0.13)	−0.28(0.14)	0.03(0.11)
Retail	−0.07(0.16)	−0.25(0.15)	−0.36(0.17)*	−0.13(0.13)
Banking	−0.05(0.14)	−0.30(0.13)*	0.20(0.13)	−0.15(0.11)
Australia	−0.45(0.42)			
Austria	−0.58(0.29)*		−0.22(0.25)	
Belgium	1.66(0.16)***	1.12(0.18)***	1.44(0.17)***	0.12(0.15)
Bulgaria	−1.07(0.26)***	−1.89(0.24)***	−0.79(0.23)***	−0.50(0.16)**
Cyprus	−1.43(0.46)**	−1.69(0.43)***	−1.03(0.43)*	1.47(0.24)***
Czech Republic	−0.62(0.39)	−2.14(0.47)***		0.49(0.29)
Estonia	−0.66(0.40)	−2.93(0.63)***	−0.48(0.41)	1.24(0.23)***
Denmark	−0.36(0.20)	0.67(0.17)***	−0.38(0.18)*	−1.05(0.15)***
Finland	0.20(0.32)	−0.35(0.26)		
France		−0.34(0.28)	−0.67(0.30)*	
Germany	0.49(0.18)**	0.43(0.17)*	−0.73(0.23)**	−0.61(0.13)***
Greece		−1.61(0.26)***	1.25(0.42)**	0.49(0.17)**
Hungary	1.61(0.37)***	1.51(0.42)***		0.19(0.40)
Israel		0.55(0.31)		
Japan	0.72(0.20)***		1.07(0.20)***	0.85(0.20)***
Lithuania	−1.58(0.45)***	−2.34(0.39)***	−1.07(0.36)***	1.14(0.26)***
The Netherlands	0.86(0.22)***	1.24(0.24)***		0.94(0.30)***
Norway	−0.67(0.34)*	1.08(0.30)***	−1.14(0.40)**	−0.89(0.24)***
Russia		−1.89(0.53)***	−0.94(0.59)	
Serbia	−0.65(0.49)	−3.53(1.06)***	−1.25(0.67)	
Slovakia	−0.09(0.25)	−0.71(0.26)**		
Slovenia	−1.31(0.28)***	−1.04(0.23)***	−0.67(0.22)**	
South Africa	−0.81(0.29)***	0.32(0.21)	0.53(0.24)*	
Sweden		0.34(0.16)*	−0.38(0.21)	0.97(0.14)***
Switzerland	−1.00(0.46)*			
Taiwan	−17.41(0.15)***	−3.70(0.48)***	−2.06(0.34)***	−0.85(0.17)***
Turkish Cyprus	−0.49(0.38)	−1.37(0.42)**	−1.06(0.51)*	0.64(0.36)
United Kingdom	1.07(0.26)***	0.82(0.26)***	1.03(0.25)***	−0.23(0.24)
United States	0.74(0.17)***	0.78(0.17)***	1.46(0.15)***	−0.45(0.14)**
Constant				
Log pseudolikelihood	−2810	−3504	−2913	−4203
Wald Chi^2	32853***	601***	535***	406***
F–test				
Pseudo R^2	0.096	0.112	0.092	0.043
R^2				
N	3056	2974	2993	3036

1 Model numbers correspond with correlations table. Displaying unstandardized betas, standard errors (in

Ordinary Least Squares Regression Results for Overall Outsourcing Construct[1]

5	6	7	8	9	10
0.23(0.10)*	0.17(0.08)*	0.37(0.07)***	0.24(0.09)*	0.16(0.12)	0.80(0.23)***
0.00(0.00)	0.00(0.00)	0.00(0.00)	0.00(0.00)	0.00(0.00)	0.00(0.00)
0.00(0.00)	0.00(0.00)	0.00(0.00)	0.00(0.00)	0.00(0.00)	0.00(0.00)
0.00(0.00)	0.00(0.00)	0.00(0.00)	0.00(0.00)	0.00(0.00)	0.00(0.00)
0.44(0.17)**	0.23(0.12)	0.14(0.12)	0.05(0.13)	−0.46(0.15)**	−0.49(0.35)
0.25(0.10)*	0.05(0.08)	−0.02(0.08)	0.11(0.10)	0.10(0.12)	0.39(0.25)
0.16(0.04)***	0.08(0.03)**	0.17(0.03)***	0.17(0.04)***	0.10(0.05)*	0.59(0.09)***
−0.11(0.06)	−0.08(0.05)	−0.05(0.05)	−0.15(0.06)	−0.05(0.08)	−0.22(0.15)
0.02(0.03)	0.03(0.02)	−0.04(0.02)	0.02(0.02)	−0.01(0.03)	−0.10(0.07)
0.08(0.26)	−0.34(0.24)	−0.34(0.22)	−0.51(0.28)	−0.21(0.37)	−0.57(0.73)
−0.22(0.15)	−0.16(0.12)	0.11(0.11)	−0.14(0.14)	−0.12(0.19)	−0.11(0.35)
0.00(0.15)	−0.09(0.12)	0.21(0.12)	0.00(0.14)	−0.12(0.29)	−0.56(0.38)
−0.28(0.17)	−0.07(0.14)	−0.08(0.13)	−0.12(0.16)	0.12(0.19)	−0.66(0.40)
−0.10(0.15)	0.00(0.12)	0.00(0.12)	−0.28(0.15)	−0.42(0.21)	−0.56(0.37)
0.93(0.35)**	−0.20(0.33)	0.96(0.25)***		−0.79(0.75)	
−1.30(0.34)***	−0.94(0.25)***				−1.29(0.58)*
2.36(0.22)***	0.79(0.15)***	0.54(0.17)**	1.33(0.17)***	1.15(0.22)***	7.08(0.59)***
−0.77(0.26)**	−0.32(0.17)				−3.19(0.45)***
	0.59(0.27)*	0.03(0.37)		0.59(0.40)	
−15.45(0.18)***	0.93(0.29)***	−1.71(0.39)***			−2.09(0.69)**
−0.54(0.39)	1.19(0.22)***				
0.26(0.19)	−0.83(0.17)***	−0.35(0.14)*		−0.62(0.29)*	−1.14(0.42)**
−1.21(0.41)*		−0.31(0.25)	−0.33(0.28)		−1.00(0.63)
		0.65(0.18)***	0.40(0.24)		
	−0.76(0.15)***			−0.54(0.26)*	
−0.82(0.23)***	0.32(0.18)		0.54(0.18)**		
−0.80(0.56)	−0.03(0.33)				
−15.23(0.20)***	−0.34(0.43)		0.76(0.43)		
		0.54(0.23)*	−0.83(0.27)**		1.96(0.64)**
−1.42(0.40)***	0.35(0.23)	0.60(0.25)*			−1.51(0.59)*
0.67(0.26)**	0.41(0.27)	0.31(0.27)	0.41(0.26)	2.01(0.25)***	4.16(0.83)***
−1.70(0.48)***	−0.48(0.27)	−0.48(0.25)			
−0.92(0.54)					−3.44(0.80)***
−2.25(1.05)*	−0.69(0.42)	−1.10(0.50)*	−0.75(0.50)		−3.66(1.08)***
−1.07(0.28)***			0.20(0.20)	0.96(0.22)***	
−0.55(0.23)*			−0.50(0.22)*		−1.70(0.44)***
−0.33(0.25)			−0.94(0.29)**		
0.93(0.17)***	1.11(0.17)***	0.75(0.14)***	1.04(0.17)***	−1.13(0.43)**	2.67(0.56)***
1.05(0.33)**	−0.65(0.32)*			−0.69(0.59)	−0.07(0.78)
−2.13(0.38)***	−0.50(0.19)**	−1.48(0.20)***	−2.23(0.38)***	−2.49(0.73)***	−5.79(0.35)***
−0.40(0.48)					−1.27(0.90)
		−0.19(0.26)	−0.39(0.33)		1.97(0.90)*
0.42(0.19)*		−0.49(0.14)***	−1.27(0.22)***		
					6.11(0.60)***
−2453	−3608	−3676	−2315	−1555	
15497***	314***	298***	328***	177.8***	
					29.02***
0.119	0.037	0.040	0.074	0.061	
					0.220
2968	3012	3046	2796	2913	2521

brackets) and significance levels. Significance levels: *** 0.1%; **1%; *5%.

observation that few of the activity, firm and industry effects included as control variables seemed to explain much variance in the levels of outsourcing of the organizations in the sample. This is interesting, as it apparently runs counter to the main predictions of TCE (Williamson, 1985) and RBV (Barney, 1999) and economic arguments about competition on the role of activity, firm and industry characteristics respectively.

We suggest two key potential reasons for these results. First, they could be a result of measurement issues. The measures contained within the survey were not created with a view towards including important antecedents of outsourcing choices. For instance, our measure of specific resources is some way removed from measuring specialized resources for the specific tasks that firms can outsource and is rather more reflective of resource strength of the firm as a whole. Likewise, there is no real measure for asset specificity here, although one could perhaps be assigned to the different activities, given what is known about their characteristics. This could then potentially be used to explain differences in outsourcing levels from one activity to the next, but it would not help us in explaining differences in outsourcing from one firm to the next. And we measure industry through dummies. In principle these should pick up underlying dimensions, such as the extent of competition in the industry, but competition takes place at a much more detailed level than we have here, with broad sector dummies. These sector dummies bundle two-digit industries, where realistically we might need to go down to the level of single three-digit or even four-digit industries to pick up these effects.

There is, however, a second and much more benign conceptual explanation for this lack of significant findings, which is that the various activity, firm and industry level variables we include in our model have different effects, depending on the country. In other words, and purely hypothetically, it may be that having an HRM board member has a positive effect on outsourcing choices in the United States of America, where these individuals may speed up outsourcing processes, but a negative effect in France, where they might hold up those processes. This would require further refining of our theories of outsourcing, to discuss how transaction, firm and industry effects are actually contextually dependent and perhaps to introduce elements of agency and individual choice. It would go to the heart of long-standing discussions around the extent to which theories of firm behaviour are universal or particularistic (Rosenzweig, 1994), i.e. is TCE a more helpful theory for explaining governance choices in the United States of America, where it was invented, compared to France, with its different institutions and cultures? And it might address concerns about such theories taking on a normative dimension and shaping practice in various ways, some of which may be undesirable (Ghoshal, 2005). Clearly, this is also an interesting further step for empirical research, although it extends well beyond the scope of the current chapter.

As can be seen from the other chapters in this volume, there are, in many areas of HRM, strong relationships between capitalist archetypes and the relative incidence of specific HRM practices. However, when it comes to the outsourcing of HRM functions, these patterns break down. Why would this be the case? First, even within the coordinated markets, there is much variation in areas such as relative national training provision and inter-firm ties (Amable, 2003). Both will affect the relative development of independent providers tendering for outsourced services.

For example, both adversarial competition and strong inter-firm ties may encourage outsourcing of training. In the former, this will be to gain insights into best practice not otherwise attainable and, in the case of the latter, it will be to deal with gaps in (generally developed) industry level vocational training and to benefit from economies of scale. Second, each area of possible HRM outsourcing (e.g. training, wages, etc) comprises both routine and more strategic areas of activity. In short, firms may outsource HRM activities within a general functional area either to rid themselves of a standardized routine function (e.g. payroll administration) and/or to gain advanced capabilities (e.g. strategic reward systems).

It also may be the case that high outsourcing countries share some other common characteristics. For example, broadly they tend to have higher GDPs and are often small open economies. The former could be explained by an increasing division of tasks between firms, meaning ever greater specialization and focus by each individual firm and economic development going hand in hand, almost in the sense implied by Adam Smith. The latter might be an indicator that an economy is highly competitive. As noted above, at the industry level competition and outsourcing often seem to go hand in hand and this may be the case at the level of entire economies as well. In addition it could be the case that organizations operating in open economies have access to a wider global supply base, which facilitates outsourcing (Mol and Brewster, 2013).

Finally, using Cranet data, Goergen et al. (2013) found that the relative proclivity of firms to make use of redundancies was associated with the relative political orientation of the government. Under right wing governments, firms were more likely to lay off staff. As outsourcing often entails job cuts, the political orientation of governments may also result in an intensification of outsourcing activity. Unfortunately, it was not possible to replicate the methodology of the Goergen et al. study in this chapter, as the former was based on earlier waves of Cranet data and an index of political orientation that has not been updated and, hence, is not comparable with the latest Cranet wave. However, comparing the ideological orientation of governments and HRM practices would constitute a fertile area for future research.

In concluding, we return to our leading question. The answer to the first part of the question appears to be straightforward, as we found significant and fairly consistent cross-national differences in the use of HRM outsourcing. The second part of the question is harder to answer though, as no dominant explanation of those differences readily appears from our theorizing. We would suggest that future research therefore ought to look more explicitly at a variety of explanatory variables, instead of country dummies, to better answer this question. In doing so, an interesting route could be to explore to what extent country level factors interact with activity and firm level factors in shaping outsourcing decisions.

References

Amable, B. (2003) *The Diversity of Modern Capitalism*. Oxford: Oxford University Press.

Arrow, K.J. (1974) *The Limits of Organization*. New York: John Brockman Associates.

Barney, J. (1991) 'Firm resources and sustained competitive advantage', *Journal of Management* 17(1): 99–120.

Barney, J.B. (1999) 'How a firm's capabilities affect boundary decisions', *Sloan Management Review* 40(3): 137–45.

Cachon, G.P. and Harker, P.T. (2002) 'Competition and outsourcing with scale economies', *Management Science* 48(10): 1314–33.

Chiang, F., Chow, I. and Birtch, T. (2010) 'Examining human resource management outsourcing in Hong Kong', *International Journal of Human Resource Management* 21(5): 2762–77.

Coase, R. (1937) 'The nature of the firm', *Economica N.S.* 4: 386–405.

Collings, D. and Wood, G. (2009) 'Human resource management: a critical approach', in D. Collings and G. Wood (eds) *Human Resource Management: A Critical Approach*. London: Routledge.

Delios, A. and Henisz, W.J. (2003) 'Political hazards, experience, and sequential entry strategies: The international expansion of Japanese firms, 1980–1998', *Strategic Management Journal* 24: 1153–64.

Durvasula, S., Netemeyer, R.G., Andrews, J.C. and Lysonski, S., (2006) 'Examining the cross-national applicability of multi-item, multi-dimensional measures using generalizability theory', *Journal of International Business Studies* 37(4): 469–83.

Galanaki, E., Bourantis, D. and Papalexandris, N. (2008) 'A decision model for outsourcing training functions', *International Journal of Human Resource Management* 19(12): 2332–51.

Gerhart, B., and Fang, M. (2005) 'National culture and human resource management: assumptions and evidence', *International Journal of Human Resource Management*, 16(6): 971–86.

Ghoshal, S. (2005) 'Bad management theories are destroying good management practices', *Academy of Management Learning & Education*, 14(1): 75–91.

Gilley, K.M., Greer, C.R. and Rasheed, A.A. (2004) 'Human resource outsourcing and organizational performance in manufacturing firms', *Journal of Business Research* 57(3): 232–40.

Goergen, M., Brewster, C. and Wood, G. (2009) 'Corporate governance and training', *Journal of Industrial Relations* 51(4): 461–89.

Goergen, M., Brewster, C. and Wood, G. (2013) 'The effects of national setting on employment practice: The case of downsizing', *International Business Review* (in print).

Gooderham, P., Nordhaug, O. and Ringdal, K. (2006) 'National embeddedness and calculative HRM in US subsidiaries in Europe and Australia', *Human Relations* 59: 1491–513.

Hall, P. and Soskice, D. (2001) 'An introduction to the varieties of capitalism', in P. Hall and D. Soskice (eds) *Varieties of Capitalism: The Institutional Basis of Competitive Advantage*. Oxford: Oxford University Press.

Hancke, B., Rhodes, M., and Thatcher, M. (2007) 'Introduction: beyond varieties of capitalism', in B. Hancke, M. Rhodes and M. Thatcher (eds.) *Beyond Varieties of Capitalism: Conflict, Contradictions and Complementarities in the European Economy*: 3–39. Oxford: Oxford University Press.

Harcourt, M., Harcourt, S. and Wood, G. (2004) 'Do unions affect employer compliance with the law?', *British Journal of Industrial Relations* 42(3): 527–41.

Harcourt, M. and Wood, G. (2007) 'The importance of employment protection for skill development in coordinated market economies', *European Journal of Industrial Relations* 13(2): 141–59.

Hofstede, G. (1980) *Culture's Consequences: International Differences in Work-related Values*. Beverly Hills, CA: Sage.

House, R.J., Hanges, P.J., Javidan, M., Dorfman, P.W. and Gupta, V. (eds) (2004) *Culture, Leadership and Organisations: The GLOBE study of 62 societies*. London: Sage.

Ippolito, R.A. (2002) 'Stayers as "workers" and "savers": Toward reconciling the pension–quit literature', *The Journal of Human Resources* 37: 275–308.

Jacobides, M.G. and Winter, S.G. (2005) 'The co-evolution of capabilities and transaction costs: Explaining the institutional structure of production', *Strategic Management Journal* 26: 395–413.

Khanna, T., and Palepu, K.G. (1999) 'Policy shocks, market intermediaries, and corporate strategy: Evidence from Chile and India', *Journal of Economics and Management Strategy* 8(2): 271–310.

Klaas, B.S., Gainey, T.W., McClendon, J.A. and Yang, H. (2005) 'Professional employer organizations and their impacts on client satisfaction with Human Resource outcomes: A field study of Human Resource outsourcing in small and medium enterprises', *Journal of Management* 31: 234–54.

Klaas, B.S., McClendon, J.A. and Gainey, T.W. (1999) 'HR outsourcing and its impact: The role of transaction costs', *Personnel Psychology* 52: 113–36.

Kotabe, M., Mol, M.J., Murray, J. and Parente, R. (2012) 'Outsourcing and its implications for market success: Negative curvilinearity, firm resources, and competition', *Journal of the Academy of Marketing Science* 40(2): 329–46.

Lane, D. and Myant, M. (2007) 'Introduction', in D. Lane and M. Myant (eds) *Varieties of Capitalism in Post-Communist Countries*. London: Palgrave.

La Porta, R., Lopez-de-Silanes, F. and Shleifer, A. (2008) 'The economic consequences of legal origins', *Journal of Economic Literature* 46(2): 285–332.

Lazear, E.P. (1990) 'Pensions and deferred benefits as strategic compensation', *Industrial Relations* 29: 263–80.

Lincoln, J. and Kalleberg, A. (1990) *Culture, Control and Commitment: A Study of Work Organization in the United States and Japan*. Cambridge: Cambridge University Press.

Mol, M.J. (2007) *Outsourcing: Design, Process and Performance*. Cambridge: Cambridge University Press.

Mol, M.J. and Brewster, C. (2013) '*The outsourcing strategy of local and multinational firms: A supply base perspective*'. Working paper. University of Warwick, Coventry.

Norman, T.J. (2009) *Outsourcing Human Resource Activities: Measuring the Hidden Costs and Benefits*. Unpublished PhD dissertation. University of Minnesota.

Porter, M.E. (1985) *Competitive Advantage*. New York: Free Press.

Quinn, J.B. and Hilmer, F.G. (1994) 'Strategic outsourcing', *Sloan Management Review* 35(4): 43–55.

Rangan, S. (2000) 'The problem of search and deliberation in international exchange: Microfoundations to some macro patterns', *Journal of International Business Studies* 31(2): 205–22.

Richbell, S. and Wood, G. (2009) 'Reward management', in D. Collings and G. Wood (eds) *Human Resource Management: A Critical Approach*. London: Routledge.

Rosenzweig, P. (1994) 'When can management science research be generalized internationally?', *Management Science* 40(1): 28–39.

Shy, O. and Stenbacka, R. (2003) 'Strategic outsourcing', *Journal of Economic Behavior and Organization* 50(2): 203–24.

Smith, P.C., Vozikis, G.S. and Varaksina, L. (2006) 'Outsourcing human resource management: a comparison of Russian and US practices', *Journal of Labor Research* 27(3): 305–21.

Sorge, A. (2004) 'Cross-national differences in human resource management and organization', in A.-W. Harzing and V. Ruysseveldt (eds) *International Human Resource Management* (2nd ed.). London: Sage.

Thelen, K. (2001) 'Varieties of labour politics in the developed democracies', in P. Hall and D. Soskice (eds) *Varieties of Capitalism: The Institutional Basis of Competitive Advantage*. Oxford: Oxford University Press.

Toulan, O.N. (2002) 'The impact of market liberalization on vertical scope', *Strategic Management Journal*, 23(6): 551–60.

Williamson, O.E. (1975) *Markets and Hierarchies: Analysis and Antitrust Implications*. New York: Free Press.

Williamson, O.E. (1985) *The Economic Institutions of Capitalism*. New York: Free Press.

Index

Page numbers in **bold** refer to figures, page numbers in *italic* refer to tables.